AF888577

THE CORRESPONDENCE

OF

IU. SAMARIN AND BARONESS RAHDEN

(1861-1876)

Translated from the Second Edition of D. Samarin,

Moscow, 1894

by

Terence Scully
(from the French)

Helen Swediuk-Cheyne
(from the German)

Loren Calder
(from the Russian)

With Editing and an Introductory Essay on Iu. Samarin

by

Loren Calder

1974

UNIVERSITY OF BRISTOL

WITHDRAWN

ISBN—0-88920-004-1
(paper)
ISBN—0-88920-005-X
(cloth)

© 1974

Wilfrid Laurier University
Waterloo, Ontario, Canada

UNIVERSITY
OF BRISTOL
LIBRARY

W.M.L.

INTRODUCTION

One well might ask, why read the *Correspondence* of Iuri Samarin and Baroness Rahden, two little remembered representatives of nineteenth-century Russia and a bygone era? A general answer is that Samarin and Rahden were intelligent and cultured people who moved easily in Russian and European society and whose comments on leading personalities, religious, political and social questions still have relevance for today. Another answer is that the *Correspondence* introduces one to a side of Russian intellectual life, which deserves more attention than it has generally received, if only because it opens the door to a broader view of Russian society. A more specific answer, and certainly the most important one, is that Iuri Samarin was one of the most prominent and effective Slavophils, exerting a powerful influence on the development of Russian society in his lifetime as a political reformer and publicist. His work deserves attention, and this *Correspondence* reveals much about the quality of his learning, his personality and character, and his philosophy of politics and religion.[1] A brief sketch of Samarin's biography gives support to these assertions.[2]

Iuri Samarin was a member of the same generation of Russians as Leo Tolstoy, Fedor Dostoevski, Mikhail Katkov,

[1]Samarin wrote on many subjects, but especially on the peasant question, the borderlands, and philosophical and religious problems. However, his major works were essentially compilations of articles written to achieve more or less specific objectives and comprise a number of volumes in each case. For this reason the *Correspondence*, spanning fifteen years and touching on a number of problems and subjects, emerges as a valuable, and perhaps even the best, single representative work.

[2]Biographical information on the Baroness Rahden is found in

Alexander Herzen, Nicholas Chernyshevski, and the Tsar Alexander II. He was privileged to enjoy all the advantages of noble birth, being born in St. Petersburg on April 21, 1819 into a family that moved in the highest court circles. Enormous patrimonial estates held near Moscow, Tula and Samara were the basis of the family's affluence, and long associations with the court were the guarantee of its social and political privileges.[3]

In 1826, when Iuri was still only seven years old, his father moved his family to Moscow. In view of the depth of Irui's future Russian patriotism, it is worth noting that his father's main reason for leaving St. Petersburg was to break his children away from the French atmosphere of its court. As an indicator of how pervasive this atmosphere was, Iuri spoke only French at this stage of his development.

The elder Samarin's main concern when he reached Moscow was to superintend the education of his children. To this end he established a very good household school, setting high standards and employing only the best teachers. Iuri Samarin obtained all of his basic education in this family school. When he entered the University of Moscow, in 1834 at the age of fifteen, he had an excellent knowledge of Russian, French and Latin, and a good grounding in Greek, German, geography and arithmetic.

On entering the university Iuri elected to study in the Faculty of Arts (*slovesnoe otdelenie*). His favourite subject was history and his favourite professor, the famous historian and exponent of "official nationalism," M. P. Pogodin. Certainly Samarin was pushed towards Slavophilism by Pogodin's teachings, for he said of him:

the Preface, see pp. 25-34.

[3]Baron B. E. Nol'de, *Iuri Samarin i ego vremia* (Paris, 1926), pp. 8-9. This is the one full-length biography of Samarin available. It is an excellent work, rich in factual detail and penetrating analysis. Another useful work is Dmitri Samarin, "Biograficheski ocherk Iu. F. Samarin," *Sochineniia Iu. F. Samarina*, IX (Moscow, 1898), ix-xxiv.

> He had an independent direction of thought . . . warmed by a deep sympathy for Russian life . . . . He brought us to a completely new view of Russian history and Russian life in general. Western formulas were not applicable to us; in Russian life there was some kind of particular beginning foreign to other people; her development proceeded by another law, as yet undetermined by science. Pogodin said this to us fairly awkwardly, without proof, but in such a way that his conviction became a part of us.[4]

These ideas Samarin would express repeatedly as a mature Slavophil politician and polemicist. He finished his course at the university in 1838 at the top of his class.[5]

It was at the university that Samarin met Konstantin Aksakov,[6] his closest and most influential friend of the period. These two young men, their respective courses completed, began to study for the master's degree together. Through diligent study, writing and discussion they gradually consolidated their views on religion, Russia and Europe. One of the immediate consequences of this friendship for Samarin was that it brought him into contact with literary and progressive Moscow. Gogol and Lermontov frequented the Aksakov home, as did Stankevich, Belinsky, Herzen, Bakunin and Granovsky. It was during this period also that he and

[4] Iu. F. Samarin, "Iz vospominanii ob universitete 1834-1838," *Rus'*, No. 1 (November 15, 1880), p. 19.

[5] Among his classmates was S. M. Solov'ev, the outstanding historian, and M. Katkov, the influential conservative journalist of the 1870's and 1880's. Nol'de, p. 13.

[6] Konstantin S. Aksakov (1817-60) became one of the most prominent Slavophils. A son of the writer S. T. Aksakov, he was the Slavophil historian and philologist. In his work he developed the belief that religious and moral factors determine the historical process, that the true religion was Orthodoxy, and that only on the basis of Orthodoxy could durable political and social forms be created. See K. S. Aksakov, *Polnoe sobranie sochinenii*, ed. I. S. Aksakov (3 vols.; Moscow, 1861-80).

Aksakov met and joined the group of people which later became known as the Slavophils. First among them were Aleksei Khomiakov and Ivan Kireevski, the principal founders of the Slavophil movement.[7]

In the spring of 1840 Samarin began work on his master's thesis, a project which had a decisive influence on his future career.[8] His assigned topic was to work on Stefan Iavorsky and Feofan Prokopovich, preachers and administrators of the Russian Orthodox Church during the Petrine era. Already convinced that religious questions were of vital importance and finding them of absorbing interest, he decided that in writing his thesis, he would seek to establish his position on religion and on the religious conflicts that had rent history. On this foundation his thesis took shape. In the

[7]Alexei S. Khomiakov (1804-60) was a public-man, poet, and philosopher-theologian. He had roots in the old aristocracy, was a wealthy landowner, and was a founding member and leader of the Slavophil movement. In the late thirties he began to enunciate Slavophil doctrine. He proclaimed that Russia had a unique course of development opposed to that of the West with its individualism and materialism. He valued the commune (*obshchina*) because it embodied the principle of brotherhood, and he was a convinced monarchist and defender of autocracy, even while he favoured political and social reforms. He believed in the superiority of Orthodoxy and in the primacy of faith and religion. See A. S. Khomiakov, *Polnoe sobranie sochinenii* (8 vols.; Moscow, 1900-1904).

Ivan V. Kireevski (1808-56), a prominent philosopher and publicist, was also one of the founders of Slavophilism. As an active propagator of Slavophil ideas he exercised a powerful influence on the movement. He was convinced of the superiority of the Russian experience based on the commune (*obshchina*) and Orthodoxy. He emphasized the importance of revelation and was sceptical of rationalism. See *Polnoe sobranie sochinenii Ivana Vasil'evicha Kireevskogo*, pub. A. I. Koshelev (2 vols.; Moscow, 1861).

[8]The most detailed account of Samarin's life during this period is to be found in D. Samarin, "Dannyia dlia biografii Iu. F. Samarina za 1840-1845 gg.," *Sochineniia*, V (Moscow, 1880), xxv-xcii: also in *Russkii biograficheskii slovar'*, XVIII (St. Petersburg, 1904), 133-46.

first part, "Stefan Iavorsky and Feofan Prokopovich as Theologians," he tried to establish the place of Orthodoxy as a religious teaching. In the second part, "Stefan Iavorsky and Feofan Prokopovich as officials of the Church," he studied the relationship of the Orthodox Church to the Russian state. In the third part, "Stefan Iavorsky and Feofan Prokopovich as Preachers," he examined the literary content of their writings. This third part had little real interest for Samarin, but had to be written to satisfy university requirements.[9]

This period saw the youth pass through a crisis arising from a conflict between faith and reason. Essentially he tried to prove, using Hegel, that Orthodoxy was the only true religious doctrine. His deliberations led him into a morass of confusion and doubt from which Khomiakov extricated him, by bringing him to the view that belief cannot, and should not, be demonstrated rationally. Khomiakov's strength lay in his unshakable faith in Orthodoxy and this characteristic Samarin came to share with him. Certainly the mature Samarin was distinguished by a deep and abiding faith in the Russian Orthodox Church as an institution, and as an "organism of truth and love."[10]

The second part of Samarin's thesis—a study of church-state relationships in Russia—merits special attention for it foreshadows the direction of his future career. In this work he set himself a political question, thus for the first time entering into a field of thought and action in which he would distinguish himself later. The privileged environment in which Samarin grew up and his family's long tradition of close relations with the court all but guaranteed that he would become

[9]*Sochineniia*, V: *Stefan Iavorski i Feofan Prokopovich* (Moscow, 1880). Part 3 was published separately by the University of Moscow as *Stefan Iavorski i Feofan Prokopovich, kak propovedniki* (Moscow, 1844). Samarin's collected works were published in eleven volumes (I-X, XII) between 1877-1911.

[10]Nol'de, p. 31: see P. K. Christoff, *A. S. Xomjakov* (The Hague, 1961), p. 56.

a monarchist. And in fact autocracy became, for him, the foundation of Russian society. He would say as late as December, 1867:

> that it is still not time for Russia to think about a change of the existing form of government . . . autocracy was never so strong morally as now . . . at this minute no other power could inspire such faith, could dispose so easily of such voluntary, unanimous, and unqualified co-operation from the nation; I conclude from this that the historical calling of autocracy has still not been fulfilled and that it is still destined to do much for Russia.[11]

However, conservative as Samarin's belief in autocracy might seem, he revealed strong liberal tendencies early: while working on this part of his thesis he modified his monarchical principles to argue that "absolute power . . . must be founded on the acknowledgement of a wide sphere of freedom for the subject."[12] He also argued that a free church in a society recognizing freedom of religious conscience for every one of its members was mandatory for human fulfillment.

Samarin presented his thesis in the fall of 1843, and defended it brilliantly the following spring. He now had to decide on a direction for his future career. While his personal inclination was to pursue a life of scholarship, his father was anxious for him to enter the government service, so that Samarin, accepting his father's wishes, left for St. Petersburg and an appointment in the Ministry of Justice (August, 1844).[13]

In all he spent two rather depressing years in St. Petersburg, moving to various governmental departments but always doing the same thing—copying and correcting reports.

[11]Samarin, *Sochineniia*, VIII (Moscow, 1890), 4.

[12]Nol'de, p. 27.

[13]D. Samarin, "Dannyia dlia biografii Iu. F. Samarina za 1840-1845 gg.," *Sochineniia*, V (Moscow, 1880), lxxix-lxxxiii.

His response to his work and to the deadening bureaucratic atmosphere of the capital was positive, however; for we see him in a letter of this period reproaching Konstantin Aksakov for his "Moscowism," that is, for his tendency to denounce St. Petersburg, and yet make no positive contribution to the improvement of affairs. Samarin himself began a serious study of Russia's history for the purpose of gaining a clearer understanding of her present political, cultural and religious situation.[14] On this basis he would soon be active in defending Russia's traditions, and in reforming her institutions, for he was already convinced that theory must be wedded to practice. Time and again in his career he used theory based on research as an adjunct to practice, and habitually urged others to take an active line. As this period advanced there was a steady growth in his interest in social and political questions. It culminated in two events signalizing active involvement in politics. First, in May, 1846, he was posted to Riga, in the service of the Ministry of Internal Affairs, to work on a commission established to draft a plan for reform of the administrative structure and economy of the city. Second, his article *On the Historical and Literary Opinions of 'Sovremmenik'* was published in the Slavophil journal *Moskvitianin.*[15]

This article contains Samarin's first clear formulation of some basic Slavophil teachings. To summarize briefly he asserted: (1) that Western individualism leads nowhere; (2) that the idea of man in society under law does not grow out of individualism; (3) that Europe was searching for such an idea; (4) that the Russian experience was relevant because it provided such an idea in the "commune"; (5) that Christianity had brought "consciousness and freedom" to Russian life; (6) that the problem of Russia's "internal history" had been "to enlighten the national communal principle by the

[14]*Sochineniia*, XII, 149-57.

[15]Nol'de, p. 35. Khomiakov and Samarin were the most active Slavophil polemicists during the 1840's. Christoff, p. 85.

communal principle of the Church"; and (7) that the aim of Russia's "external history" had been "to defend and to protect" this enterprise "by the creation of a strong state structure" in harmony with it.[16]

Samarin's work in Riga involved writing a history of that city's institutions as part of a series of steps towards far-reaching administrative reforms.[17] With the scholarly thoroughness which so typified him, he examined Russia's relations with the whole Baltic area in the process. His finished work, "an excellent, undated, historical and juridical monograph,"[18] was published by the Ministry of the Interior for distribution among the highest members of the government. As so often happened the projected reform was dropped: as for the publication, it was subsequently lost or destroyed, probably by fire.[19] His work was not barren, however, for he took a few dominant ideas from his research and experience in Riga. First, he acquired an abiding distrust of constitutionalism because of the way in which the privileged German landholding element had used constitutional guarantees to protect their narrow class interest—insofar his faith in the virtues of a responsible monarchy were con-

[16](Sochineniia, I (Moscow, 1877), 63-64.)

[17]Riga, located at the mouth of the Western Dvina river, was for centuries the chief commercial and administrative centre of Livonia, the indigenous homeland of Latvians and Estonians. Russia has had a long involvement with the region, going back at least to Kievan times when Vladimir (980-1015) tried to establish his authority there. In the twelfth and thirteenth centuries, settlement and conquest under the auspices of the Livonian and Teutonic orders established political and economic power in German hands—a situation which continued under successive conquests of the region by Poles (sixteenth century), Swedes (seventeenth century), and Russians (eighteenth century). See A. Bilmanis, *A History of Latvia* (Princeton, New Jersey, 1951); and E. Uustalu, *The History of the Estonian People* (London, 1952).

[18]Nol'de, pp. 40-41.

[19]*Sochineniia*, VII, cxxxv.

firmed. Second, he came to an important decision concerning the peasant question, which he already considered of paramount importance in Russia. His work in Latvia convinced him that the abolition of serfdom must be engineered by the government under conditions guaranteeing peasant rights, and especially their right to land.[20]

Samarin's service in Riga ended in turmoil. By the end of it he had become so angered by the direction of Russian policy in the Baltic region that he wrote a long pamphlet, *Letters from Riga*, denouncing it. Something of his aim and mood is contained in the following quotation from a letter to Konstantin Aksakov (April, 1848):

> The systematic oppression of Russians by Germans is an hourly insult to Russian nationality before the eyes of many of her representatives—this is what stirs the blood in me and I work for only one thing—to bring the fact to people's attention . . . .[21]

Even before his return to St. Petersburg, he began to circulate manuscript copies of his pamphlet. His attack on government policy, erupting in the hermetically sealed atmosphere of Nicholation Russia, created a small storm in court circles. Its principal effect was to provoke the powerful German party to take reprisals. Nicholas was pressed for action, and Samarin was promptly lodged in the Peter-Paul fortress. After a twelve-day imprisonment he was taken to Nicholas, who administered a sharp rebuke, accusing him of divulging state secrets and of stirring up enmity between Germans and Russians. The affair ended with what was, in effect, banishment from the capital—first to Moscow, and later to the provinces.[22]

After a three-month stay in Moscow, Samarin was posted

[20]Nol'de, pp. 42-43.

[21]*Sochineniia*, XII, 200.

[22]*Ibid.*, VII, xc ff. Samarin recorded Nicholas' rebuke verbatim.

to Simbirsk on the Volga. From there he was shortly sent to Kiev, where he was placed at the disposal of Governor-General Bibikov. Much of this period, brief as it was, was devoted to study of the peasant question. As pointed out above, he was already convinced that a just solution to this question would have to be enforced and guaranteed by the government.

Fortuitously, Samarin's arrival in Kiev coincided with the introduction in the south-western region of inventories designed to determine the land relationships between landlords and peasants. Samarin did not play an active part in this process, but he studied it closely and wrote about it, gaining thereby a knowledge of the peasant question that he was able to turn to account later.

By 1850 Samarin was in charge of Bibikov's chancellery. However, civil service work was seriously impeding his new research and reform interest, so that when the need to manage the family estates because of his father's illness arose, he retired, settling once again in Moscow (1852).[23]

He was now convinced of the need to abolish serfdom. Characteristically he began a full-scale study of peasant-landlord relationships, village agriculture and peasant life in general.[24] The next five years were spent in this pursuit. The summers were passed studying and working on the family estates in the Tula and Samara regions: the winters were passed in Moscow, in study and discussion with his Slavophil friends—Cherkasski,[25] Khomiakov, Koshelev,[26] and

[23]Nol'de, pp. 59-60.

[24]V. N. Bochkarev, "Iuri Fedorovich Samarin," *Velikaia reforma*, V (Moscow, 1911), 94.

[25]Prince Vladimir A. Cherkasski was a politician and reformer. He played an important role in bringing the peasant reform to fruition and was a key figure in preparing the peasant reform in Poland (1864). He was elected mayor of Moscow in 1869 and was active in preparing the municipal statutes of 1870. See *Kniaz' Vladimir Aleksandrovich Cherkasski. Ego stat'i, ego rechi i vospominaniia o nem* (Moscow, 1879).

Konstantin and Ivan Aksakov.[27]

The articles which he wrote during this period played a decisive role in shaping his future career. In 1853 he began to write a series of papers on the peasant question which, distributed among his friends and in highest court circles, played an important role in setting the stage for emancipation.[28] But recognition didn't come as quickly as it might have, because his Slavophilism made him suspect.[29] The situation changed when the reign of Alexander II began, and the Slavophils won permission to publish their own journal, *Russkaia beseda*, and later *Sel'skoe blagoustroistva*, a journal devoted exclusively to peasant affairs. While Samarin devoted much time to these journals including writing two articles on nationality and science, he concentrated most of

[26]Aleksandr I. Koshelev (1806-83) was a prominent Slavophil and publicist. He issued a number of Slavophil publications including *Russkaia beseda* (Russian Conversation), 1856-60. He stood for the establishment of representative institutions at the local level and the convoking of a consultative assembly. He played an active role in preparing the peasant reform and wrote extensively on political questions: see, for example, *Konstitutsiia, samoderzhavie i zemskaia duma* (Leipzig, 1862).

[27]Ivan S. Aksakov (1823-86) was a brother of Konstantin Aksakov, and a prominent Slavophil publicist, especially during the later stages of the movement. His strongly nationalistic political creed was expounded in the Slavophil journals which he published, namely: *Den'* (1862-65); *Moskva* (1867-68); *Moskvich* (1867-68); and *Rus'* (1880-86). Aksakov was always viewed with suspicion by the government and *Den'*, *Moskva* and *Moskvich* were all suppressed by the censor. See I. S. Aksakov, *Polnoe sobranie sochinenii* (7 vols.; Moscow, 1886-87); and *Ivan Sergeevich Aksakov v ego pismakh* (4 vols.; Moscow-St. Petersburg, 1888-96).

[28]Bochkarev, V, 96-97: see M. T. Florinsky, *Russia*, II (New York, 1961), 885.

[29]Samarin said in a letter to K. Aksakov (1844): "We . . . have attracted . . . strong undeserved suspicion from the government side and distrust from the side of society." *Sochineniia*, XII, 150.

his attention on the peasant question, advocating a reform programme which was moderate. His central concern was to find a way to destroy serfdom, and at the same time preserve the communal basis of Russian agriculture.[30] His connections, especially with the Grand Duchess Helen and the Grand Duke Constantine (influential reform-oriented members of the Royal family), his literary gifts, and scholarly analysis established him as an authority on the peasant question.[31]

Samarin was first and foremost a doer. The Imperial Rescript of November 20, 1857, commanding the nobility to prepare proposals for the "improvement of peasant life" (a circumlocution for emancipation), gave him the opportunity he was waiting for. Under the terms of the Rescript, committees of landlords were formed in every province of the empire. He was asked to represent the government on the Samara provincial committee. With hope and enthusiasm he welcomed the opportunity, and for the next five years worked, almost without interruption, on the peasant reform. This would prove to be the most difficult, and perhaps the most praiseworthy, period of his life.[32]

[30]Bochkarev, p. 95.

[31]The Grand Duchess Helen Pavlovna (1806-73) was born Frederika-Charlotte-Maria Princess of Würtemberg. In 1823 she married the Grand Duke Michael Pavlovich and settled in Russia where she played a prominent role as a patron of the arts and as a creator of welfare and educational institutions. During the Crimean War she helped to lay the foundations for the Red Cross. In the late 1850's she was a passionate and enlightened proponent of peasant reform.

The Grand Duke Konstantin Nikolaevich (1827-92) was a brother of Alexander II. For many years he was commander of the fleet and chairman of the state council. An able man with an eye for reform, he was a key factor in bringing the peasant, judicial and censorship reforms to fruition. After the Crimean War, he was a powerful force in modernizing the Russian fleet and in re-establishing Russian sea power on the Black Sea.

[32]Bochkarev, p. 98.

From the very beginning, the provincial committees were rent with disputes between a large majority defending the interests of the landlords, and a small minority working for the well-being of the peasants. Samarin was among the small minority. He rejected unconditionally the proposal that every peasant should be given freedom without land. He stood for a moderate programme of reform, maintaining communal land ownership, and guaranteeing each peasant a land allotment sufficient to support himself and his family. He held a key position on the Samara committee; in fact, as a literary man and a theoretician with a clearly articulated programme, he did the bulk of the work. It is interesting to note that relations on the committee were so strained and the opposition of the landlords so impassioned that Samarin never went out of the house unless he was armed and accompanied by a bodyguard.[33]

In the spring of 1859, an Editing Commission, headed by Ia. I. Rostovtsev, was established in St. Petersburg to examine the proposals of the various provincial committees and to draft the emancipation statute. Samarin was invited to participate in the work of this Commission as an expert. By mid-summer he was working in St. Petersburg, where he quickly discovered that he was in disagreement with the basic principles of the reform as set out by his more conservative colleagues. While he considered resigning, he was prevailed upon to stay, and continued to serve the Commission until its work was completed in October, 1860. He worked mainly on the question of obligations, but also played an active part in compiling the proposals of the south-western region. There was a brief interruption of three months in his service, because of a nervous breakdown, brought on by the heavy strain of his work, for this was a very difficult period for the members of the Commission—not only was there great social animosity, but the work was very strenuous, especially for

[33]*Ibid.*, p. 100.

someone like Samarin whose great writing capacity was exploited.[34]

After the preliminary drafting of the Emancipation Statute, Samarin remained in St. Petersburg for consultation with the Grand Duke Constantine, while it was being discussed by the Main Committee. During this period he wrote several notes refuting arguments against the proposals of the Editing Commission. He also wrote a first draft of the Emancipation Manifesto. The planning and drafting of the Emancipation Statute was over: Samarin was certainly one of its "principal authors."[35]

Samarin's work on the peasant question did not end with the publication of the Emancipation Manifesto (February 19, 1861). The reform still had to be implemented, and Samarin, even though he had some reservations about its final form, worked hard to put its measures into effect. In March, he was again in Samara, this time serving the government as an Arbitrator (*mirovoi posrednik*) on the provincial commission responsible for introducing the reform. During this period agreements were drawn up between the landlords and their peasants, fixing land allotments and obligations. Samarin's task was to verify these agreements. Because of the illiteracy of his assistants, however, a much greater volume of work fell on his shoulders. He was, in fact, a "leading executor"[36] of the reform, and his impartial and diligent service did much to improve the government office's standing among the peasants.[37]

[34]Nol'de, pp. 112-31.

[35]Nicholas V. Riasanovsky, *Russia and the West in the Teaching of the Slavophils* (Cambridge, Massachusetts: Harvard University Press, 1952), p. 57. V. I. Semevski, *Krest'ianskii vopros v Rossii v pervoi polovine XIX veka*, II (St. Petersburg, 1888), 417, credits Samarin with making a "significant" contribution to the reform.

[36]Riasanovsky, p. 57.

[37]Bochkarev, p. 103.

When most of the agreements were completed, Samarin considered his task done, and retired for a second time (summer, 1863). The nobility of Samara, who had followed his career closely, and had come, despite earlier differences, to value his stirling qualities, fêted him.[38]

Samarin was not, however, destined to take his ease, at least not for a while yet. Revolt had broken out in Poland in January, and he was soon caught up in government attempts to deal with it. In October he was asked by Nicholas Miliutin[39] to take part in a commission being established to work out a solution for the peasant question in Poland. Miliutin, who was head of the commission and who had worked with Samarin on the Emancipation Statute, chose him because of his theoretical knowledge.[40] Samarin, who had already revealed his deep concern over the borderlands in his Riga days, accepted. Then he, Miliutin and Cherkasski, the third member of the Commission, spent six weeks in Warsaw, and a few days in a lightning tour of south-western Poland. Samarin's observations and impressions were expounded in a comprehensive note to the Tsar, and contributed to a new programme for the reconstruction of Polish peasant life and village government. This programme, based on the Slavophil point of view, was ratified by Alexander (February 19, 1864) and remained the government programme for Poland over the next half-century.[41]

Samarin's attitude to Poland was complex. He was sympathetically inclined towards the Poles as members of a Slavic nation, but he hated Polonism, which he viewed as the "armed propaganda of Latinism [Catholicism] . . . a sharp

[38]Nol'de, p. 145.

[39]Nicholas A. Miliutin (1818-1972), a prominent statesman of Alexander II's reign, was close to the Slavophils. He was an exponent of enlightened absolutism and played a leading role in preparing the peasant and administrative reforms of the reign.

[40]Bochkarev, p. 104.

[41]Florinsky, II, 916.

wedge . . . driven into the heart of the Slavonic world . . . ."[42] To Polonism he opposed Eastern Slavonic Orthodoxy. While anxious to irradicate Polonism, he did not advocate Russification, including the imposition of Orthodoxy, because he believed that the Poles had a right to cultural and national self-determination, i.e., freedom of religious instruction, a national language, and independent civil government. His final aim was to achieve, through a gradual mingling of Poles and Russians, complete reconciliation in a greater Slavic unity. His method of achieving this objective was to suppress the revolt, and then to win the support of the Polish peasantry by emancipating them on favourable terms. In all fairness it should be pointed out that Samarin's programme, eschewing Russification, was implemented more harshly than he envisaged.[43]

When, at forty-five, he returned from Poland, Samarin found his health broken. However, he was far from despairing for he felt he could still look forward to useful work. In fact, he was to live another twelve years, and to accomplish an outstanding amount of work in that period. These last years of his life were devoted to public and literary activity, following a uniform pattern. Almost every year he went abroad, both for reasons of health, and for the publishing of his literary work. The fall usually found him on the Volga, where he saw to the management of his estates and the schools which he had founded on them. He also hunted for he was a passionate hunter. The winters he spent in Moscow working in *duma* and *zemstvo* councils. As this period coincided with the sterile second half of Alexander's reign, Samarin became increasingly estranged from governmental circles. He was remembered only once, being entrusted with the presidency of the Samara Provincial *Zemstvo* conference (December, 1865).[44]

[42]Quoted from Bochkarev, p. 105.

[43]Bochkarev, p. 105.

[44]Nol'de, p. 193.

As suggested above, Samarin's public activities were concentrated in Moscow. The laziness, the sloth, the ignorance, that he had come up against in the provinces after the reform of 1861 had brought him to the point of despair, but it had been instructive. It had convinced him that the proper task for the moment was, eschewing constitutional reform projects like those of Koshelev and other liberals, to concentrate on creating efficient organs of local self-government, i.e., on the *Zemstvo* programme.[45] It is not strange then, that from 1866 onward, he should serve as an elected representative on both the Moscow City *Duma* and Moscow Provincial *Zemstvo* Council. He was a very active representative, and his clear, logical exposition was both impressive and effective. He served on various commissions, frequently as chairman, and drafted many reports. His most noteworthy work went into drafting a reform of the poll-tax. Samarin proved to be a reliable leader and a diligent worker, accepting all manner of assignments—whether locating cemeteries or planning for the removal of garbage, no task was too humble. "It was a time," he said, "for stonemasons, not architects."[46]

Samarin's literary activity during this final twelve-year period was impressive. To this period are related his best-known works. In 1865 he began to publish a long, hard-hitting attack on the Jesuits—*The Jesuits and their Relation to Russia*[47]—which won him considerable notoriety. In 1867 he edited and published the first Russian edition of Khomiakov's philosophical writings. For this work he wrote a long preface evaluating the role of Khomiakov as philosopher and theologian. It was "superb . . . expressing the character of the teaching and the point of view of Khomiakov . . . ."[48]

[45]Bochkarev, p. 106.

[46]Nol'de, p. 145.

[47]Samarin, *Sochineniia*, VI (Moscow, 1887), 1-326.

[48]Prince V. Odoevski, an outstanding Schellingist, as quoted in Christoff, p. 37 n.

Samarin was ambitious to continue the philosophical work of Khomiakov (his friends, especially Ivan Aksakov, hoped that he would), but he became convinced that he lacked the philosophical depth required. Peter Struve has remarked apropos: "as distinct from Kireevski and Khomiakov . . . the mind of Samarin was not a philosophical-constructing, but a civil-servant arranging and regulating [one] . . . the mind of Samarin was the mind of a statesman and political thinker."[49] There are two other examples of Samarin's philosophical writing from this period: an analysis of K. D. Kavelin's book, *The Problems of Psychology*, and a brief study of Max Mueller's *History of Religion*.

Samarin was a great Russian publicist—some of his Russian contemporaries called him the greatest publicist of all times. While this latter opinion is exaggerated, there is no doubt at all that Samarin was among the best. His publicist work is distinguished by scholarly analysis, precision, lucidity and power. Certainly, his most important work of this kind was *Borderlands of Russia*, an extensive publication stretching into three volumes, which began to appear in 1867, and continued to appear regularly until his death in 1876. In *Borderlands*, he returned to the study of Russia and the Baltic states, which had occupied his attention during his stay in Riga twenty years earlier. It was written to combat the autocratic, class character of Russian policy in the 1860's, which Samarin feared would provoke a centrifugal or separatist movement in the borderlands—in Finland, the Baltic states, Poland, and even in the Ukraine and the Caucasus.[50] It was published abroad as was almost everything written during this period. The first two issues of *Borderlands* provoked the Tsar's displeasure, leading Samarin to write a personal explanation of his position. It provoked a heated debate in Germany and made the author famous in Europe.

[49]Peter Struve, "Iuri Samarin. Opyt kharateristiki i otsenki," *Vozrozhdenie*, No. 376 (June 13, 1926). *Sochineniia*, VI, xi.

[50]Nol'de, pp. 202-204.

It received a mixed response in Russia: nationalists, who favoured a strongly pro-Russian policy, welcomed it; while less committed Russians accused him of chauvinism. It is a measure of his influence that his programme was adopted by Alexander III.

One of Samarin's last publications was the booklet, *Revolutionary Conservatism* (Berlin, 1875). This booklet was a long letter to General Fadeev, attacking his constitutionalism. Samarin still regarded constitutionalism as a gentry device for the perpetuation of their class interests. When General Fadeev, who had roots in the highest government and court circles, appeared as the exponent of a new constitutionalism, and at the same time disparaged the basic foundations of the Great Reforms, Samarin felt compelled to speak out against him.[51]

Samarin enjoyed an enormous reputation, and the signs of it took a tangible form during these last years. Among the distinctions bestowed on him was the creation of five scholarships bearing his name, and his enrolment as an honorary member of both the University of Moscow and the Moscow Ecclesiastical Academy. After his death, the University created a special prize to be granted in his name to the best composition on peasant and *Zemstvo* affairs.

During this period his health was generally poor, partly because he was troubled by a chronic nervous condition. Over the summer and fall of 1876, however, his health seemed sound and his energy unabated, so that his death came quite unexpectedly from a minor cause. Late in December, he went to Berlin to have the sixth issue of *Borderlands* published, as well as to study the institutions of local government and the tax system in Prussia. Early in March, he insisted on having a small swelling about the size of a hazel-nut removed from his right arm. As a result of this minor operation, he contracted blood poisoning and died (March 19, 1876).

[51]Bochkarev, p. 106.

In summary, a few very basic ideas emerge as the underpinning of Iuri Samarin's Slavophilism. First, he believed in Christianity, and especially in the superiority of the Russian Orthodox Church as a manifestation of that faith. Second, he believed that Russian autocracy was still a just and viable political institution. Third, he was a Moscovite who looked on the West with circumspection; certainly, he repudiated Western individualism in favour of collectivism as exemplified in the traditional Russian commune. Fourth, he was an enemy of arbitrariness, corruption and irresponsibility in government, and a friend of reform, his sole proviso being that reform be consistent with the national experience. Finally, he believed in religious liberty, and the freedom of thought, of press and of conscience which it implies.

Samarin ranks very high among the Slavophils. Only one or two—Khomiakov and perhaps Kireevski, both theorists and older than he was—could be ranked higher. He earned this distinction by writing, and by participating in practical reform work. The volume and range of his writing made a powerful impact on his contemporaries, including government. In volume his written work comprises fifteen heavy tomes, including four of letters. In range he wrote on philosophical and religious questions (two volumes), the peasant question (three volumes), literary and historical questions (one volume), on nationality and borderland questions (four volumes), and on financial and educational questions (one volume). The impact of his work can be documented and has been acknowledged by authority: he was a prime mover in conditioning the government to accept peasant reform, and played a big role in drafting and implementing that reform; he was active in establishing local government under the *zemstvo* system; and finally, he established the basis of Russian policy towards the borderlands in the last quarter of the nineteenth century. Samarin was certainly an important Slavophil, he was without doubt the most important Slavophil statesman.[52]

This contribution to Slavophilism and to the development of Russian society in the nineteenth century make it desirable that English readers have an opportunity to acquaint themselves with Samarin's thought and character. This present work, comprising his correspondence with the Baroness Rahden, is particularly suitable for that purpose—in fact, no other single work so adequately presents the man.

This present edition is translated from: *Correspondance de G. Samarine avec La Baronne De Rahden, 1861-1876*, published by D. Samarin, 2nd edition, Moscow, 1894. It faithfully reproduces the original, including a long preface about the Baroness Rahden and her friendship with Iuri Samarin. Dr. Terence Scully has translated the French which was the language of the original correspondence, Dr. Helen Swediuk-Cheyne has translated the German sections and phrases scattered throughout, and I have handled Russian sentences and phrases where required. In transliterating we have used the Library of Congress system, except that we have reduced the -ii endings in proper names to a single -i. More familiar Russian names like Herzen have been reproduced in the current fashion. The original spelling of German and Russian words has been retained.

Finally, my colleagues and I would like to express our appreciation to the Humanities Research Council of Canada for the subvention, using funds provided by the Canada Council, which helped to make publication of this

[52]Paul Vinogradov calls Samarin "... the greatest Slavophil statesman" ("A Prophetic Career," *British Review*, XII [October, 1915], 3). A. D. Gradovski ("Pamiati Iuriia Fedorovicha Samarina [1876 g.]," IX [St. Petersburg, 1904], CXLVI) says: "While Kireevski, Khomiakov and the Aksakovs tried to apply their principles to purely cultural questions (religion, science, art, philosophy) it fell to Samarin to apply them to political questions, and not only to theory, but also to practise." Baroness Rahden describes him (1869) as "... the head and the standard bearer of the national movement." See p. 128 of this text. A full exposition of his political creed can be found in "Borderlands," *Sochineniia*, VII, IX and X (Moscow, 1890-98).

manuscript possible. We would also like to thank Mrs. P. L. Barber for typing it.

Loren Calder

PREFACE[1]

The name of the Baroness Edith Fedorovna of Rahden, well known in St. Petersburg society, is almost entirely unknown to most Russian readers. In order to give an idea of this remarkable person we shall cite the lines which I. S. Aksakov devoted to her on receiving word of her death in 1885.

> During the night of October 9th there died in St. Petersburg the Baroness Rahden, one of the most remarkable women of our age. Together with a lofty, broad intelligence, a brilliant and enlightened mind, she possessed a great strength of will which balked at nothing as soon as she saw there was a duty to perform; endowed with an unshakable firmness in her moral convictions, nothing could weaken the nobility of the religious feelings pervading her soul. Whoever had the opportunity of meeting her or chatting with her felt his spirit strengthened, her nature was so noble. For a long time she was attached, as lady-in-waiting, to the late Grand Duchess Helen Pavlovna who, as is known, liked to gather together in her soirées all that was then the cream of St. Petersburg wit, scholarship and talent: learned men, writers and statesmen. It was in the salons of the Grand Duchess that the two Miliutins and a good number of young people who afterwards became champions of the great reforms of this past reign made their first appearances at the outset of their careers. It was there that, at the time of the emancipation of the peasants and even before, all of the initiators of, and later the principal workers for, the greatest of the reforms came together: Iuri

[1]This Preface was originally written in Russian for the first edition of the *Correspondence* (1893) by Iu. Samarin's younger brother Dmitri, editor and publisher of the *Sochineniia.* It was subsequently translated into French for the second edition (1894) and has been translated from the French for this third edition. (Ed.)

> Fedorovitch Samarin, Prince Cherkasski and many others. Independently of the Grand Duchess, Baroness Rahden formed one of the principal attractions of these historic soirées. She was intimately connected with the elite of the habitués and in particular with Iu. Samarin. After the death of the latter, she collected their correspondence with care and put it into order. . . . We have had a chance to read some of the letters of Samarin; they are brilliant articles which strike the reader with the depth of their ideas, the accuracy of their expression and that accent of warm sincerity which is ordinarily missing in most works intended for printing. It is to be hoped that the correspondence of these two exceptional people, both so highly gifted in mind and character, will not remain for long in obscurity. Furthermore, Baroness Rahden herself indicated her desire that, after her death, the letters of Samarin should be published.
>
> After the death of the Grand Duchess, Baroness Rahden was elevated to the dignity of lady-in-waiting of the late Empress, a title which she kept with the present Empress. Her Majesty deigned to entrust to her care the exercise of a special surveillance over the educational institutions founded by the Empress Mary, a function to which she devoted herself with all of the passionate energy of her temperament . . . . In spite of the illness that preceded her end, the terror of death had no hold on her courageous soul which, throughout her entire lifetime, had never ceased to burn with the fire of faith.
>
> She leaves an empty place in St. Petersburg society and in the circle of her friends and her acquaintances. . . .[2]

To this accurate appraisal it is fitting to add that Baroness Rahden, a person of firm convictions, was devoted with her whole soul to her native country, Courland.

The relations between Baroness Rahden and Iu. Samarin go back to the years 1859-61; at this time he was a member of the Editorial Commission charged with working out the

[2] *Rus'*, 1885, No. 15. (D. S. = Dmitri Samarin.)

bill on the peasant question, and he often met the Baroness at the soirées of the Grand Duchess Helen Pavlovna. The similarity of their ideas and aspirations on this question, which at that time formed the principal object of the government's attention and about which the interests of the whole of Russian society were concentrated, gave rise to a durable relationship between them; this was as yet, however, neither friendship nor even reciprocal sympathy. Such at least is the impression which emerges from the lines which Baroness Rahden wrote a long while afterwards, in 1873, at the time when Iu. Samarin was gravely ill. Alluding to a sickness which had struck her friend during the period of the Editorial Commissions, she told him: "Apart from your groundless fantasies, I have known you to be sick only once, when you upset me a great deal; at that time your friends' anxieties surrounded you with a sort of exaggerated mystical halo, which I rather made fun of to myself."[3] This can be understood; at that time Iu. Samarin was known in St. Petersburg not only as a partisan of the emancipation of the peasants, but also as the declared enemy of the customs and privileges of the Baltic Provinces. St. Petersburg society still remembered clearly his *Letters from Riga* in 1848 and Baroness Rahden did not hide her sympathy for the Baltic Provinces. This explains why, up until the year 1864, Iu. Samarin and Baroness Rahden wrote to one another only once, and even on that occasion the Baroness was but an intermediary between Samarin and the Grand Duchess.

It was abroad, during the stay which they had in Ragatz in 1864, that their relationship took on a warmer tone. In one of the soirées spent at the Grand Duchess Helen Pavlovna's, a conversation on the subject of the Baltic Provinces was begun between Samarin and Baroness Rahden during tea. The Baroness accused Samarin of being deliberately hostile to the Baltic Provinces, and this provoked a reply from her companion. But, at that moment, the Grand

[3]Letter of September 14, 1873, on p. 230 (Trans.)

Duchess having approached the table, Samarin's reply was terminated brusquely with these words: "*und dennoch.*"[4] Nevertheless, taking leave of the Baroness, Samarin reserved the right to justify himself in writing and to set forth his view on the question of the Baltic Provinces, which he did in two long letters dated September 16 and October 5, 1864. The reader will find an allusion to this circumstance in a letter written by Iu. Samarin on September 12, 1864.[5] From that moment on, over eleven and a half years, their correspondence continued without break up until the death of Iu. Samarin. Each time he came to St. Petersburg he went to see Baroness Rahden, so that their relations developed gradually into so profound and sincere a friendship that it withstood the divergence of their opinions on the question of the Baltic Provinces and on that of religion.

When Samarin published the first two fascicles of the *Borderlands of Russia (Okrainy Rossii)* abroad the friendship was severely strained. Baroness Rahden saw in the publication of this work an act which she was unable to approve; she considered it to be a calumny inspired by racial hatred of the Germans. In a fit of anger she wrote to Iu. Samarin (November 12, 1868) a letter couched in angry language, in which she said, "I feel myself at one with each of my brothers when it is a matter of honour, nationality, and faith," implying to her correspondent that she was writing to him for the last time.[6] This incident gave rise to a correspondence in which one can clearly trace on both sides the sharp struggle between the desire to preserve a friendship based on mutual esteem and the feeling that each one of them had his obligations towards his country and his church. However, Baroness Rahden was not long in becoming convinced that she had made a mistake about the moral significance of Iu. Samarin's action; she realized that he had not,

[4] And nevertheless. (Trans.)

[5] See p. 40 (Trans.)

[6] The passage is on p. 88 (Trans.)

when expressing his views, orally or in writing, upon the question of the Baltic Provinces, acted from a feeling of bias or hostility. She even believed it to be her duty to declare in a piece published abroad that the accusations brought against Samarin, "which were circulated against him, springing from a barbaric, destructive, nationalistic hatred,"[7] were absolutely false. Realizing how much it must have cost Baroness Rahden to declare herself openly for him against the prejudice of her compatriots, Iu. Samarin wrote to her in this regard: "I think I am right in guessing that the act of justice which you have courageously performed on my behalf must have cost you a great deal of anguish."[8] This regard for Baroness Rahden and the desire to respect her natural sympathy for her compatriots made Iu. Samarin avoid touching upon this sore question in his letters or sending her those works of his which were published abroad. This consideration did not escape Baroness Rahden; she reproached her friend for not having noticed how the bad impression produced by the *Borderlands of Russia* had subsided and changed to his advantage. She blamed him for failing to trust her and, after having compared him ironically to a "fixed star," she wrote him (August 3, 1870): "You have not yet understood that I accept beforehand any attack from your good sword because I *believe* that it has not been *dipped in the poison of the redskins*, and that one recovers or one dies without bitterness from clean, honest wounds."[9] And so the issue was set aside which threatened to break forever the friendly relationship which had become established between Baroness Rahden and Iu. Samarin. In fact, once the conduct of the latter had been presented in a moral context and the quarrel reduced to a

[7]The phrase is in German. (Trans.)

[8]Letter of October, 1869, p. 128 (Trans.)

[9]The passage is on p. 164 (Trans.)

simple difference of opinion on the Baltic question, Baroness Rahden saw the principal reason disappear, not only for severing the bonds of friendship which drew her to Iu. Samarin, but even for breaking off any association with him. An inflexible Protestant, she insisted to such an extent upon liberty of opinion and liberty of conscience that she could not help but allow her friend the right to express his point of view upon the Baltic question freely, whether this point of view was distasteful to her or not. Nevertheless, that did not bring about a solution to the struggle which had been going on in her mind ever since the appearance of the *Borderlands of Russia.* Setting truth above all, she felt obliged to resolve the question of what side truth lay on, and who was right in this debate: was it Iu. Samarin, for whom she professed a profound esteem and on whose opinion she set the highest value, or was it her compatriots with whom she was united by the bonds of blood and religion? For her it was an insoluble question. That is why she followed with concealed emotion and anguish Samarin's polemic upon the Baltic question, without being able to stifle "the almost painful interest"[10] which the writings of her friend aroused in her. Yet the love of truth compelled her to judge this polemic with all possible impartiality and to yield forthrightly to the evidence of the facts. Thus, after having read the reply of Iu. Samarin to Schirren and Bock,[11] Baroness Rahden wrote to him (September 25, 1870): "I have still to thank you for the

[10]The passage is on p. 188 (Trans.)

[11]Messrs. Schirren and Bock, Baltic German polemicists, responded to Samarin in: C. Schirren, *Livlandische Antwort an Herrn Juri Samarin (The Livonian Answer to Iuri Samarin)* (Leipzig, 1869); and W. von Bock, *Russische Bekennungen wie sie . . . G. von Samarin enthüllt und bekennt. Von einem Beobachter (Russian Confessions as they are Revealed and Avowed by G. Samarin. Notes of an Observer)* (Leipzig, 1874). Samarin's answer is in "Otvet gg. Boku i shirrenu po povodu *'Okrain Rossii'*" ("The Answer to Messrs. Bock and Schiren on *The Borderlands of Russia*"), *Sochineniia Iu. F. Samarina,* VIII (Moscow, 1890), 315-418. (Ed.)

brochure which you sent me; it is written with a nobility and moderation which make the truths it contains very powerful."[12] But if natural sympathies prevented Baroness Rahden from facing the Baltic question in a completely impartial way, they gave her on the other hand the ability to observe and trace in artistic form certain aspects of the life of the Baltic Provinces which had escaped the attention of Iu. Samarin or to which he had not attached enough importance. Thus did Baroness Rahden bear herself with regard to the polemic of Iu. Samarin on the Baltic question. As for Samarin himself, he preserved his full freedom of action and of opinion, and did this to the degree that his awareness of his duty required; but in the name of friendship he sacrificed what most offended the sensitive feelings of the Baroness, that is, the bitterness and the passionate tone of his polemic with his foreign adversaries. Moreover, understanding how difficult it was for her to consider the Baltic question in an impartial way, he did his utmost to spare the innate sympathy she felt for her compatriots; that is why he never sought to make her declare on what side, in her opinion, truth lay in this controversy. "It is not always a happy thing to have been right," he wrote to the Baroness on August 23, 1870, "and an extorted confession can be just as painful for the person who receives it as for the person who, in making it, renders homage to truth in the face of his personal sympathies."[13]

If the Baltic question had not been able to break the bonds of friendship which linked Samarin with Baroness Rahden, by the same token the religious question was not to prove an obstacle to this friendship. Without at all thinking of exercising any sort of pressure upon the conscience of his friend, Iu. Samarin endeavoured to reveal to her the doctrine of the Orthodox church as Khomiakov had expounded it. For her part, she admitted that, in her words, "Protestantism

[12]The passage is on p. 171 (Trans.)

[13]The passage is on p. 167 (Trans.)

lays itself open to a thousand attacks, but it is strong with a holy arm which overcomes every misery: it seeks, it desires truth for its own sake";[14] as a result, she sought in good conscience to go thoroughly into whatever Samarin communicated to her on the subject of Orthodoxy. These communications, showing her the Orthodox religion in a new light, woke in her soul a sympathetic echo. Without renouncing Protestantism, she showed a profound respect for the Orthodox religion and loved the ceremonies of the Orthodox service which satisfied the religious impulse of her soul. In January of 1870 she wrote to her friend:

> As a Christian woman, everything that is Christian has a right to my most ardent sympathy—what, then, when it is a matter of the Church of the country that I belong to, a church which I venerate because I have learned to know it, and whose strength I value because of its gentleness! It is misunderstood, it is judged wrongly out of ignorance; how eagerly would I not seize upon every chance to show it in its true light. How gratifying would it not be for me to bring my grain of sand to a work of truth, which, in enlightening minds, must necessarily spark fraternal charity in men's hearts?[15]

Spurred by these feelings she attempted to spread among Catholics and Protestants accurate ideas about the Orthodox church. To this end she translated into German and published in Berlin the preface written by Samarin[16] for the theological works of Khomiakov, as well as the essay on the Church by the same author.

One may wonder just why, differing in opinion as they

[14]The passage is in the letter of November 12, 1868, on p. 87 (Trans.)

[15]The passage is on p. 142 (Trans.)

[16]"Predislovie k bogoslovskim socheneniiam A. S. Khomiakova," *Socheneniia Iu. F. Samarina,* VI (Moscow, 1887), 327-70. First edited and published in Prague, 1867. (Ed.)

did upon such essential questions, Samarin valued the friendship of Baroness Rahden so very highly. The explanation is that he experienced first and foremost a feeling of profound veneration for the high moral qualities of her soul; "he bowed before her rigid, inflexible conscience which he often consulted mentally in order to illuminate his own."[17] He was sincere when he wrote to his friend: "Ever since that terrible reprimand I once received with regard to the *Borderlands of Russia,* I have been a little afraid of you, and I cannot tell you just how happy I am to have this feeling. It is healthy and has nothing painful about it. If I did not experience it, I should be missing something that is necessary; ever since the death of Khomiakov I had lost all fear of anyone."[18] He enjoyed "her lucid and vigorous intelligence," upon which, he said, he had no hold. When Baroness Rahden proposed to translate into German the preface which he had written for the theological works of Khomiakov, he sketched the ideas of this writer and ended his letter in these words: "Pardon the length and lack of order in my letter. All those with whom I used to discuss these matters are now dead, and I experience an immense satisfaction in being able to come back to them with the private conviction that your intelligence will by itself make up for what I have not been able to say, or will set aside whatever I have said that is superfluous."[19]

Finally, Iu. Samarin greatly appreciated the literary talent of the Baroness, the astonishing faculty she had of tracing the slightest movements of thought, without effort, with a constant facility whether she was writing in German, her maternal tongue, or expressing herself in French; that is why he urged her many times to embrace the career of letters.

Shortly before her death, Baroness Rahden gave us

[17]An adaptation of a passage in the letter of November 20, 1868 on p. 91 (Trans.)

[18]The passage is on p. 159 (Trans.)

[19]The passage is on p. 101 (Trans.)

possession not only of the letters of Iu. Samarin, but those too which she had written to him. It goes without saying and one can easily understand that we could not publish the first without appending the second. The letters of Baroness Rahden are a complement to those of Iu. Samarin: without them, the correspondence of the latter would offer many obscure points and the counter view would remain unknown to the reader. Moreover, the letters of Baroness Rahden are remarkable in themselves: they cast a clear light upon the moral nobility of this exceptional woman.

Apart from a few passages concerning foreign personages and two or three expressions which are intemperate, we have felt obliged to publish *in extenso* and without any modification all of the letters which have been handed over to us.

The years and the dates placed in parentheses do not appear in the original; they have been added later by Baroness Rahden, when she set her correspondence with Iu. Samarin in order.

D. Samarin

CORRESPONDENCE

IU. SAMARIN TO BARONESS RAHDEN

Moscow, March 1 (1861).

Here, Mademoiselle, are the papers which Her Imperial Highness the Grand Duchess deigned to entrust to me. I append to them the outline of the communiqué for the newspapers, so as to publicize the information necessary for those who should like to enter into the community.[1] I have similarly written down a few observations upon the proposed rule.

If I have taken so long in fulfilling my obligations, it is because I have been short of time. No sooner had I arrived in Moscow then I saw myself assailed with questions and almost obliged to open a sort of public course upon emancipation. I have drawn up more than twelve "*Ustavnyia gramoty*."[2] People are beginning to think that emancipation might well come about some day, and to concern themselves with the plan that was worked out at Petersburg. This is in itself an indication of an awakening for which we should be thankful. Nevertheless, most people still seem to have certain doubts, so as to have an excuse for not shaking off this desperate torpor which is seen around here in the Biblical proportions of a plague sent by Providence to a corrupt people.[3]

Allow me to set at your feet the respectful homage of your very obedient servant.

[1]Probably a welfare or educational institution being established by the Grand Duchess Helen. (Ed.)

[2]Charters fixing peasant land allotments and obligations as a part of the Emancipation settlement of 1861. (Ed.)

[3]The phrase is in German. (Trans.)

BARONESS RAHDEN TO IU. SAMARIN

Petersburg, April 24 (1861).

Sir, I should have answered you and thanked you a long time ago on behalf of the Grand Duchess; if I did not do so, it is firstly because I was convinced that you were certain in advance of the grateful reception which would be given to your works—and, besides, laziness! You are not the one to excuse it, I know, but a frank admission, if it does not lessen faults, at least disarms anger and that is all that I need. Now shall I tell you that your rule or programme—the name does not matter—has been confirmed without any changes? No; it is still undergoing changes and I think that you will possibly be astonished to see the grooming your creation is undergoing and which is taking on quite a clerical style. As for the cassock, I can, thanks to my quality of heretic, quite properly decline to give an opinion; I even abandon the outposts and close myself away in the fortress of general principles, of which you are not ignorant and which will be better guarded, I hope, than Gaeta or Sevastopol.

Ah! how sad the Easter celebrations are for some of us at Petersburg! The unexpected nomination of a new minister of the interior makes little difference to me; I cannot say the same for the release of Miliutin[4] which causes me exceptional anguish. He needs a rest, he needs the leisure of a trip even for the sake of his political development; I have wanted this for him for a long time. But the way in which all of it has been done, that retirement into the senate, from which the ungrateful Roman people will have to go and fetch him some day, that disgrace and neglect after the complete, absolute,

[4]The dismissal of the minister of the interior, S. S. Lanskoi, and of his adjutant, N. A. Miliutin, immediately after the publication of the manifesto of February 19, 1861 was a move to placate the conservative party of the nobility. P. A. Valuev was named minister of the interior replacing Lanskoi. (D. S.)

disinterested sacrifice of so many years, oh! that is hard, and we, his friends, we feel it doubly, both for him and for ourselves.

I was also more affected than I can say by the tragedy which is happening in the C.[5] family; you probably know that he is in a mental home, and his wife, his poor young wife, is going to follow him there according to the way things look! The children break my heart. . . . Good God, what a lot of sadness and irremediable ills there are in this world! I leave you with this last reflection: may you never apply it to those whom you love; that is my very sincere and very cordial Easter wish. Kind regards.

IU. SAMARIN TO BARONESS RAHDEN

Lausanne, September 12, 1864.

Do not be afraid, Mademoiselle, it is not yet the "nevertheless"[6] which I have reserved for myself. The "nevertheless" will come later; for the moment it is a matter of St. Gothard. Permit me to pass on to you the results of my explorations and to beg you to please submit them to Her Imperial Highness the Grand Duchess, if you should judge it necessary.

The stone which bears the inscription pointed out by Mr. Chichachev is found at several hundred steps from the hospice. It is a block of granite, completely apart, a ready-made monument. Several steps behind (down the slope), the former road, which used to lead to the hotel, splits in two; from above, you can still make out the trace of two paved paths, one of which goes to the left and the other

[5]It has not been possible to identify the family referred to here. (Ed.)

[6]The word here and in the following sentence is in German: *dennoch.* (Trans.)

to the right of a hillock which dominates the entire area and which the French occupied. It is probably from this point that Suvorov directed the attack. To understand clearly what the men whom he called giants (*bogatyri*) did you have to see the site. The approach to the heights is so difficult that a battalion occupying them would seem enough to frustrate the efforts of an army. The stone bears two inscriptions. The first is the older; I can decipher only

"...................... 1804

"*Suvorovius victor* ....

......................."

The second was ordered much later, according to what my guide told me, by a Russian General (whose name I was not able to find out) for the price of 70 francs, from a stone mason who is still living. It is impossible to decipher a single word of it. The letters, which were barely traced out by the chisel, have become obliterated beneath the moss and the lichens which cover the rock. I believe, too, that the stone itself is not hard enough and that the best thing would be to set a plaque of marble into the block. As far as the inscription is concerned, it seems to me that it ought to be simple, short and precise, as for example: "In memory of Suvorov who, at the head of 0000 Russians, forced the St. Gothard pass defended by 0000 French, on such-and-such a date in the year of grace. . . . This plaque was set through the care of Her Imperial Highness the Grand Duchess Helen of Russia on such-and-such a date in the year of grace. . . ." Once the text has been drafted in French or in Russian, in order to translate it into good Latin you should go to Professor Kossovich in Petersburg or to Leont'ev in Moscow. These are practically the only people around here who are incapable of committing a barbarism.

To come back to the locale: a little higher than the block

and quite close to the hospice can be seen a ruined chapel which dominates the road. I do not know if Mr. Chichachev spoke about it, but it is this that is particularly worthy of attention. This chapel already existed at the time the Russians passed; it rested upon a vault, and it is beneath this vault that, after the victory, those of our soldiers who paid with their lives were buried pell-mell. Since that time the chapel has fallen into ruin; the wall, on the side which faces the road, has split right down to the vault, which has collapsed, leaving the bones bare and allowing in snow and rain. Looking through the crevice, I saw a heap of skulls, broken ribs and all sorts of bones whitened by the rain and sun. The guide who was following me proposed carrying off a skull as a souvenir. This is what he said to me while contemplating with a melancholy air these abandoned bones: "Poor people! They came from very far to die for a cause which after all was foreign to them, and they were certainly mourned more among their own people than they were appreciated among us. The federal government has not even accorded them a suitable burial place!" Since the happy idea came to the Grand Duchess to consecrate the feat of arms of Suvorov by means of a commemorative inscription, will she not also be willing to restore the chapel and to have the bones of our soldiers covered over with a little earth? In any case, before undertaking anything, I think that it would be wise to consult the work of Miliutin[7] upon the campaign of Suvorov. All of the necessary information must be there. As far as I am concerned, I can only vouch for what I have seen and repeat what my guide told me.

I took a charming trip on foot to the valleys of Grindelwald and Lauterbrunn, but you will certainly believe me when I add that the magnificent sights which I admired did not prevent me from clearly remembering the charms of our stay at Ragatz. Shall I dare beg you to lay my respectful

[7] D. A. Miliutin, *History of the War of 1799 between Russia and France.* (D. S.)

homage at the feet of the Grand Duchess and to please keep a kindly memory of your devoted servant.

IU. SAMARIN TO BARONESS RAHDEN

Ostende, September 28/16, 1864.[7a]

I present myself to you now, dear lady, as a defendant, with my "nevertheless" which is conditional and unfortunately comes a bit late. I am willing to risk it, for I am not aware of any ill will. I owe you the whole truth, or more precisely, what I believe to be the truth. Just listen to me and let me hope that, even if you should not absolve me of every accusation, my sincere confession will perhaps still contribute to removing the misunderstanding which is between us, for, in the final analysis, it is a misunderstanding and nothing more.[8]

In order to simplify the question, let me restrict it. Let us first take the Baltic Provinces in themselves, *an und für sich* (as Hegel would say), not taking into consideration the bond which holds them to Russia and the relationships which spring from this. Let us forget about Russia and suppose these three provinces completely independent, or else connected by some sort of hyphen either to Prussia or to Sweden. Let us first speak of the Germans in their own country; later if you wish, we shall get to the Germans in our country, or to the position which they occupy at the heart of the government.

The order of things which holds in Livonia, in Estonia and in Courland rests upon a vault of privileges, whose inviolability has been proclaimed quite clearly. This is the strong

[7a]West European countries dated by the Gregorian calendar (new style) which was 12 days ahead of the Julian calendar (old style) being used in Russia when this correspondence took place. (ed.)

[8]The paragraph is in German. (Trans.)

side, the entrenched position of the three provinces, and it is still on these favourite grounds that questions, which daily necessities gave rise to, have been based. Every time one has tried to reform the communal organization, to free industry of the shackles which the wardenships and masterships have fastened upon it, or to touch the laws which restrict the right to acquire real estate outside of the city, the opposition, from which the government has always backed away, has never done anything but skate over the essential problem, leaving aside the opportuneness and the justice of what was desired, restricting itself to the question of strict legality. "Your bill trespasses upon our privileges, therefore it is condemned." Generally there was no progress beyond that point! Had discussion once been accepted upon this terrain there would have been a chance to begin, by realizing the value and the extent of privileges *en masse* and with individual persons. Yet this work still remains to be done. I am not the one, of course, to undertake it. I shall limit myself, in passing, to two observations: firstly, among what are conventionally called privileges, there are a number whose authenticity is completely beyond doubt: such, for example, is the famous diploma of King Sigismond-August, rightly called the Grand Charter of the Livonian nobility, yet whose authenticity the Swedish government (which knows something about it) has never been willing to recognize. Secondly, if you were to look a little more closely at it, you would discover that many privileges embrace something quite different from what they seem to. For example, the corporation of businessmen or the great guild of Riga appropriates, by virtue of a privilege of the twelfth or thirteenth century, exclusive grazing rights on a piece of land abutting on the town; however, in this privilege it is not a question of the guild, but of the entire town as a corporation, or in other words, of the totality of the bourgeoise. It would be easy to multiply the examples, but this would, I admit, be a fastidious and pointless job. What does the legal value of such and such a sheet of parchment matter anyway, if it turns out that during a number of years and even during our own days the sense which is attributed to it rightly or wrongly serves as a basis for rights recognized by the law which governs the country? I am therefore completely ready to accept privileges *en bloc*, as a starting point, but I tell you that I would be quite unable to recognize in principle that a privilege, even undisputed, should be accepted as an insurmountable barrier to any progress.

What, after all, is a privilege? Whoever says privilege says exception to the common law, a favour or exemption for certain people, an overburden or restriction for most; in other words, whoever says privilege says a trampling of private right upon the domain of public right or of free activity. Such are in effect the general features which make of the Baltic Provinces an exception to everything that can be seen in Europe. I realize that in the Middle Ages, when servitude and arbitrariness were the general rule, liberty could scarcely see the light of day but by way of privilege, so no one can question the historical legitimacy of the fact; but is this a sufficient reason to perpetuate the sixteenth century right into the nineteenth? The same authority which justified privilege in the past, and I mean by "authority" the law of historical necessity, condemns it today. Since the end of the last century, in all of the states of Europe, including England, has internal legislation been anything else but a revision of the rights acquired by privilege, with a view to submitting them to the grand principles which govern modern societies? Alone in the entire world the Baltic Provinces have not followed the general movement. Furthermore, taking the term privilege in the sense which it acquires in opposition to the general law, nothing is truer than to say that even today you do not see anything there but privileges and privileged people.

What strikes you in the first place is the great line of demarcation which splits Baltic society in two. On the one hand the Germans, who are of *the good German Nation:*[9]

[9] The phrase is in German. (Trans.)

these are the privileged people. On the other hand what do you find? These are neither Russians, nor Finns, but the totality of those to whom Providence has refused the favour of being born Germans. Juridical language and local custom designate them with the very revealing name of *Undeutsche.*[10] This single word is particularly revealing in itself. In actual fact, they are not even distinct races, albeit of an inferior order, or recognized as distinct races, but rather they constitute a purely negative element, a nothingness which cannot be defined except as opposed to the German race, a foil, created to set it off in all its brilliance. And please believe that if I insist upon underlining the significance of the word, the fact is that here the word stands perfectly for the thing. As the Germans say: *the concept is embodied in every respect in practice.*[11] There you have, then, a nationality *par excellence* which proclaims the negation of every other nationality. This is the first aspect of privilege—the privilege of race.

Let us go on and take firstly a look at the towns. At the head of each municipality there appears a corporation which exercises justice and directs the public weal—*der Rath.*[12] It does not receive any mandate and is self-generating; therefore, it governs and itself judges its aptitude to govern. The bulk of the bourgeoisie has nothing to do with it. This is the exercise of power, the right of judging and administering, by right of privilege. What do those being governed think of this? In the seventeenth century the bourgeois of Riga gratified their borough masters with the rather un-parliamentary title of great harpies (*the great harpies who sit in the town hall and gorge themselves with public property*);[13] since that time the language has softened, but the relations are basically the same.

[10]Non-Germans. (Trans.)

[11]The phrase is in German. (Trans.)

[12]Council. (Trans.)

[13]The phrase is in German. (Trans.)

Further down you will again come across the wardenships and masterships of the Middle Ages in full bloom. This is privilege exploiting the domain of industry to the detriment of the consumers and especially the working class. We know full well that attempts have been made to mitigate the excessive harshness of the regime which, in order to make a small number of select people prosper, shuts out from any career those who have not had the good fortune to be sheltered by any privilege whatsoever—but unfortunately the law has remained a dead issue. In practice it is the statutes, the rulings, the local customs (*the commendable habits*[14]) which prevail. Furthermore, it must be said, the law itself, while setting up principles that seem quite broad, has done nothing to assure their realization; and, moreover, in leaving the corporations of privileged people with their almost discretionary power, it has assured them of the possibility of making their self-centered mind predominate, which is what legislation seemed aimed at combatting. So, for example, the law abstains from promulgating in principle that, in order to obtain a benefice (a sort of sinecure with remuneration), or in order to be qualified to fill a public function, it be absolutely necessary to be German and to belong to the Augsburg confession. This is an immense step forward. Nevertheless, even though businessmen of Russian origin, settled at Riga and bourgeois of the city, are numerous enough, even though there are among them a goodly number of rich men, enlightened and perfectly honourable, there is no instance of any of them ever having obtained a benefice or been called to a public function. People have even had the candour to let them realize that it was their quality as Russians, or rather as non-Germans, which constituted their incompetency. Even though this systematic exclusion was contrary to the spirit of the law, it was perfectly invulnerable on legal terrain, and I shall show you why.

In order to obtain a benefice or to occupy a public

[14]The phrase is in German. (Trans.)

charge, it is not sufficient to enjoy the right of citizenship and to bear its obligations; it is further necessary, and absolutely so, to be accepted as a member of a *confrérie* (*Bruderschaft*). Brotherhood means a clique of privileged persons at the head of a body of privileged persons. However, the brotherhood of a great guild, while it does possess the rights of a political corporation which represents the entire class of businessmen, passes itself off as a semi-religious congregation, or rather as a charitable organization having as its mission to comfort the poor and to watch over the interests of the Protestant cult. What then is more natural than the article of this brotherhood's statute which sets the Protestant religion as a condition for eligibility? Here you put your finger on privilege. Repulsed by their fellow citizens, the Russian businessmen appealed higher. Then began the trial about which I have spoken to you and of which the following dialogue will give you the substance.

The Russians: For almost 180 years our ancestors and ourselves have been carrying on business in Riga; we are bourgeois of the town and, by this right, we bear equally with our fellow citizens the share which is ours of the communal burdens; however, we are still on the footing of foreigners and we have no part in directing public affairs. Try to pull us out of a position which seems wrong to us and which we find humiliating.

The government: What are you complaining about? The law recognizes that you are qualified for any public function, it places you on exactly the same footing as your fellow citizens of German origin and does not accord to them any privilege from which you are excluded.

The Russians: Yes! The law! But apart from the law there is quite a pronounced *parti pris* which it seems not to have foreseen. It is the means of admission to the brotherhood which serves as a pretext to shut us off from any access to public life, and since the law has not touched upon it, it has done nothing for us.

The government: What do you expect! The brotherhood

is concerned with its privileges and we would not dare infringe upon them.

The Russians: All right, fine! If, because there is privilege, you accept that a coterie which passes itself off as a private association should handle public functions, if you insist so strongly upon remaining within the limits of historical tradition, please remember that the privileges which are in force today did not spring into being all at once. History teaches us that as a new group gradually formed itself within the heart of the municipality or separated itself from the mass, it had itself recognized as a distinct corporation and obtained a privilege. Why should it not be the same today? We are not wanted in the existing brotherhood, we are isolated against our will. Well, we are resigned to it; but in that case do for us what formerly the grand masters, the archbishops and the kings of Poland did: grant us a charter and let us constitute ourselves a corporation. If it is not asking too much, we should like to obtain at Riga rights which are analogous to those enjoyed by the Tartars at Kazan and by the Jews in all of the towns of the empire where entry is not forbidden to them (*this is textual*).

The government: You must be joking! Russians as a distinct corporation in the very center of German provinces! But that would be stirring up a storm. Resign yourselves and leave us in peace . . . .

That is how things go on under the regime of privilege. Notice that I do not stress the arguments which the petitioners might have used as members of the nationality which dominates in the state; suppose, instead of them, Frenchmen or Spaniards having the rights of bourgeoisie and the essence of the question will remain the same.

If ever you should leaf through the code of the Baltic Provinces, you will not find either that, in order to earn one's bread by mending clothes, it is absolutely necessary to be received by the mastership as a master tailor, or that it is almost indispensable to marry the daughter of a tailor (*to marry in one's guild*[15]). But customs speak louder than law. I recall a poor workman whose tale I wrote of before. As an apprentice tailor he had the misfortune to displease his master in baring his heart elsewhere than at the feet of his daughter; the master put him out, and since among three privileged tailors understanding is easy, it was impossible for him to get a job in another workshop. In order to live he was reduced to seeking furtively for some button to sew on or to work in hiding. The police trailed him like a rabbit at bay (*Bönhase*, a technical term), and every time that he was caught with a needle in his hand, he was made to pay a fine. Every craft being considered as a privilege of a certain corporation (*als Bürgernahrung*), it follows that, under the regime of privilege, he who wishes to may not be able to work.

Let us pass on now to the towns in the country. Here you will find privilege armed from tip to toe, helmet on head and lance in hand. It is land which, in the absence of free competition, constitutes the hereditary prerogative of a closed corporation; moreover, it is the exercise of authority as a seigniorial policy, which, by virtue of privilege welded to landed property, is presented in the guise of private right. I shall not stress the characteristic traits of institutions with which you are more familiar than I; but to show how far the assumptions which derive from it can go, let me cite you an example. Quite recently the idea came to the government to sell to the highest bidder some of the domains belonging to the Crown; I think it was in Estonia. It was a matter, naturally, not of the land possessed by the peasants and already bought back by them (*Bauerland*), but solely of farms, forests, pasturages and cultivated land which constituted *Hofland* or Crown land. The nobility protested against the admission to bidding of purchasers who were not members of the nobiliary body, and the governor-general became its spokesman. Here is the essence of the reasoning which was put forward. All real estate belonging or having belonged to a lord (the state too is considered to be a lord) constitutes

[15]The phrase is in German. (Trans.)

UNIVERSITY
OF BRISTOL
LIBRARY
W.M.L.

forever an administrative unity which nothing can dissolve and at whose head is the lord. This unity includes not only the royal land (*Hofland*) but also that which the peasants possess, even if it were to be *bought back by them* and cleared of all debt. In the same way the peasants, proprietors of this land, even though free and even though released, *as far as the land is concerned*, from all obligation vis-à-vis the lord—the peasants remain nonetheless forever subject to his jurisdiction. It is, as you can see, the perpetuity of serfdom under another name. However, if, by the fact of an act of sale, a capitalist who was not a member of the body of the nobility (as for example a bourgeois or a Russian nobleman) should happen to acquire some Crown land, one of two things would necessarily result. Either he would acquire at the same time seigniorial rights as far as policy is concerned, which would be a flagrant infraction of the prerogatives of the body of nobles, or on the other hand these rights themselves would be extinguished. But then the peasants housed within the sight of the manor would find themselves freed from all patrimonial jurisdiction, they would become independent in fact; a small group of *Undeutsche* would come no longer to feel the pressure of the lord. That would mean the ruin of the entire social order. I do not know how the question was settled.

The peasants of the Baltic Provinces are free, aren't they? This freedom, this right to carry their work wherever it may please them, I have heard it proclaimed quite loudly in order to make it be understood that there was no occasion for the law to intervene in the agrarian question. But would you like to know what the freedom of the peasants is becoming in the face of the omnipotent interest of the privileged class? Two or three years ago a few Livonian peasants, after having fulfilled all the required formalities, left the country to come and establish themselves in Russia. I believe there were Russian proprietors who, fearing a scarcity of workers, engaged them to establish themselves in Russia. Others, apparently, prepared to follow them. As soon as the news spread, the nobility became alarmed. The phantom of a mass emigration was set before the eyes of the governor-general, he was shown the people in movement, the country depopulated, the proprietors ruined and all of the things which ordinarily are shown to the authorities when it is a matter of bringing about an iniquitous action. This was not done in vain. The governor-general took a broad jump over the law and by his own authority established a personal tax of the heaviest sort which any peasant had to pay before passing the frontier of the Provinces. The effect, as you can see, was to make this liberty, which was supposedly already acquired, be bought once more. The ordinance was published in the gazette of Riga, but care was taken not to submit the matter to Petersburg; it was only later and by accident that the measure taken by the governor-general came to the knowledge of the government, and it was, I believe, the senate which did away with it. Certainly this was expected, but what does it matter? The end was achieved, the emigration had ended.

Whatever may be my personal sympathies or antipathies, I am quite willing to recognize that an aristocratic government may, like any other, have its reason for being and its historical legitimacy, but I believe that it is only on one condition, and that is that it be popular. It is necessary that the masses, kept in trusteeship by a minority in power, recognize themselves in it and accept it as the personification of their instincts and their wishes; this minority must feel itself supported, if not by sympathies, at least by the confidence it inspires. I scarcely dare to ask if such are the connections between the corporations of nobles and the Finnish populations subject to their domination. Almost fifty years ago a Livonian author (Merkel or Ianau?) said in speaking of his country: "*The Russian bayonets only protect German despotism in Livonia.*"[16] Would this phrase not be true even in our own days? I am inclined to believe so, when I think of the terrors which periodically besiege this so proud nobility, and the cry of alarm which it sent from Mitau to Petersburg when it happened to catch a priest of the Church chatting

[16]The quotation is in German. (Trans.)

with a peasant, or when, for example, an employee of Russian origin arrived on a mission in the Provinces. Is this the attitude, is this the bearing of an aristocracy set square upon its base and sure of its authority?

Can this order of things last?

Ever since the day when the abolition of serfdom was promulgated here, the peasants have gone back under the regime of common law and every privilege has ceased; they fully enjoy an absolute autonomy in the direction of their communal affairs; almost a third already enjoy the ownership of their ground without any debt whatsoever; finally, a new law admits rural populations on a perfectly equal footing with the bourgeoisie and the nobility into the provincial assemblies, which have been called to take into their own hands the directing of local affairs. But nothing of what is being done here is penetrating into the Baltic Provinces: statute labour, servitudes and seigniorial rights are perpetuated in the shadow of privilege; there, people speak enough about repurchase of land to prevent a legislative intervention, but without seriously wishing any; there is certainly a semblance of communal or parishional organization, but we know, however, that it is all only so much pretence as long as seigniorial power weighs upon the commune; as far as admitting peasants to the provincial assemblies, the person who spoke of it would risk being stoned.

I am possibly wrong in establishing this parallel. Care has been taken to inculcate in us that the principles which direct the legislation of the empire have nothing to do with the essentially German institutions of the Baltic Provinces; we have even been told that it would be doing violence to the historical tradition to wish even to take into consideration what is being done here, when it is a question of deciding what should be done in Livonia or in Courland. Never mind that. Let us again forget Russia and look elsewhere. Let us turn our eyes towards Germany, let us glance over it in every direction; let us question Prussia, Saxony, Bavaria, Austria, even Hungary. Everywhere common law and free competition have done away with privilege; scarcely anyone remembers anymore the wardenships and masterships; as far as servitudes and seigniorial rights are concerned, you will find them now only in the form of debris marking the route which the nations have followed in the way of progress.

Do you want one last test? Question the privileged people themselves. Certainly, I do not expect that the property owners should come and take action against seigniorial rights which constitute them judges and parties in their suits; neither will it be the three privileged boot makers of a small town, who today possess the exclusive privilege of deforming the feet of their fellow citizens, who will set themselves up, as far as boots are concerned, as the apostles of free enterprise. But try to bring the privileged people into confrontation: ask the petty bourgeoisie what it thinks of the directing of public revenues by a privileged body; interrogate the manufacturers and the proprietors about the regime of the masterships; find out what the bourgeois think of the privileges of the nobility. Each time I have tried the test, I have found myself in the centre of a crossfire, and the revelations that I have heard always went much beyond what I might have supposed. Nevertheless I must add that the war privileged people make among themselves ceases, giving way to a tacit truce, the very instant that the shadow of the government can be perceived in the distance, or the moment they sense themselves facing the interest of the *Undeutsche*.

Again, can all that last?

Many a time I have heard it said that the Baltic Provinces should recognize their mission of initiating Russia to the advantages and benefits of civilization. Generally we are still considered to be unable to draw from other resources. I will agree! But then why not preach by example? Above all why allow oneself to have been overtaken on the agrarian question? I shall tell you. It is instinctively felt that any reform, any progress, would have as an inevitable result the lowering of two barriers: that, firstly, which closes public life to the mass of the indigenous people, and that, too, which separates the three Provinces from the rest of the empire. Even so, however, there is a staunch opposition to any fusion. You can quite properly say that it is not the originality of the present-day institutions which brings isolation as a consequence; it is, on the contrary, isolation which is sought as an end, and it is to maintain it that they cling to vicious and worm-eaten institutions. Separated forever from the great Germanic mainstream, the colony of Germans which reigns over the three Provinces wishes neither to raise the mass of the *Undeutsche* to its level, nor to condescend to fraternize with us. I must say that in my opinion it is a wrong and a mistake, possibly even more in its own interest than in ours. It means shutting oneself off from any political future.

That is what I said in 1848[17] and what gained me the reputation you know of. I repeat it today calling on you to be my judge. See if that is the language of an enemy. My subject has not been exhausted, but that is quite enough already for a first time. If you want me to continue, give me a word of encouragement, addressing it General Delivery at Paris. Above all tell me if you still consider me hostile with premeditation.

I beg you to accept the expression of the profound respect of your devoted servant.

BARONESS RAHDEN TO IU. SAMARIN

Lausanne, September 28/October 10, (1864).

You are very good, Sir, to have kept your word so fully—and I am very grateful to you for doing so. I shall await with impatience the continuation which you make me hope for: does that not show you what complete confidence your sincerity of judgment inspires in me? That is where I ought to

[17] Letters written from Riga (*Pis'ma iz Rigi*). See Vol. VII of the *Works of Iu. Samarin.* (D. S.)

stop if I were wise, *und dennoch*—I must add a few comments to what I have just written. Nations in their childhood speak in allegories and allow themselves to use imagery which philosophic precision of a more advanced age no longer admits. The intelligence of women will, I fear, always keep this taste of young peoples; I claim it for myself today in order to express my thought such as I *feel* it. Have you ever seen a skillfully traced portrait of a person who is dear to you or even only well known, whose features are reproduced with complete unimpeachable fidelity, and which you look at nevertheless without, in the face of this inflexible truthfulness, finding any fault, but you are left with the possibly mute but very vital protestation of your heart, which repeats ceaselessly: Yet that is not how it is! By dint of striving to understand instinctively what is missing in the portrait, one could manage little by little, I imagine, to rationalize his interior contradiction and he might say to himself: this portrait has everything, except *life*; in drawing it the painter did not experience for his model the sympathy which establishes bonds of clairvoyance between individuals, consequently he *was not able* to conceive and reproduce the *true life* of the person whom he was drawing, to conserve in it his own originality, to give to it the expression of his soul . . . . Will you pardon me, Sir, if I add that that is the impression which your letter made upon me? It is beyond me to challenge the exactitude of the facts which you record in it, I believe as you do that there is such-and-such a privilege which has become an anachronism, such-and-such an age-old injustice which it would be desirable to reform; I am even persuaded that, with you and me, the small handful of impartial men scattered throughout the Provinces will say without hesitation that these abuses, which are contrary to the spirit of the age and of human justice in its absolute sense, are approaching their end, condemned by their very principle and swept irresistibly by the force of circumstances. But, they will still say, let us not consider the Baltic Provinces from the point of view of a party or of an age, let us look at them in the conditions which *are theirs alone*, and which, consequently, determine the *only* really fair point of view to be taken with regard to them. Forgotten, so to speak, in the midst of the great European movement, cast from one foreign suzerainty to another, these three little German provinces have, by extraordinary efforts of concentration, kept their national character, their historic rights and their feudal organization intact. This concentration has not managed to avoid a natural though lamentable excess: it has to a large extent become a caste egotism carried to the blindest obstinacy. On the other hand, however, the wealth of honesty, culture, perseverance, loyalty and rectitude which is found generally in the provinces is due only to their isolation up until now; and in this respect the instinctive terror with which the aristocracy defend their privileges is not merely a matter of nobiliary and nationalist coemption: they *feel* and they *know* what they have saved of the *moral heritage* of their forefathers, and with the strength of a somewhat narrow-minded but respectable Germanic passive resistance they cling to the ramparts which have defended them for six hundred years. There is one other virtue that plays a greater role than is realized in the combined action of the three provinces, and that is the sincere respect for legal right. From their point of view, they *are within their rights.* In order not to anger what it best in them, in order not to upset the most solid bases of the public conscience, they *themselves* must be left the task of reforming, *slowly*, *in keeping with the character of their nationality*, without shocks and without violence, all that is backward and iniquitous in their traditional customs. You think that they would show more political sense in freely amalgamating themselves with Russia. I do not think so. The *political* future of the Germans of our Baltic provinces is really just a myth. It seems to me that I made a very frank admission to you on this subject at Ragatz. With very rare exceptions, the level of intelligence in our provinces is very mediocre, it is exceptional to find a capable person there. The humble conditions[18] in which my compatriots are born and are brought up reinforce so to speak the good and the bad sides of their natural aptitudes and make of them a nursery of useful mediocrities. I have never considered the provinces other than as a ballast (should I say an indispensable ballast) to the great Slavic ship which we see cleaving the agitated waves of the century with a boldness which is close to audacity. It is from this point of view that the virtues which privilege shelters ought to be looked at with a more lenient eye. Baltic aristocracy is of a mediocre calibre: names that are old but obscure, ordinary fortunes but generally rather diffused, capabilities which are solid, persevering, clear, though neither broad nor brilliant—is that not the natural element to fill the immense gap which exists between the great Russian political organizations at the top of things and the as yet undeveloped mass at the bottom of the social ladder? It is exclusivism of race, language and religion which has produced through the centuries the result we see; an exceptional position has inordinately prolonged a few historic anachronisms: is it fair to look only at them? Would it not be more fair to consider them as the regrettable flaws of precious qualities? Are you quite sure that in violently breaking down the dikes you are not going to wash away the qualities along with the flaws? Is it not more consistent with the wisdom of a true governmental policy, wherever no danger threatens, wherever good services are rendered tacitly, to let events develop according to the character and habits of the interested parties without *cutting* the Gordian knot for the pleasure of being done with it all the sooner? Never will you be able to communicate to a German population the proverbial carefreeness, the rash capacity for self-sacrifice, the indifference for traditional law, the breadth of views, the innate tolerant geniality of the Russian people. These characteristic traits are more likeable and much more attractive than anything that the German character offers. But is it a matter of knowing what one *loves the best*, or rather what *is*

[18] *Kleine Verhältnisse.* (Trans.)

and what it would be fair to accept as it is, shrugging one's shoulders and laughing if you wish, but without hatred and without envy? Do not forget that Germany has always had an almost sentimental piety toward ruins; it has always let those buildings crumble which it could no longer hold up, without knocking them down violently or artificially razing them; it admires with pride their splendid proportions right up to the moment of their collapse. Slowly built, stone by stone, the castles of the Middle Ages seem to call for a decent end, and they fall beneath a hand of time which produces other works which are more powerful. Build beside the outdated privileges of the Baltic provinces a real, serious, honest liberty, as pure as it is strong, and soon you will no longer have anything feudal to deplore; what you call shadows must imperceptibly give way to light, if it is a real light. But until that time, respect a half-light which has a bit of good in it. I am reproducing to some extent the arguments of those who preach against liberty of conscience, I fully realize. But have I not heard myself told a thousand times on behalf of the Orthodox church what I argue more or less for the Baltic provinces: be careful not to open the gate, the real life there will perhaps escape. Except I do not go that far, I do not object to having the gates opened, but I would like to see those who have closed them accorded the right to turn the key in the lock themselves, without having too zealous benefactors come and smash them down with axes.

It is extremely late, Sir, I have let myself be dragged on to such a string of commentaries that I am almost ashamed. The very rapid résumé of what we have said to one another would possibly be this: you are Russian and I am German. Permit me to add again that Russians and Germans can meet, in spite of their most diverse opinions, in the sincere desire to arrive at the *truth*; and does not the truth lie in the goodwill with which one faces men and things?

I was almost forgetting a serious reproach which I have to address to you: you do not say anything of your health. Do not overlook it the next time you send me a word, I beg you. My best wishes.

We are leaving on the 3/15th from Lausanne, we will spend the 6/18th and the 7/19th in Baden and we shall be in Russia on the twentieth of October according to our calendar.

IU. SAMARIN TO BARONESS RAHDEN

Brussels, October 17 (1864).

Your kind letter, Mademoiselle, reached me yesterday; I had it sent on from Paris, my stay at Brussels being prolonged more than I had planned. I owe you new evidence of a truth that I am always happy to be able to note even though it is as old as the world and even though it may seem quite banal: that is, that one does not completely understand the spirit of an institution, a society, just as for a person, except when one loves it and only to the extent that one loves it. The fathers of the Church in insisting upon the difference between what they call exterior knowledge and interior knowledge, the only type which to their eyes has any merit, do not understand anything else. I have been able, from my point of view, more or less to diagnose the Baltic Provinces (to use medical terminology), or in other words to indicate what is abnormal and sickly in their constitution; you have felt and shown what makes them live. In this respect, I can only agree with you, with nevertheless a few reservations. That is, for example, it seems to me that you make too light of the political future of the Baltic Provinces and particularly of the individual value of the men which they have furnished us and which they can still furnish us. It can be seen that the local conditions[19] will not form great citizens for the very reason that the notion of homeland is foreign to the German colony. The three provinces in themselves do not constitute a country, they are only a possession; they will have none of Russia

[19]*Local-Verhältnisse.* (Trans.)

as a homeland. As far as Germanism[20] is concerned, this is only an abstraction which can be cherished and caressed as an idea but has no hold on the person. On the other hand, for many reasons which it would be too long to enumerate, these same conditions favour more than any others the developing of great personal capabilities especially in the domain of practical action. Let it suffice to cite as examples Sievers as an administrator, Fersen, Barclay, Todtleben and so many others as men of war.

To give you the essence of my thought, I would still have to place before you several observations on the position of the Germans among us, on the political principle that they represent in the heart of the government. Here it is impossible to refer to palpable facts; it would be necessary to specify tendencies and I confess that in thinking about it I wondered how to manage to avoid the suggestion of exaggeration or even of malevolent interpretation. The task seemed difficult to me but fortunately I discovered that someone else had accomplished it for me. You will surely have had in your hands the latest brochure of Schédo-Ferotti[21] (the eighth study: "What will be done with Poland?")—that famous brochure about which Golovnin[22] has made so much noise. Read over again, I beg you, pages 210, 249, 292 and 293. You will find there firstly a declaration of devotion together with an allusion to the services which the natives of the Baltic Provinces would render to the dynasty in lining up with crossed bayonets around the throne

[20]*Deutschthum* connoting German primacy. (Trans.)

[21]Schedo-Ferotti was the pseudonym of an engineer and publicist, F. I. Firks (1812-72), who gained some fame for his works on Russian domestic affairs including the peasant and Polish questions. On the peasant question he advocated very gradual emancipation extending over a twenty-year period. (Ed.)

[22]A. V. Golovnin (1821-86) was the Minister of Education (1862-66). As Minister he pursued a moderately liberal educational policy towards the universities and secondary schools. In 1866 he was replaced by the reactionary D. A. Tolstoy. (Ed.)

in the supposed case of a struggle between the dynastic interest and the interest of the country. Further on, there is the cherished ideal of a grand denationalized empire which would no longer be, in its ensemble, either Russian or Polish or German, but in which all the nationalities, remaining completely foreigners to one another, would live each in his corner, without anyone of them being authorized to consider itself as *the* nation;[23] it would be, so to speak, the reproduction on a very large scale of the hotel Ragatz, where Russians, Americans and French would come, without knowing one another, and sit at the same table. The great merit of the author is in having completed the nomenclature of the provinces which are a part of the empire but which we Russians ought forever to consider as foreigners for us. That is the term that the author uses. To Livonia, to Poland and to Finland he is careful to add the Caucasus. Finally, you will see rise above the denationalized state the great figure of the sovereign who, while being quite willing to let himself be worshipped by his Russian family like a legitimate father, would not give himself to it body and soul but would retain the advantage of possessing moreover a half-dozen other families of German, Polish and even Circassian origin. That is what might be called polygamy raised to the level of a duty and set up as a political system. This system, you know, is not the invention of the author; he found it ready-made. It is a doctrine, a school, represented by our most highly placed people, patronized by at least two ministeries,[24] protected by censure and which it is unwise to attack. To grasp its implications fully it is sufficient to apply it in principle to another country. Instead of Russia, its sovereign, Poland, Finland and the Caucasus, let us suppose the British Empire, the king of England, Ireland, the Indies and Australia; let us suppose a group of Irish representing England in Paris,

[23] *Als Stamm.* (Trans.)iginal. (Trans.)

[24] Iu. Samarin is certainly alluding to the minister of the interior (P. A. Valuev) and to that of public education (A. V. Golovnin). (D. S.)

Vienna, Berlin and Petersburg, commanding at least half the English regiments, occupying a third of the most important posts in all branches of the public service, and coming to urge the king to make pure-blooded English understand that it is wrong for them to consider themselves, by virtue of being the creators, as the masters of the British Empire, and that after all in Ireland, in the Indies, and in Australia an Englishman is only a foreigner. Let us add that in order to make themselves heard these same Irishmen are careful to insinuate to the seat of authority that the less one values the country the more one feels himself apt to serve the dynasty in face of and against everyone. What would the English think of that?

What they would think of it is exactly what explains the all too regrettable antagonism which we see among us between what is German and what feels itself to be Russian. It is sad, but whose fault is it? One has to get used to it: we Russians claim to be in Russia what the French are in France and the English are upon all of the territory of the British possessions.

To close my profession of faith upon this subject let me say this to you once again: I bow with respect and grateful acknowledgement before the great German figures who have served my country and are still serving it; as far as the system begun and represented by the Germans is concerned, inasmuch as it is a politial party, it is a razor blade passed between the nation's heart and head, it is a poison injected into the most sensitive fibres of the social body, a solvent which is far more dangerous than the propaganda of Herzen,[25] and possibly the only solvent which we have to fear.

Now that I have finished my confession, permit me to lead you onto completely different, but less slippery and more solid, ground. I have had translated into English and

[25] A. I. Herzen (1812-70), the outstanding Westernizer, philosopher and publicist, was very close to the Slavophils, including Samarin and K. Aksakov to 1844, when the conflict of their political and religious views (Herzen was a revolutionary and atheist) proved to be an irreconcilable obstacle to continued friendship. (Ed.)

printed up one of the theological essays of the late Khomiakov.[26] It is a statement of our Church's doctrine about itself, about the manner of understanding unity in matter of faith and the different manifestations of divine grace. Permit me to offer you a copy of it, and to ask you to deposit another one in the library of Her Highness, the Grand Duchess. I shall not be able to send them to you before you leave Baden so they shall be sent directly to Michael Palace in Petersburg.

A thousand most sincere thanks for the interest you take in my health. In spite of the cold I have persisted in taking sea baths up until October 10 and have greatly benefited from them. In any case one would have to be moribund not to revive in contact with the sea. In four or five days I am leaving for Paris.

Let me set at your feet the respectful homage of your completely devoted servant.

P.S. Please excuse my scribbling: I have a pin instead of a pen, and watered coal instead of ink.

IU. SAMARIN TO BARONESS RAHDEN

Moscow, November 11/23, (1865).

It was only yesterday, Mademoiselle, on my arrival in Moscow that I received your letter of September 17 from Ragatz. Let me first of all give a word of explanation for this long delay. Prince Odoevski, to whom the package containing your letter was addressed, thought it best to keep it at his house for a month and a half; this time having passed and after careful consideration he seized his courage in his two

[26] Treatise on the dogma of the Church by A. S. Khomiakov. This treatise was published in Vol. II of the complete collection of his work. (D. S.)

hands and sent it mysteriously, though by the agency of two persons, to my sister who seeing the notes upon it did not dare to send it to me at Samara but kept it under lock and key until I came back.

Since Mr. Belaev[27] undertook the work which I was directed to propose to him, I have followed its fulfillment as closely as I have been able; unfortunately, other obligatory work (a thesis to write and defend to obtain the degree of doctor, etc. etc.) have not permitted the author to finish it in the agreed time; at the present moment there remain only a few pages to be added on the new municipal institutions of 1864 with which the country has just been endowed. The

[27]The Grand Duchess Helen Pavlovna had expressed the desire to see a study published upon the origins of representative institutions in Russia. Iu. Samarin edited the plan of this study and following his advice this work was handed over to Ivan Dmitrievich Belaev, a professor at the University of Moscow. This outline was found among the papers of Iu. Samarin; we give the French translation which he himself had made, probably to submit for the approval of the Grand Duchess. (D. S.)

Programme of a study on the origins of representative institutions in Russia.

The purpose of the work is to set forth the participation of the Russian nation in the direction of public affairs at the different ages of our history. It is a matter of showing who was participating in this (whether it was the entire nation or certain classes of society); what were the circumstances which provoked, facilitated or impeded it; what were the acts by which it was manifested and what were its consequences for the public welfare.

I. The first stage, up until the death of Prince Iaroslav I. The constituent elements of Russian society in the ninth to eleventh centuries: (1) the prince, (2) his retinue (*Kniazheskaia Druzhina*) as the origin of the nobiliary body in the service of the state, (3) the nation (*Zemstvo, das Land*).

II. The age of apanages up until the establishment of autocracy under the first of the czars. (1) The princes, (2) their retinue, (3) the nation (*Zemstvo*): the municipal and provincial assemblies (*Vechi*);

those elected by the nation (*Vybornye*). The triple role of the nation and of its representatives in public affairs: *consultative* action, when called upon by the prince himself; *opposition* action, as a limit to the omnipotence of central authority; *constitutive* action in troubled times and following the dissolution of authority: appeals and expulsions of princes agange, participation in their intestine wars, etc. etc. Detailed survey of the more precise relations between the municipalities of Novgorod and Pskov and the princes.

III. Age of the czars of Moscow up to Peter I. (1) The czar, (2) the nobiliary and the clergy, (3) the nation. Dissolution of the provincial representative institutions and foundation of a system of general representation: the *Zemskiia Dumy*. Historical survey. Double action of the general assemblies: *consultative* participation, provoked by the sovereign, in the questions of legislative reforms, of peace and of war, etc. etc.; *constitutive* action for the purpose of re-establishing power when it should weaken or be extinguished (elections of the czars and the general movement of 1612). What was the manner of convening the *Zemskiia Dumy*?—Of what elements were they composed? The influence of serfdom.—What was the manner of representation: by classes (*Stand*), by regions?—What was the established order for discussions and votes?

IV. The last period since Peter I. Influence of the reform of Peter I on the development of our representative institutions. Cessation of every kind of participation in the action of the supreme authority. Impossibility of a general and homogeneous representation as the result of serfdom and of the scission introduced in the social body. Fruitless tendency of the upper nobility to isolate itself and to limit supreme authority to its own interest (abortive try for an oligarchic constitution in the time of the Empress Anne). Another equally fruitless attempt of the Empress Catherine II with the purpose of having society participate in the legislative reforms planned by the government. The last vestiges of representative institutions in the organization of our rural communes.

The work can be finished in one year *at the latest.*

The dimension of the work will be from 6 to 10 printed sheets, the printed sheet corresponding to two and a half sheets of manuscript.

The payment sought would be 85 rubles silver per printed sheet; the entire work would come to 510-850 rubles payable when the whole is finished and presented.

If the programme is approved and conditions accepted, Mr. Belaev will set to work immediately.

whole thing will be finished and will be handed over to me at the latest on the first of January. I shall still need almost a month to read it, to touch it up, fill it in and have it copied; towards the end of January I hope to be able to present the work completely finished to the Grand Duchess. It remains to be seen whether Her Highness will judge it necessary to have it translated into German.

I am very grateful to you for your kindness in giving me news of the health of the Grand Duchess; three times I had asked different people for detailed news of her and I see that the information which had reached me was far from being exact. I thought that Graev had completely reassured Her Highness on the state of her eyes. God grant that the cure at Wiesbaden will do her some good. As soon as I hear of your arrival in Petersburg, I shall go there immediately.

It remains for me to add, since you are good enough to be interested in my health, that thanks, I believe, to the stay at Ragatz, I have had somewhat of a return to youth and energy, to which I was very far from being in a position to lay claim and which has just stood up to the test of 600 versts made in *perekladnaia.*[28] Before leaving Samara I was called to take part in a district assembly (*Uezdnoe zemskoe Sobranie*), where I had to struggle against a general movement to pervert the spirit of the masses by means of flattering them and by arousing exaggerated hopes which the resources of the country in no wise justify. In two days the session of the nobiliary assembly of Moscow will open. Here that will be something completely different to judge by the rumours that are making the rounds. The government is going to great expense to win over the leaders and to obtain even a postponement; unfortunately all these approaches and exhortations only flatter our little agitators by exaggerating their importance in their own eyes and by making them believe that it is only up to them to become a serious obstacle.

Since you will be passing through Berlin, may I dare

[28]Post-chaise. (Trans.)

address a request to you? This is to bring with you a book on the Eastern church which has just been published bearing as an epigraph "Ex oriente lux" (*Vom Oriente das Licht*) of a certain Overbeck. According to what little I know about it, it is a most remarkable book, one of the most conscientious attempts to evoke the early Church of before the schism with Rome.

I hope to see you again in a month then. In the meantime permit me to lay at your feet the respectful homage of your devoted servant.

IU. SAMARIN TO BARONESS RAHDEN

Moscow, December 12/24, 1865.

On the point of leaving for Samara I am directing one of my friends to communicate to you two copies of my brochure on the Jesuits.[29] Allow me, Mademoiselle, to offer you one and to beg you to put the other into the library of her Imperial Highness the Grand Duchess. Since you have rejected the kindly advice I tried to give you, I have only to beg your indulgence for the prodigious number of printing errors which you will find in my brochure.

Accept, I beg you, the respectful homage of your devoted servant.

IU. SAMARIN TO BARONESS RAHDEN

Moscow, March 21, 1866.

Excuse me, Mademoiselle, for having kept so long the

[29]This brochure is probably only an extract from the journal *Den'*, since the first edition of the letters of Iu. Samarin on the Jesuits did not appear in print until 1866 (see the following letter). (D. S.)

book and the two notes which you sent me.[30] Before giving you my opinion I wanted to have a long chat about them with Mr. Gulliarov-Platonov, who has been particularly concerned with the subject. He approves wholeheartedly of what has been done and of what Mr. Ossinin proposes to do. As far as the programme of Mr. Pobedonostsev is concerned, it embraces so much material that the only thing to do is to draw lots for collaborators on whom you will be able to count.

Enclosed you will find a note on what I would propose to add and a few observations on the rule to be followed for the juridical party. It would be my opinion not to embrace too much material, to give only very precise information and such as would be of general applicability, and especially not to touch upon the yet indeterminate part of our legislation. However, anything that bears upon the communal organization, on the method of assessment of taxes, on statute labour and on payment in kind, and so forth, is still on a very uncertain foundation and, as it were, in the process of developing.[31] I have written my brother to get detailed information on the parish council over which he presides; since for the past six months I have not received any sort of information about what is being done there I do not know whether the results that have been obtained are worthwhile publishing; as soon as I have a reply I shall send you word of it immediately.

Let me say something about Mr. Ossinin who, unless I am mistaken, will be charged with the religious part of the calendar. I do not know him personally but his academic standing leads one to suppose that he possesses more than the

[30]It is a question here of the plan formulated by the Grand Duchess Helen Pavlovna to publish an orthodox calendar for the people. Unlike the usual contents of calendars it was intended to set forth information that was religious, juridical, agricultural and so forth, adapted principally to the needs of the peasants. (D. S.)

[31]The end of the sentence is in German. (Trans.)

necessary knowledge for the work he shall have to do. I was surprised therefore to see, in an article just published by him in the Moscow *Gazette* on the tendencies of the Anglo-American church towards orthodoxy, that he has fallen into an error of interpretation which is common among ordinary people but which is not to be expected on the part of a theologian. There is in our liturgy a versicle, where we ask the Lord for the *union of churches* (*soedinenie tserkvei*) which, according to Mr. Ossinin, would mean the union (*Vereinigung*) of the different Christian communions. However, it is a fact that this versicle antedates the schism with Rome, that *soedinenie* in Slavic means union, accord, unity of faith and love and not re-union of disjointed parts, and that the term *churches* (in the plural) means simply dioceses (as for example the Church of Ephesus, the Church of Antioch, etc.) and is never used in theology in the plural in the sense of confession, since according to all Christian doctrine there is and can be only one single confession which is the Church. Do not think that it is just to quibble with the author that I pick out this inadvertent error, but when it comes to teaching and especially when one is addressing a public that can only take one at one's word an excess of precaution is never out of place.

Mr. Belaev has delivered to me the work with which he was charged. It contains the material of nine to ten printed sheets, which according to the conditions agreed to by the Grand Duchess gives him right to a remuneration of 800 rubles silver. I should be very obliged to you to send me the amount before Easter. It is up to me now to review the work and to make the necessary additions in it; I am going to set to work immediately, undertaking to do my best and to conclude it as soon as possible, but I should point out to you that there will be a great deal of work and that I shall have to work through a complete study of our legislation since Peter I.

One of my friends is going to publish the new edition[32] of my letters on the Jesuits. Since the first one is riddled with mistakes I hope that you will allow me to replace the two copies which I sent you with the two new and, at least as far as appearances are concerned, more presentable copies.

Please receive the respectful homage of your devoted servant.

BARONESS RAHDEN TO IU. SAMARIN

April 26, (1866).

I must thank you so much, Sir, for your having sent your letters; one of the copies was passed to the Grand Duchess, and I'm keeping the other according to your authorization. The consultations for the calendar have taken on a positive shape, there has resulted a sort of compromise between the original programme and your remarks. After long conversations with Mr. Semenov, who kindly undertook an article on the different zones of Russia and the agricultural and manufacturing industries which are connected with them, I appealed to the goodwill of Pobedonostsev, Ossinin and Turgenev.[33] The two first were *sure*, and the last was quite encouraging without, however, *promising on his honour*, which makes me tremble at the possibility of not obtaining the funds I am expecting. Mr. Dahl[34] has had his services offered to the Grand Duchess by Mr. Redkin; one of these days he is going to be answered with a request for some short

[32]The first edition was published in 1866 by the *Russki Arkhiv* under the title *Iesuity i ikh otnoshenie k Rossii.* (D. S.)

[33]I. S. Turgenev (1818-83), the leading novelist, was approached about writing "a work of art of three pages." I. S. Turgenev, *Pis'ma, 1865-1867,* VI (Moscow-Leningrad, 1963), 380. (Ed.)

[34]V. I. Dahl (1801-72) produced a monumental *Dictionary of the Russian Language* (1861-68). He was also a writer of tales and a collector of proverbs. (Ed.)

story or a half-dozen proverbs.—Ah! sir, can you not see that I am greatly upset in telling you what the *Pravoslavnyi Kalendar'*[35] expects of you. I am so much involved in it that I feel it intercedes for me, and that is what embarrasses me. Mr. Semenov claims that there is no way of doing without an article on emancipation and that no one in the world could write it like you. —More than ever we need healthy food for people upon whom every sort of poison is being tried. Think of the importance which the historical account of emancipation is acquiring, and of the influence which this great reform ought to exercise on the life of the nation. I know that you have a great many tasks, but you would have three months ahead of you, and the subject that you would be dealing with is so much a vital part of your thought that in reality you would have only to let yourself re-live this age of glorious struggle. This is the title under which the article is designated in the programme: "Istoricheski ocherk krepostnogo sostoianiia po ego vozniknoveniiu i vliianiiu na narodnyi byt, i zatem ob osvobozhdenii krest'ian i o znachenii etoi peremeny v narodnoi zhizni."[36] I add nothing more for fear of appearing indiscrete.

The Grand Duchess is again suffering greatly from her eyes; following the emotional stresses and the toils which she has undergone, her Highness had a congestion in her eyes, it was necessary to put cups on her, and for three days she has been a recluse in a room as dark as night. Tomorrow I hope they will relieve the darkness around her. This relapse troubles me and makes me anxious about the future. The impending war will be probably an obstacle to her taking a very

[35]Russkii Pravoslavnyi Kalendar' was published in 1865 and 1866 by the Krestovozdvizhenskii Sisters of Mercy, a charitable organization founded by the Grand Duchess Helen. It contained verse and pieces on the Church, Russian history, literature and agriculture. Turgenev, *Pis'ma, 1865-1867*, VI, 482. (Ed.)

[36]"An historic sketch of serfdom, as regards its origins and influence on the life of the people; on the emancipation of the peasants and the significance of this reform for the national life." (D. S.)

necessary cure. What do you think about the *attentat* against Bismarck? Five bullets at point-blank range, his frock cloak riddled, himself lightly wounded. The assassin is a citizen of Würtemberg named Wild. Bismarck arrested him with his own hands and handed him over to the police. It seems to me that he will gain in popularity, for the public conscience will be greatly shaken.

I could write you volumes if I wanted to tell you about what is going on around here, but I have a feeling that you are going to be coming to us. It would be a real pleasure for your friends. Many kind regards.

IU. SAMARIN TO BARONESS RAHDEN

Moscow, April 12/24, (1866).

A thousand apologies, Mademoiselle, for all the trouble caused by the confusion in addresses on my parcels to you, and a thousand thanks for the volume and the kind letter of Baron Haxthausen[37] which you were good enough to send along to me. The package sent to you contained only two copies of my brochure; if they have been lost, then that is so much the better. But I shall return to the attack and send you two more copies which this time I hope will reach their destination.

Enclosed in this letter you will find the receipt of Mr. Belaev which I should have sent to you a long time ago. To my shame I admit that for fear of misplacing it I had hidden

[37] A. F. Haxthausen (1792-1866) was a German political economist who was hired by Nicholas I to do a study of peasant relationships in Russia (1843). The results of his investigations were published as *Studien über die innern Zusfände des Volkslebens, und insbesondere die ländlichen Einrichtungen Russlands* (Studies of the Internal State of the Life of the People, and Especially of the Rural Institutions of Russia) (Hanover, 1847-52). From this he went on to write a number of books on Russia including *The Russian Empire* (1856). (Ed.)

it so well that I had difficulty in finding it again.

What is going on here[38] is full of significance, a good deal of which unfortunately is lost. In many passages the Bible talks of Israel prostrate before the Lord; to realize that this sort of personification of a whole people which moans or cries out blessings can be literally true, it is enough to have seen Moscow these last few days. Once you were in the street you felt yourself borne along as if by an electric current which was rising from earth to heaven and whose strength was totally irresistible. Incredulity, nihilism, the whims of political opposition—everything has gone by the boards, everything has melted away. I doubt if such a unanimous and spontaneous impulse could be seen anywhere else. A day like that one supplies a victorious answer to a great many shortcomings. Well, this truly Biblical eruption of love and gratitude, which in particular circumstances would have produced thousands of martyrs, was unable to resist the temptation of three casks of wine which some merchants, badly inspired by a deplorable custom, had taken it into their heads to offer to the crowd. The day before yesterday it was being said at the governor's that up to forty people had been trampled in the crowd and taken to the hospital, the half of them practically in a hopeless state. It seems to me that a pastoral letter from the higher clergy addressed to the whole city would have been apropos but its tradition has been lost and to find antecedents it would have been necessary to go too far back. A veritable hecatomb! . . .

Besides, I do not know if there is not as much brutality, although of a different sort, in the avalanche of ovations which the public of Petersburg is raining upon the head of the man whom Providence used to accomplish its ends. Is it not to be disrespectful to him at the very hour in which, out of a feeling of moral modesty, he is seeking to slip away,

[38]The author is alluding here to the stir produced in Moscow by news of the *attentat* committed against the person of His Majesty, the Emperor Alexander II, April 4, 1866. (D. S.)

feeling himself sagging beneath the grandeur of the mission which he has just fulfilled? And what do you say of the traditional platitude and the desperate uniformity of all those addresses which follow one another copied like soldiers in a line. So much sincerity, so much emotion, and not one line which seems true. Between the heart and the word there is something of a gap. All that proves many things, which you know quite well anyway and which you can feel better than I.

Please receive this respectful homage of your completely devoted servant.

P. S. I have just learned of the nomination of General Trepov[39] to the post of Military Governor of St. Petersburg. A more fortunate and more apropos choice was impossible to make.

IU. SAMARIN TO BARONESS RAHDEN

Moscow, May 9/21, (1866).

And here I am again found wanting, Mademoiselle, and, what is more, doubly so. I thought I had sent you the receipt of Mr. Belaev and yesterday I found it on my table while I was straightening up my papers. If I have not yet answered your kind letter of April 26, it is because I have been waiting for my brother so as to be able to give you a definite answer. Let me begin with what I can promise without fear of breaking my word. The article on parish assemblies (*Prikhodskiia Popechitelstva*) will be written by my brother, reviewed and corrected by me, and will be sent to you in due time. Regarding the second article (on emancipation) frankly, in spite of the rhetorical care you took not to frighten me too much, I should like to believe you have no doubt that I would have

[39]General F. F. Trepov, who was subsequently shot and seriously wounded in 1878 by the revolutionary Vera Zasulich. (Ed.)

seized with joy the chance of taking part in a work in which you are interested, so if I do not engage myself formally it is because there are two neverthelesses[40] from which your absolution is necessary right at the outset. Let me therefore send you my answer in a few days' time. Friday the 13th I am leaving for Petersburg and Saturday I shall come knocking at your door. The news you give me of the Grand Duchess is extremely alarming; God grant that what might be feared will not come about. Please receive the respectful homage of your completely devoted servant.

IU. SAMARIN TO BARONESS RAHDEN

Moscow, August 12/24, 1866.

Just as debtors often do whose business is becoming tangled, I have dragged along right up to the last moment and here I am reduced, Mademoiselle, to the sad necessity of laying my balance sheet at your feet with the admission of my insolvency. This admission is all the more painful for me in that the commitment which I had contracted was very close to my heart and that it was the first time that an opportunity had been presented to me to bring my pocr contribution to a work under the patronage of Her Highness the Grand Duchess and in which you had an interest. After one month of work, I have not been able to do anything that is worthwhile. If I were to show you what I have written, your indulgence would not go so far as to contradict me. I know full well that this is not an excuse, but rather my literary condemnation which I am pronouncing. However, since I insist that my goodwill be beyond question, let me tell you what the difficulties are that I have not been able to overcome, and then judge for yourself.

My idea was to present a complete picture of our rural

[40]*Dennoch.* (Trans.)

way of life,[41] which would permit one to take in at a glance the results of emancipation from the economic and social points of view. To succeed in this somehow or other it was necessary firstly to gather a certain quantity of statistical facts which were as general as possible and entirely unquestionable; it was then necessary to characterize the tendencies and to appraise the wishes of the parties interested in reform, avoiding as much as possible anything that might have given to the work too pronouncedly polemical a character. However, the first of these conditions was completely missing, and I could not manage to fulfill the second. Following the progress of the agrarian question[42] as I have only from a distance, I was far from supposing that those who are directing it are not concerned with establishing the achievements by figures. It is unbelievable, and yet that is what has happened. In the matter of general statistical facts we possess only the figures furnished by the bank on the repurchase operation. To go into details with any matter of certainty as to how and to what degree the condition of the peasants had been improved, I wanted to know: (1) how many new farmsteads[43] had been established since 1861 (I believe the number has almost doubled); (2) how many peasants had acquired licenses for commerce and exemptions from being drafted; (3) how many courts had registered acts of sale for real estate acquired individually by peasants; (4) how many villages had passed from an organization based on communal possession to one of hereditary landed property; (5) what was the average salary set by the communes for their mayors and clerks. I cite only the most simple problems; the pro-

[41]*Ländichen Verhältnisse.* (Trans.)

[42]By "agrarian question" Iu. Samarin means the introduction of statutory charters (*Ustavnyia Gramoty*) and in general the agrarian organization of the peasants under the Ruling of February 19, 1861. (D. S.)

[43]*Bauernwirthschaften.* (Trans.)

gramme which I had framed for myself when I was back from Petersburg covered about fifteen; well, within that programme I have not found a single general fact which has been duly verified. With regard to raw materials I have gleaned only a few scattered observations of questionable soundness and which still hold only for very restricted localities. How can one dare make any sort of general deduction upon the basis of individual, and almost always contradictory, affirmations?

When, passing from tangible facts into the realm of ideas, I tried to evaluate the different ways of judging the present situation which have currency in our social regions, and to reduce the tendencies which can be seen there to their true worth, another type of difficulty arose. You are aware that the bases of agrarian reform seem to be becoming again matter for dispute; far from becoming simplified by pure and simple acceptance of the *fait accompli*, the question tends on the contrary to become more complicated with claims which, while they do pretend to have a new form, are not really anything but belated bitter recriminations against the carrying out of what certain people were unwilling to combat bare-facedly.[44] Certainly the difficulty of discussion in this area would not be any reason to avoid it, but there would have been an abuse of confidence and poor taste in carrying the debate over into a publication, which is directed to our whole people *en masse* and which appears under the patronage of Her Highness the Grand Duchess. I am far from claiming that the risk was inevitable, but I have not found how to avoid it. If on your return you will cast a glance over what I have written—you can judge of the difficulty.

The opportunity remained for me to get caught up on the article that I had asked my brother for, but a rest cure

[44]In this passage Iu. Samarin is probably alluding to the rumours that were then going around concerning a reform of the *volosti* of the peasants (a group of rural communes forming a district), including in the term *volosti* all classes of inhabitants. (D. S.)

which his health required and many pressing affairs have taken up all of his summer. Now that I stand convicted of having failed in my promises, for which I had already received thanks, it would be improper for me to take on new engagements; let me only hope that, if later I manage to do something even slightly passable, you will not refuse me the chance of rehabilitating myself.

In two or three days we are expecting the Americans and the city is making many preparations to receive them; if they are not spared something from the programme of all the dinners they are threatened with, I very much fear that in the end they will have to experience the regimen of our hospitals. Apropos of hospitals, as the probability of seeing cholera develop in Moscow diminishes, the zeal displayed by the administration to combat it seems to increase. The persecution directed against cucumbers and currants is taking on colossal proportions and we have already, to watch over the sanitary state of the city, three special committees one set on top of the other.

The immense popularity acquired by the justices of the peace since the first days of their installation still continues to grow. Public opinion is unanimous with regard to them, and the prodigious quantity of business which comes their way goes beyond anything that had been foreseen. You hear expressions of touching *naïveté* which are inspired in the ordinary people by the unforeseen appearance of a free, swift and honest judicature. In order to fully understand the public reaction you must consider that nine-tenths of the lawsuits taken to the magistrates' tribunals consist of claims about violated rights which, under the old regime, would not even have been moved in court. It is not simply an amelioration of our institutions, it is a whole social milieu which has been newly conquered for justice and into which the notion of the inviolability of law is penetrating for the first time. This beginning would lead one to believe that legislative labour may at last have succeeded in finding the desired form and in rooting the drifting seed of our social renovation. Here again is a curious fact. A justice of the peace has become especially concerned with pursuing the indecent language which all too often strikes one's ears in our streets, and the inhabitants of his quarter are already perceiving that the ordinary people who have business with him are beginning to take notice and to get rid of this detestable habit which no one had thought of combatting. That is a purely moral effect of a series of public sentences, because the fine which accompanies them is nothing by itself.

Knowing that you are in Berlin, I cannot help but envy you. Has the unforeseen logic of events ever played in a more cavalier manner with all of the diplomatic claims of mastering the course of things? In the immense successes of Prussia,[45] what seems to me very much more admirable than success in itself is the hidden work which preceded it and the mass of every sort of preparatory measure which made it certain. Here at home public opinion is not yet clear about what to think of German unity under the Prussian regime. I have difficulty in understanding why we ought to fear it more than any other political re-alignment. In short, the general tendency of all great political nationalities to constitute themselves into bodies is far from being opposed to our interests, provided that it be frankly accepted on the Balkan question as elsewhere. As far as united Germany is concerned, nothing seems to suggest that it might be called to make a great thrust of invasion beyond itself, as France and England. If anything should worry us it is not so much a direct blow as an infiltration of the German element; however, political splitting-up does not seem to me much of a guarantee against this type of action.

Forgive me my interminable scribbling and do not deny to the sincerity of my confession the benefit of the attenuating circumstances. If you should have a spare moment, a word of absolution on your part and news of the health of

[45]During the war with Austria, which was finished by the Battle of Sadowa and the peace concluded at Prague in 1866. (D. S.)

the Grand Duchess would fulfill the wishes of your very humble and very devoted servant.

BARONESS RAHDEN TO IU. SAMARIN

Ragatz, September 4/16, (1866).

Your letter came to me here and I shall not hide from you that I was very much pained by it. It had never entered my mind a single moment that you and your brother could ever refuse us your collaboration. Nevertheless your reasons are so serious and the impossibility of working without raw materials is so obvious that I must yield, although with some protest about the "inexorable logic of facts."

Her Highness the Grand Duchess remembers you with tenderness. She happily recalls the time that you spent here several years ago and regrets that your *séjour* has never been repeated. We are being very poorly treated by the weather, it is teaming so *very* often; I recall the Falkniss rather like a tradition from the era of Mr. Titov, so heavily covered is it with mist and inaccessible even to admiration. Happily this has no ill effect upon Her Highness' cure. She is decidedly improving. Carlsbad, while tiring her, did her a great deal of good; Ragatz is giving her back her strength and her air of freshness. I cannot tell you how pleased the Grand Duchess is that your political views concerning Prussia and Germany correspond so perfectly with her own. More than in any other matter one must be able to set aside the personal element when it is a question of safeguarding the real interests of one's country, and consider the position in an objective manner—that triumph of philosophy—or else quite simply obey a phrase of the Gospel whose inexhaustible significance is not reflected upon enough: "Whosoever will save *his* life shall lose it."[46]

[46] *Wer sein Leben lieb hat, der wird es verlieren. Sein* is underlined in the text. (Trans.)

We shall spend a fortnight more here; after a short rest Her Royal Highness will set off home again. Shall we see you in Petersburg in November? I clasp your hand cordially and without spite. Best wishes.

IU. SAMARIN TO BARONESS RAHDEN

Friday (1867).

I was sorry, Mademoiselle, in returning home yesterday about one o'clock to learn that the palace servant had been looking for me and that it had not occurred to my servant, who is not up on my habits, to direct him to the Miliutins. Hoping that the Grand Duchess would be willing to allow me to present my respects to her I have made no engagements of any sort for the five days I am to spend here. I am therefore completely at the disposal of Her Royal Highness whose orders I shall await without budging from here. You will not be angry with me if I do not come knocking at your door until I do have the chance of seeing you again.

Receive, I beg you, the expression of the profound respect of your devoted servant.

BARONESS RAHDEN TO IU. SAMARIN

(1867).

I deeply regret not being able to say goodbye to you before you leave. It seems to me that I said nothing offensive to you at our last meeting, and yet I should have liked to repeat to you that if our opinions are occasionally very divergent, I believe that we are in complete agreement on the *true basis* of things. This concern for friendly clarity may seem childish to you, it is very important to me. Spider webs are spun so quickly and veil the horizon so wretchedly! Kind regards, and *bon voyage*.

My greetings to the Cherkasskis and to your sister.

IU. SAMARIN TO BARONESS RAHDEN

Moscow, March 30, (1867).

A thousand thanks, Mademoiselle, for the last lines that you were good enough to send me before I left. All my things were packed and that is why I had to put off my reply until arriving in Moscow. Certainly I had nothing to reproach you for; on the contrary, I am the one who was afraid of having strained your tolerance, and that is why I was anxious for a last handshake.

You are aware that the *Moskva*[47] has just received its third warning together with a three-month suspension. What is most curious is that this measure is motivated above all by the regrets and the disapproval which the editorship allowed itself to show with regard to the rigorous measures with which Pastor Deubner and the consistory of Livonia have just been struck. It is considered bad that we should prefer a free discussion with courtly weapons.

My sister and the Cherkasskis extend through me their very best wishes. Allow me to join to them the homage of your devoted servant.

[47]*Moskva* was a daily edited and published by I. S. Aksakov during 1867-68. It treated political, economic and literary affairs and was finally suppressed for its attack on the pro-German administration of the Baltic Provinces and the bureaucratic formalism of the regime. During its short life it received nine warnings and was three times suppressed by the censor. See p. 13 fn. (Ed.)

IU. SAMARIN TO BARONESS RAHDEN

Berlin, May 11, (1868).

I have taken the liberty, Mademoiselle, of sending you from here the latest publications of the Baltic press to have appeared beyond its borders: the *Livländischen Beiträge*[48] (by Bock), four fascicles, a special lecture by the same,[49] and the brochure of G. Sievers (*Appel an die Oeffentlichkeit*).[50] Whatever impression the reading of all these works makes on you, I urge you to persevere right to the end. I am possibly wrong to keep coming back to these questions but you know full well that I have never for a moment harboured the ridiculous idea of modifying your views, especially when they spring from a way of feeling. I appeal only to your impartiality and I do so possibly for the purpose of a preliminary personal excuse, that is my justification. In two or three days I am leaving for Petersburg, where, quite certainly, I shall come knocking on your door; but since my stay in Petersburg will be very short and since I may possibly not manage to see you I have thought it wise to inform you of my parcel so that you may take the necessary measures for it to reach you. I believe the whole thing is prohibited by censorship.

Allow me to set at your feet the respectful homage of your devoted servant.

BARONESS RAHDEN TO IU. SAMARIN

Kamennyi-Ostrov, May 27, (1868).

By a queer stroke of fate your letter from Berlin came to me at Riga where I was spending several weeks with my

[48] Livonian contribution. (Trans.)

[49] Following the colon the sentence is in German. (Trans.)

[50] Appeal to the public. (Trans.)

sister. It was with sadness that I read it; I shall not offer against it either arguments or explanations. The troubles I have had during these last years have possibly tired me a little; possibly, too, they have made me take a more accurate point of view in considering the true value of things of this world. It seems to me that I am no longer disposed to get worked up about an aggression or a resistance affecting ephemeral interests, as, moreover, I have acquired the unshakeable conviction that moral interests—the only ones which are worth the trouble of fighting for—cannot be vanquished or cannot triumph except by the weapons of light. Saint Paul has engraved this faith in my soul. The weapons of light, what are they if not the brilliance of divine reason, the warmth of a heart which loves—the one penetrates the shadows of ignorance, the other dissipates the frost of hatred, of mistrust, of indifference . . . . Apart from these weapons, we possess others which can obtain great momentary success, but destruction alone accompanies them; they will never build or cure. Forgive me these reflections which may seem untimely to you, and do not hold it against me either if I do not just yet read the brochures which you sent to me: I am barely back and I am hemmed in on all sides by duties of convention. However, in order to safeguard your good faith in which I have complete trust, I shall warn you that Mr. de Bock has expatriated himself as a consequence of his disagreement with all classes of his compatriots, that he aspires somewhat to the role of a Baltic Herzen, and that I saw no one at Riga who was willing to be associated with his elucubrations.

When will you be passing again through Petersburg? I should have liked so much to have seen you. Her Highness the Grand Duchess will not be leaving until the beginning of July; she is going to Carlsbad as usual and then later to Switzerland. I clasp your hand very warmly; think kindly of me.

IU. SAMARIN TO BARONESS RAHDEN

Berlin, June 18/30, (1868).

To my very great regret, Mademoiselle, I saw myself forced to pass through Petersburg without being able to thank you for the kind letter which I received in Moscow. I had scarcely arrived when I had to set out immediately again for Berlin in case I should miss my brother, with the result that I saw no one in Petersburg.

My parcel of books arrived inopportunely; I suspected as much even before receiving your letter, but it was already too late, and I deeply regretted the unfortunate idea that I had of offering you reading which, after all, could only leave you with a painful impression. If it was at my request that you undertook that reading, let me beg you to abandon it; throw Mr. Bock into the fire and let us not speak about him any more. All I should like is for you to take seriously what I told you once, and what you shrugged yours shoulders at: namely, that I mean well, not only with regard to my native country in the narrowest sense of the word, but also with regard to every constituent part of the same as well.[51]

I have one further request to address to you: when you are established at Carlsbad, and when you find out exactly how and where you will be spending the summer, would you be so kind as to send a word to me in Prague, at the hotel Zum Schwarzen Ross, to let me know if I can without indiscretion come and present myself to Her Highness the Grand Duchess. Let me set at your feet the respectful homage of your devoted servant.

[51]Following the colon, the sentence is in German. (Trans.)

IU. SAMARIN TO BARONESS RAHDEN

Prague, August 5/17, 1868.

This letter, Mademoiselle, is accompanied by a parcel.[52] It is not without some feeling that I address it to you; I will not hide it, and I do not blush for it, whatever confidence your impartiality may inspire in me. To make me run the risk of producing quite a different impression than that which I should have wished to leave in people's minds, those people upon whose opinion I depend the most, a series of offensive publications and of almost direct provocations would possibly not have sufficed. It needed the positive feeling of a duty to be fulfilled, not only towards my country as a whole but particularly as well towards the three provinces which I see entering upon a road which is completely wrong and full of dangers. Profoundly convinced that they have an historically legitimate and possible future only in an intimate, cordial and fraternal union with Russia, I know also that with regard to them this conviction itself imposes upon me certain moral obligations which I willingly accept, in my soul and conscience, without any reservations whatsoever. I do not believe that I have violated those obligations, but they do not go so far as to impose silence for fear of wounding with truths which absolutely must be expressed. Anyhow, you can read and you can judge for yourself. A thousand thanks for the two fine days for which I am very much obliged to you. Permit me to set at your feet the respectful homage of your devoted servant.

P. S. Since my works will not be published and put on sale until I have returned to the fold, I am very anxious that the small number of copies which I am now distributing should not circulate for a couple of weeks.

[52]The first two fascicles of the *Okrainy Rossii* and probably the second volume of the works of A. S. Khomiakov, published in Prague in 1868 by Iu. Samarin. (D. S.)

IU. SAMARIN TO BARONESS RAHDEN

Prague, August 8/20, (1868).

Permit me, Mademoiselle, to bother you once again before my return to Russia has brought our correspondence to an end. You told me a couple of days ago that you did not know too much what to think about the sincerity of the opinion professed by what is called the national party on the matter of liberty of conscience. The article in the *Moskva* marked in red, which I found on my return to Prague, seems to be written in reply to your doubts. I believe it is difficult to be more explicit and I will add that in colliding head-on with the prejudices of our high clergy the editor knew full well that he was risking the alienation of the sole party which up to now has supported him with its sympathies.

One other word. Friends in Petersburg have told me, and Her Highness the Grand Duchess repeated it to me at Carlsbad, that Prince Gorchakov[53] disapproved of my work on the Baltic Provinces since it would disturb the *entente cordiale* prevailing between the cabinets of Petersburg and Berlin and prevent Count Bismarck from supporting us on the eastern question, as he is supposed to be doing at the present moment. It is a condemnation pronounced in advance, given out by a party whose methods I know from long experience and which will certainly gain ground. Well, I affirm that *today*, well ahead of the release of my publications, the harm feared by Prince Gorchakov (and which will be imputed to me) *has already been done*. Permit me in proof to set in front of you the underlined passages of the *Moscow Gazette*.[54] Thanks to a series of slanderous and provocative publications, coming from the opposition party, which our government has pretended to ignore and to which no one on our side has replied, the German public has risen against us;

[53]A. M. Gorchakov (1798-1883) was an outstanding Russian diplomat. He was Minister of.Foreign Affairs, 1856-82. (Ed.)

the calumny has produced its effect, and much has remained of it; we are believed to be in the wrong, and moreover we are believed impotent and cowardly thanks to our stubborn silence. That is what we have to thank the pamphlets of Messrs. Bock, Sievers, Eckhardt,[55] Nolcken, etc., etc., etc., for, and for which the responsibility, a moral one in the eyes of Prince Gorchakov and the government, is going to fall upon your very obedient and very devoted servant.

P. S. The two sheets enclosed do not belong to me. Would you have the great kindness to send them on to Prague: Herrn von Kisseleff, Gärtner-Gasse No. 466. II. Once again my profound apologies.

BARONESS RAHDEN TO IU. SAMARIN

November 12, (1868).

I hesitated a long time before writing you—perhaps I lacked the courage! It seems to me though that I have to reply to your last letter from Prague which was accompanied by the shipment of your books. They have hurt me very much. God knows I wanted to read them with the sincerest impartiality, that I considered as far as possible everything from your point of view, that I have made a great allowance for the enmities of race, religion, nature . . . . This book is not good, it is not true, consequently it is of a bad political theory. I shall leave to others the trouble of refuting one by

[54] The *Moscow Gazette* (*Moskovskie vedomosti*) was founded by the University of Moscow in 1756. Generally a conservative publication, it was edited from 1863 to 1887 by M. N. Katkov, an influential and vigorous supporter of the regime's policy of "official nationalism." (Ed.)

[55] Julius Eckhardt, *J. Samarin's Anklage gegen die Ostseeprovinzen Russlands* (Iu. Samarin's Indictment of the Baltic Provinces of Russia) (1869) (Ed.).

one the accusations and the slanders which it contains, of pointing out the inexactitudes, and of speaking out about what you suppress. It is not my place to follow you on the terrain of history, to prove to you the worthlessness of your arguments or the haphazard audacity of your hypotheses, but this book makes me mistrust you, and this hurts me! You cannot believe what you write! Beginning with that childish detail of Mr. de Bock's title, which you repeat wrongly at every opportunity, right through to the shameful pamphlet which comprises the second part of your work. You can have no conviction about what you are proposing. Did I not warn you myself in the spring, and with what absolute and naïve confidence in your good faith, about the peculiar situation of Mr. de Bock vis-à-vis his compatriots and his country? It seemed to me so natural that once you had been warned you would readily accept anything which might tend to temper the relations, which you assured me you wanted to be intimate, between the provinces and Russia! And it is in order to strengthen their ties that you set up Mr. de Bock as a representative of the provinces, that you suspect a vast, thoroughly Jesuit conspiracy, that you remain obstinately silent on the legislative and administrative progress of the country, that you bitterly ridicule and scoff at even the character of its inhabitants! And the second part of your publication, this libelous satire for which, it is true, you do not assume entire responsibility, but which you spew about in the world under the aegis of your name, this satire which dares to cast a slur on the protestant clergy for an open complicity with the most shameful immorality. I appeal to all consciences, or at least to all cultivated intellects, is that possible, is that believable? Protestantism lays itself open to a thousand attacks, but it is strong with a holy arm which overcomes every misery: it seeks, it desires truth for its own sake. That is the secret of its profound affinity with the Germanic character and of the moralizing strength which it exerts. You know how easily I abandon the talents and the political scope of my compatriots to the critics, but their honesty, their intrinsic moral value, never! Those are the sides which are attacked when the Protestant Church is considered, when its ministers are slandered. Must I have these insults from your hand? I feel myself at one with each of my brothers when it is a matter of honour, nationality, and faith. You know so very well my hopes and desires for the reciprocal influence to be exercised between our two races. I had confided so freely to you about the modest activity, the warm devotion which I bore to my work. Hundreds of my compatriots were doing, still do as I do, and you answer us thus in the name of Russia! Is it believable that you think you can assimilate, build, by means of violence and contempt? Is it right, is it human to claim that a person can remain faithful and dutiful, ready for any service, while someone else is throwing insults in his face and stirring up suspicion all around him? Do you really think that all a church needs in order to become all-conquering is the splendour of its service and Caesarian protection? Do you believe that someone is a Christian when he is dishonouring his brother? Why did you do that? I have already said too much. It seems to me that I am speaking to you for the last time and I should like no personal bitterness to burst into what I have written to you. Let me rather remember, as I say farewell to you, the beautiful, good hours which I owe you, in which, freely associating myself with your noble mind, I felt my heart burn for the liberation of our common fatherland. Those memories are indelible; they will, little by little, wrap my present hurt in their quiet peace.

Pardon me if I send you this letter such as it is, I could not copy it out again.

IU. SAMARIN TO BARONESS RAHDEN

Moscow, November 20, 1868.

I felt a thrill of joy as I recognized your writing. You are right: I had that letter coming to me, and if you had not forestalled me I should have provoked it. It is your silence I feared. Even after reading your three pages I still had that joy I mentioned, and I thank you for it from the bottom of my heart.

Let us understand one another, though: I do not have a single word to retract, my conscience does not reproach me about anything and I can look you in the eye as in the past. You are the one who is wrong. It is impossible to misconstrue intentions, to strike more wrongly, to deny evidence with more aplomb, to push injustice further than you have done with me. I would have to say only a word to you to convince you of this in more than one respect. Let a single example suffice. You go so far as to reproach me for having been affected in tacking on after Mr. de Bock's name his official title; you even claim that I make a mistake in it. In what way though, if you will? Evidently you do not know that it is Mr. de Bock himself who has the conceit to put it at the head of his publications. But since I am only a *slanderer* who is unworthy of any credibility, let me set the proof of what I am saying in front of you.

In order to see clearly and have a sound judgment in the Baltic question you lack one qualification and you have one too many. What you lack are the facts: you are completely ignorant of them (pardon my rude frankness). What you have too much of is your memories, your family ties, yourself in your past existence. You see reality only through that pink veil, and your intelligence refuses to perceive it otherwise. I have crossed Switzerland and Italy and I have seen nowhere that compares with the countryside where we used to spend our summers forty years ago.[56] Imagine the Moscow sky, three scrawny birch trees, a square pond, and a lonely knoll. That is my Livonian landscape. Discussion with you on this question is impossible, but there is in your letter a passage which you will soon regret and which I shall forget. You

[56]Ismalkogo, near the station of Odintsogo, on the Moscow-Smolensk line. (D. S.)

blame us for seeking the protection of Caesar. Rubbish! You are really the ones who take shelter under his wing, and it is against us that your people direct the point of his sword. I know that when you were writing to me you had not yet heard that I was already feeling it pricking my chest.[57] People will expect me to be well muzzled, and when they are fully assured of my enforced silence they will put forward proofs and facts in order to refute me; up until then insults will be enough. Look—if I were able to hold a grudge against you for having misconstrued my intentions, I would feel myself already avenged in considering the triumph which your cause will soon enjoy over an unarmed adversary; but I prefer to hope that the blush of indignation which this triumph will bring to your noble brow will perhaps bring about in your mind a return to a friend whom you misunderstand today. Until then I shall remain silent. Even if I were to feel strong enough to convince you, I should not attempt it. It is for you a matter of faith, as mine is in the future of my country; when yours is shaken I shall not, however, be able to share mine with you. But I do tell myself one thing: we are *fundamentally* of the same church, and every step that we Russians take in the way of real and true progress will move us closer to what constitutes the foundation of your beliefs and your aspirations . . . .

I know that I have been denied access to Michael Palace, which is tantamount to saying that there is no longer any possible Petersburg for me; besides, contingencies which are in the making will probably save me the trouble of having to choose my place of residence.[58] Thus I shall not see you again for a long time, even if your letter were not a sort of final farewell. You yourself said so. Do not hold it against me

[57] Allusion to the order of His Majesty the Emperor, delivered around the middle of November, to Iu. Samarin by the Governor General of Moscow. As it appears in the petition written by Samarin on the 23rd of December, 1868, the order of His Majesty contained at the same time "an accusation, a condemnation and a threat." (See *Works of Iu. Samarin*, VIII, xi.) (D. S.)

then if I try to prolong this farewell, and let me speak to you this time with an open heart.

I had for you the affection of a brother—you did not suspect this, I know. I enjoyed your vigorous and lucid intelligence upon which I had no hold; I bowed before your rigid, inflexible conscience and often consulted it mentally to illuminate my own. On more than one difficult occasion I wondered what you would have thought or done, and when I found myself almost alone on the road I had chosen I would say to myself that you would have given me your approval. I loved even your prejudices of race and caste; they made me understand and appreciate what was exalted in a way of thinking to which we are, because of our national spirit, the most absolute adversaries. That is what I lose without having deserved such a loss, and at the time in my life when more than ever I should have wished to feel the clasp of your hand.

Finally, the truth above all and no compromise with it. Tell yourself in spite of everything that, no matter what may happen and no matter what you may think of me today, I shall not change in my feelings any more than in my convictions. If later on you were to feel disposed to receive me in spite of all this, a word from you would be enough to make me come.

I set at your feet the respectful homage of your devoted servant.

BARONESS RAHDEN TO IU. SAMARIN

November 27, (1868).

It is just an hour now since I received your letter, and I want to reply to it without delay.

[58]Iu. Samarin supposed that, following the order of His Majesty which had been communicated to him and particularly following the petition which he had resolved to write, he would be exiled to the country or to some distant appointment. (D. S.)

On the printed sheet you send me, you did not take into consideration the two letters which follow the name of Mr. de Bock: *a.D.* that is to say, *ausser Diensten.*[59] You furnish me so to speak with an exhibit which I am returning to you because you have added to it words unworthy of you or of me.

Your second argument struck me with stupor. Me, reproach you with "seeking the protection of Caesar"?! Me, Edith Rahden! I search vainly for the basis for your accusation and I suppose that it must refer to what I said about the Orthodox church, for which I ask more than *Caesarian protection,* if it is to struggle with Protestantism, that is to say intelligence and virtue in those individuals who represent it. Such was my thought, I am quite certain. Is it possible that I expressed it in such a way as to give rise to a misunderstanding which is so painful for me?

These two errors on your part are nevertheless an infinite consolation for me: they prove to me to what extent your judgment can go astray, while remaining in good faith. That is the sole conviction I need. Pardon me for having doubted a single instant. I think that I shall be to the end your irreconcilable adversary, but I know I shall remain your friend forever, whatever may happen, whatever harm you may do to me. Your affectionate words have moved me very much. If you could give any thought to my plea, you would shut yourself up for a while in quiet abstention and avoid the possibility of ruffling any more feelings—my own to begin with. I shall never be the one whom you will miss in your times of sorrow or of testing! Apart from politics and inter-party warfare, let me repeat to you again that you can count upon my friendship.

[59]Retired from service. (Trans.)

IU. SAMARIN TO BARONESS RAHDEN

Moscow, November 30, (1868).

I received your letter the day before yesterday and an occasion arises today to reply to it. I have said enough to you for you to be able to imagine the infinite joy that it gave me. Please accept my deepest thanks. You are right regarding the two points you touch upon. In effect, I did not understand the sense of the two letters *a.* and *D.* and I shall publicly apologize for the involuntary error which I committed. I did not properly understand either what you told me regarding Caesarian protection; when I was reading you I still had in my ear a sort of buzzing caused by the numerous insinuations which were coming at me from all sides. Pardon the foolishness that I wrote with a pencil and be generous enough not to speak to me about it again. You were not the one I was addressing in my mind.

You may rest assured that I shall allow myself neither boastfulness nor provocation; that would no longer even be proper at my age. I shall limit myself to offering explanations which I do not believe myself entitled to refuse, and I shall act in such a way as to show that anyone is mistaken in supposing that a menace is sufficient to make an honest man renounce what he believes to be a good thing for his country.

I believe in any case that everything will calm down in a little while and I shall not even have the merit of facing up to any clash. Sincerely yours.

IU. SAMARIN TO BARONESS RAHDEN

Moscow, February 13, (1869).

The departure of my brother to foreign parts gives me the chance, which I have long been looking for, to write to you. Rest easy: there will not be a single word of politics in my letter. I am writing you solely to hear about you; I should like to know something about that area you never touch upon, either in your letters or conversations: I mean your work, your spirits, and so forth. Has the year '69 begun better for you than the year just finished? Without even suspecting it you have lately given me two sources of pleasure, for which I am grateful to you. Firstly a father, who did not know that I knew you and whose daughter attends a school you direct, has spoken very much to me about you and about your personal influence upon the masters and the pupils. Then, I learned that you had offered to put your script (which, in parenthesis, always makes me blush about my own) at the service of one of my friends[60] who was at a loss to furnish on the set day the necessary number of copies of a supportive document which he had to present. I know that he had the delicacy not to take you up on it, but I could sense from here the impulse which moved you to make this rash offer (there were I believe twenty large sheets) and nothing but at the thought of your writing in the service of ideas which are dear to me, I experienced a feeling which you will easily understand. Everything that comes to me from Petersburg leads me to suppose that you must be turning more than ever within yourself, without losing any of your serenity. Seeing you in public I have thought more than once of those personages in the Middle Ages who wore a coat of mail under their festive garments.

Prince D. Obolenski[61] sent me on your behalf the book of Jung-Stilling on the agrarian question in the Baltic Provinces. I already knew it: it is a new sort of novel in figures, which, as a work of the imagination, does not lack a certain

[60]It is probably a question here of the explanations presented by I. S. Aksakov to the Senate which was to examine the question of the suppression of his newspaper *Moskva*, whose tendencies were considered harmful by the minister of the interior. (D. S.)

[61]D. A. Obolenski (1822-81), Samarin's cousin, was a member of the State Council. (Ed.)

merit. You have possibly heard of a long letter which I wrote to the Emperor almost two months ago. Do not impute to me, I beg you, the vanity or the ingenuousness of having been able to hope to produce a conversion, or even a reaction against what is much more a question of temperament than of conviction. It was for me only a matter of pointing out, in the most polite way I could find, that I had the carefully considered intention of going on with my publications. Since it comes back to me from a reliable source that my letter did not leave the Emperor's cabinet, and that it did not provoke any sort of reaction, I believe I have attained my goal.

We are up to our necks in the elections. You probably know that we are promoting Prince Cherkasski[62] as candidate for the office of mayor. His election is practically assured, but it remains to be seen if it will be confirmed. There will be on the one hand the fear of seeing a man who is supposed a malcontent putting himself at the head of a constituted body, and on the other, there will possibly be the idea that we are definitely getting rid of a possible contestant for other more exalted and more sought-after functions. Which of these two motives will prevail? The authorities here appear quite well disposed towards Cherkasski. The day before yesterday Prince Dolgoruki,[63] who is showering me with kindness, told me that he needed above all an intelligent man; that then, feeling themselves both on the same grounds, he and the mayor would certainly come to an eventual understanding. I agreed entirely with this idea, and I even gave him to understand that in case of need he could lend the mayor from his surplus. I have often heard it said in Petersburg that politicians are quickly spoiled at Moscow; in this connection Prince Dolgoruki presents alarming symptoms.

Have you read a curious book which Guizot speaks of in

[62]See note, p. 12 fn. (Ed.)

[63]V. A. Dolgoruki (1810-91), Governor-General of Moscow, 1865-91. (Ed.)

his *Considérations: Ecce homo*? If you have read it, could you tell me in two words what you think of it. I am in the dark about the book.[64] The second volume of the works of Khomiakov[65] which I published in Prague is making its way into the circle of our clergy. It is spoken of a great deal; several articles have already appeared and I know that others are being prepared; I am also receiving many letters. There are many doubts, apprehensions and fears; without really realizing it, people find the light too bright, but fundamentally they experience a sincere need for movement and for frankness in the realm of religious ideas. All of that makes me very happy. As I have noticed that my manner wounded and shocked many people who were inclined to give up, I keep out of the way and say nothing. It seems to me that the idea will make its way on its own. A little progress in this direction would be more than compensation for a great many disappointments in other areas. That is your opinion too, isn't it? Yours sincerely.

BARONESS RAHDEN TO IU. SAMARIN

Petersburg, February 26, (1869).

I am on the point of leaving for Riga, where my sick sister has been calling for me—I have a free hour this evening; let me use it to thank you for your letter, for which I am extremely grateful but which made me blush more than once. How can you attach any importance to so simple an offer as that of my collaboration, which, alas, is completely mechanical, in the cause of freedom of thought. In parenthesis, how can D. Obolenski possibly amuse himself telling you details of this sort! Why do you interpret my actions in their best sense while I condemn you so often in your work, in your

[64] The sentence is in German. (Trans.)

[65] See note, p. 32 of Preface.

biases, in the exaggerated inclination of your mind toward the bitterness of sarcasm, in the cold, cutting passion of your reasoning? You are too kind to me, you must know that I am giving you evil for good. Your gentleness embarrasses me, it overwhelms me; I prefer a stance of war and the truths which you speak so clearly when you set about it. *I beg you*, be absolutely sincere with me, and do not spare me ever, and let us speak of something other than me for now.

The election of the mayor seems to me impossible to refuse, although I have heard it said around here that the prince would reveal himself quickly in this post, which he will make as important as required by his spites. You have no idea of the frivolous and vulgar physiognomy of our official world. The cross-fire of all these uneasy, false, evil eyes fills me with feelings which I would sooner not qualify. Governmental action is limited to secret intrigues, minor victories, artificial triumphs. When it comes to an attack on the minister of war, there is an understanding and a mutual exchange of help. When that matter is taken care of, they play practical jokes among themselves, just to keep their hand in. Have you heard a story concerning Ogarev of the Orel government . . . . spare me these tales, so really petty that they barely qualify as conversation, but which constitute the substance of our public life.

While the heights of the social ladder becomes thinned out, our third estate is gaining in value. Thanks to an unexpected gift of Mr. Basil Narichkin I have had some fine, interesting moments and sincere pleasure in closely examining the slow but sure work which is being done in the middle classes, in perceiving the evident progress in the attitudes[66] of the parish clergy. The *Bratstvo*[67] is expanding and taking on some solidity, collective action obviously tends to make up for the defects of a paternal government. You can see ideal tendencies springing up where you would expect them the

[66]*Gesinnung*. (Trans.)

[67]Brotherhood. (Trans.) See pp. 196 and 205. (Ed.)

least. As I have the good fortune to own two copies of the second volume of Khomiakov, I shall permit myself to publicize them intensively among my ecclesiastical friends. I have already begun, for I attach the greatest importance to everything which helps at all to shed light upon eternal truths. In this respect I like your preface in spite of certain expressions which, I believe, are being criticized quite properly, and which are being unfairly exploited. I have even been undertaking for some time a translation which I intend to finish at Riga, where one of my literary friends will correct the stylistic flaws, while a pastor will review the theological expressions. I want this respectable clergy, of whom you think so poorly, to learn to know you from another point of view than that of the insult. If you will permit it, I shall send this translation to a *theologische Zeitschrift* abroad. If you are unwilling, I shall simply have put my writing at your service and that's all.

I have said nothing to you of your letter[68] which I read and reread. The silence that envelops it seems rather to be a sign of intense feeling than of forgetfulness. If it were not three o'clock in the morning, I should have explained more fully why I find it wonderful, but I am *too* tired. Farewell.

IU. SAMARIN TO BARONESS RAHDEN

Moscow, March 9, (1869).

I received your letter of February 26th the day after the funeral of Prince Odoevski. His death was for many people, even for his most intimate friends, like a belated revelation of his value and merits. With the sorrow that he leaves behind is mixed a feeling of remorse. People did not generally do him the honour of taking him seriously when he merited it in

[68] A letter of Iu. Samarin to His Majesty Emperor Alexander II dated the 23rd of December, 1868. (D. S.)

more than one respect; rather the candor with which this completely ingenuous soul exposed himself to ridicule provoked sarcasm. I feel certain that in Germany or England he would have caused less laughter at his own expense, and I wonder if the excessive, unquestionable sensitivity of our society with regard to ridicule is really a proof of superiority, as many people imagine. Is it not rather a total lack of seriousness? In this respect the country would show up Petersburg.

If you believe you need my authorization to make use of my preface, I shall give it to you completely. Do what you want with it, a translation or an extract. Possibly an extract would be better. At least I think you could prune many things from it, among them the opposition of our two theological schools in the form of a dialogue from page XXX to half-way down XXXVI. If however you think it necessary to keep this passage, let me give you some help. On page XXXIII it is a matter of *zaslugi sverkh trebuemykh*; that is the literal translation of the well-known Latin term: *opera supererogationis* (supererogatory works, those going beyond what is strictly necessary for personal salvation). One more thing: if you have at hand the French brochures of Khomiakov and if you should have the necessary time to reread them, you will feel right away the insufficiency of my preface and you might possibly feel disposed to remedy this with a few lines of introduction. The substance of Khomiakov's thought is found entirely in the versicle of our liturgy which immediately precedes the Credo: "*vozliubim drug druga da edinomysliem ispovemy Ottsa Syna i Sviatago Dukha*"—let us love one another *in order to be able* with one accord to confess Father, Son and Holy Ghost. From the day in which the disciples of Jesus Christ recognized themselves to be a *Church* (*als Kirche*) the big question which still preoccupies the world was posed: how to maintain the unity of faith (as a doctrine) without interfering with liberty of conscience. We have before us three different solutions. The Latin church realizes unity in the form of *submission* to an *authority* which is accepted by all. Faith (as faith, and not as doctrine or as the object of faith)[69] becomes consequently the apanage of him who represents the principle of authority and to whom the rest of humanity is bound only by an exterior tie, obedience. The salvation of every member of the Church is wrought not by his personal faith but by the faith of another, in which he becomes a participant, or which in other words is imputed to him through the merit of his submission. Therein lies the immense value of works in the Latin Church, for at the basis of works, as it understands them, there is always an act of submission.

What accounts for the glory of Protestantism is to have felt just how much humiliation there was for the regenerated man in asking only submission of him rather than personal faith. The reformation sets the individual so to speak again in front of his Redemptor; that is its great merit, but also its error, for the individual is isolated man, but he is not the Church. I fully realize that the first Protestants never dreamed of sacrificing unity. They were hoping to save it by binding themselves to the Bible. It was a matter of replacing the authority of man with that of a book. Later, when experience showed how illogical it was arbitrarily to impose this restriction upon a principle which was recognized and accepted in its full breadth, Protestantism saw itself forced to abandon its first position. With the book, faith (as a doctrine) slips away. It is no longer a repository to be maintained, it is something to be discovered. People hope to manage this by dint of intellectual work, by criticism, by accumulating proofs; the day will come, so they say, in which doubt and objection in matters of dogma will become as impossible as they are in matters of geometry. The lost unity will be restored by *science*. I have no need to add that the seed of pure rationalism is found in this illusory hope—which, by the way, is fading from day to day.

[69] *Als Glaube, nicht als Lehre oder als Object des Glaubens.* (Trans.)

The third solution can be summed up in the versicle which I have quoted above: faith entrusted to love. If you dig into this formula you can find three notions closely bound together. If truth is revealed by love, the degree of lucidity of a particular individual's faith is consequently a variant of the power of love and not of the degree of intellectual development. Intelligence is a natural gift which is susceptible to development up to a certain limit, and the fact of this development always presupposes a set of entirely accidental circumstances. Love on the contrary resides entirely in *intention*, in *will*, which in its essence is unlimited and of which every man is the master. The whole moral order rests on this truth. Therefore faith, too, is accessible to everyone to an unlimited degree. Here we are touching upon the true grounds of *equality*, and I confess that beyond these grounds I cannot see too clearly where else it could rest. In short, love is social by its very nature: it's a matter of man breaking down the limits of his individuality and identifying himself with his fellows; therefore it is unity as the Church understands it.

I have only one other word to add: in recognizing that faith depends upon a predisposition of the moral individual, which in turn depends only upon willpower, we place human liberty even higher than the Protestants do. And we are supposed to worship slavery, we are thought capable of accepting violence in matters of faith, we are imagined to have been caught *flagrante delicto* in a logical contradiction when we are seen speaking of liberty of conscience!

Pardon the length and lack of order in my letter. All those with whom I used to discuss these matters are now dead, and I experience an immense satisfaction in being able to come back to them with the private conviction that your intelligence will by itself make up for what I have not been able to say, or will set aside whatever I have said that is superfluous. But you are still going to protest; to satisfy you, I should have said that my reasonings will probably not be within your grasp.

You ask me always to be absolutely sincere and never to spare you. The promise costs me nothing, I shall so swear—and anyway I believe I have already proven it to you more than once in the past. I could ask you several questions which I consider important, but you have in your letter a formal prohibition which closes up my mouth. Yours sincerely.

BARONESS RAHDEN TO IU. SAMARIN

Riga, March 18, (1869).

I had written you yesterday a long letter full of theological reflections: after having reread it, I have just torn it up. What good does more antagonism do? I am always so sure of triggering it off that today I shall give myself the luxury of merely latent opposition. Besides, my arguments probably are of only very slight value; I am extremely ignorant in many areas, and especially in theology. For me Christianity is a personal experience, my doctrine could be summed up easily in the words of the man who was blind from birth: *Eins weiss ich wohl, dass ich blind war und bin nun sehend.*[70] Between seeing, thinking, and willing there still are great gulfs, I know; but in your fine definition of Christian love there is no room for grace, and it constitutes the hope of those who do not know enough how to will. What action does the Eastern Church attribute to grace? Tell me too, I beg you, what the Church teaches about that treasure of supererogatory works which I thought to be the exclusive apanage of the Roman Catholic Church. The only time I managed to make Palmer[71] really angry was on the question of that treasury of holy works—of which he ended up telling me I might have good need.

[70]"One thing I know, that, whereas I was blind, now I see." John 9:25. (Trans.)

You are very kind to have answered me so quickly concerning the preface, and since you think it is better to cut out the pages dealing with differences between schools I shall certainly do it. I had already thought of it, but I should never have thought myself justified in asking you. As for generally taking an extract from your preface, it would be tantamount to murder. For a completely foreign public it is essential to keep even in detail its original flavour, that mixture of elevation, finesse, of abstract thought and irony which is inimitable. And then there is that breath of virile, brave liberty which occasionally bursts forth all of a sudden like a ray of light. What can you want to extract from this whole? For me your preface produces the effect of a sudden eruption of the lay element in the serried rank of the ecclesiastical army. Would I be wrong in pointing out the same tendency in all churches? It is tempting to say that, weary of all paraphernalia of the job, weary of the routine exclusivism of the factory, the lay element is trying to bring back to life itself what was illegitimately taken from it, and to invite the Divine Master to sit again at the table of publicans and sinners. *Machet die Thore weit und die Thüren in der Welt hoch, dass da einziehe der König der Ehren.*[72] It bothers me to quote the Holy Scripture in French, it seems to me that I am slipping back into conversation and the German has an august gravity about it which is admirably suited to prayer.

One more word. The transition from prayer to death is so natural! I am more grieved than I can say at the death of our friend Odoevski, and your very accurate assessment of this pure soul is very heartening for me. Farewell, and please

[71] William Palmer, an Oxford theologian who showed great interest in the Russian Orthodox Church and developed a number of Russian contacts, including Khomiakov: R. Hare, *Pioneers of Russian Social Thought* (London: Oxford University Press, 1951), p. 124; and P. K. Christoff, *A. S. Xomjakov* (The Hague: Mouton & Co.), *passim* (Ed.).

[72] "Lift up your heads, O ye gates; and be ye lifted up, ye everlasting doors; and the King of glory shall come in." Psalm 24:7. (Trans.)

be assured that I understand and am grateful for the motives which determine your behaviour toward me.

IU. SAMARIN TO BARONESS RAHDEN

Moscow, April 3, (1869).

Why did you deprive me of the long letter that you had written me. I am all the more sorry in that it is impossible for me to guess what it could have been about. It is futile for me to think back over what I wrote to you, I cannot conceive what might have provoked such a radical opposition. You reproach me with having ignored the action of grace and you are right in the sense that I did not name it *while I did assume it.* Moral renovation, that *rebirth* which shocked Nicodemus, cannot be but the result of the simultaneous actions of two forces, one from below and the other from above. Even if the role of the first were only negative, even if it were a mere consenting or a non-resistance, still it would be indispensable. To set it completely aside, as is done in certain schools, would be equivalent to taking away the fundamental notion of *imputation* (*vmenenie*) on which the whole moral order rests. To try to distinguish by any sign whatsoever between the action of the will and the action of grace is impossible. The Catholics have tried it; they believe they can see up to four or five varieties of grace, but all of this futility has served only to disturb the moral sense which alone can realize the phenomena which are accomplished within a person. I do not think I am wrong in affirming that St. Paul has said on this matter all there was to be said, and that our Church acts wisely in limiting itself to merely repeating his words and not going any further. I know full well that the question of grace touches upon that of predestination, that terrible question upon which St. Paul brusquely turns his back after having set it forth in all of its rigour, but I shall be very careful not to touch upon it. Milton said that it had been imagined for the torment of the damned, and I shall take shelter behind his authority.

For want of a solution, let me draw upon my personal experience. You probably know that it is to Kant that the honour goes of having cast a floodlight upon this apparently quite simple truth, that the concepts (*Cathegorien*) of *time* and *place* are nothing other than two limits set upon human understanding. It is the distinctive feature of everything that is *finished, der Endlichkeit.* We can free ourselves from it only in a negative sense, that is in recognizing the fact of limits which are insuperable for our understanding. However, it is only after having studied Kant closely that I thought I perceived that there was a radical flaw in the manner in which the question of predestination was put. God knows and sees everything *before* it has been accomplished; what God sees is necessarily made real, therefore he *wills* what he sees before I have willed it. Is it not evident that in applying to God the term *before* or the particle *pre* (destination), we impose upon him the limits of our understanding, we lower him into the world of *Endlichkeit*, and then we wonder naively how he will go about maintaining himself here while keeping the attributes of an infinite being.[73] I feel I am expressing myself poorly and that I am abusing your good will and your capacity for understanding what is not well expressed, but you have a quite irresistible way all your own of propounding the most difficult questions in very plain terms. There is one other question about which I must say a couple of words. Our *Church* has never admitted the doctrine of supererogatory works; it is not found in any of our symbols, none of our councils has even discussed it; but one of our theological *schools* (that of Kiev in the seventeenth century) made use of it, borrowing it from the Jesuits, to react against the action of Protestantism. There was a want of weapons, people were generally ignorant, and arrows were made out of any kind of wood. It is particularly in the work

[73]*Eines unendlichen Wesens.* (Trans.)

of a certain Stefan Iavorski,[74] entitled *Kamen' Very*, that the Latin doctrine on supererogatory works is found exposed in all of its absurdity—a doctrine which was vigorously fought by us, at the very moment of its appearance, and today is completely forgotten.

The few lines in your letter about my preface have given me the warmest pleasure and I feel great gratification, which I believe to be excusable, that it is you who have been willing to present me to the German public.

You probably know that Prince Cherkasski has just been elected mayor of Moscow by an immense majority. His confirmation, which I think is quite certain, is expected from Petersburg. It seems to me that his enemies will even prefer to see him settled into a position than to know that he is still unengaged and available. Yesterday I learned that the Grand Duchess was intending to come to Moscow to be present at a concert of the philharmonic society. Will you be accompanying her? I certainly intend to present myself at her door, but I do not hope to be received.

There are many things I could tell you about what I am learning about your provinces, but I shall remain silent. The absolute silence which I impose upon myself in this respect, far from paining me, is one of the benefits which I draw from your friendship. Yours truly.

BARONESS RAHDEN TO IU. SAMARIN

April 16, (1869).

How good you are to have sent me a portrait of our friend Odoevski! I am quite touched with it and I thank you from my heart.

Your last two letters have been an almost unmixed pleasure for me; in this morning's, which came to me from

[74]See p. 6. (Ed.)

Riga, there is one sentence which I shall come back to in a moment. Everything you say to me concerning grace and predestination satisfies me completely. Reading you I experienced what one feels in the presence of very illuminating truths, whose brilliance all of a sudden dissipates the mist of half-formed ideas; it seemed to me that I had already been thinking what you write without being able to express it. I congratulate myself all the more for having torn up my answer in which I stood up for grace and St. Paul, the Holy Spirit . . . . Afterwards I changed my mind and in order to clarify myself I had the wisdom to question you on your real position instead of attacking you haphazardly. I hope that that has been an explicit confession. I am laying it completely open to your raillery.

Why do you suppose that the Grand Duchess will not welcome you as usual? She has had you told that she did not understand your doubts in this matter. Didn't D. Obolenski pass that on to you? And how many times have I myself not told you, in order to avoid any misunderstanding between you and the Grand Duchess.

"There are many things I could tell you about your provinces but I shall remain silent. The absolute silence which I impose upon myself," etc. Two lines further on you speak of my friendship. Since you mention it, that is a matter I should like to see us perfectly clear about. There is something essentially false in these obligatory reticences in association with the idea of friendship. One may deceive himself in this for a moment, being swayed by a true emotion, but in friendship as in music dissonances cannot remain without becoming painful, and in time unbearable. If there are any subjects which cause you to impose an absolute silence upon yourself with respect to me, it is because you yourself feel that I could not possibly hear them without inhibition or without revolt. Can a purely political hostility alter a serious amicable relationship? I do not think so at all. Only the profound animosities of race and faith can open a gulf between souls, and it seems to me that you are feeling them without being willing to admit them frankly to yourself. I confess I am guilty of not having clearly realized from the outset what the situation was, and for having rashly brought about an artificial relationship between us. The fact is that God himself would not discover in my heart a single thought hostile to Russia and that my feelings were blinding me to the scope of your reasoned hatred. Consequently I foresee with sorrow and certitude the time when Khomiakov and the Church will no longer serve us as lightning rods; but are peace, dignity, friendship possible without absolute frankness? I hope that you will see clearly that there is only sadness in my words, and not a shadow of reproach. I might have remained silent longer, it is true, especially in the solemn period in which we are now, but those *towards* whom I raise my eyes have the right to know the real essence of my thinking.

IU. SAMARIN TO BARONESS RAHDEN

Moscow, April 21, (1869).

I have just received your letter from Petersburg and I should like you to have my answer before you arrive in Moscow. "If there are any subjects which cause you to impose an absolute silence upon yourself with respect to me, it is because you yourself feel that I could not possibly hear them without inhibition or without revolt"—those are your words, you could add to them *or without affliction*, and you will be on the right road. If I had among my relatives someone whose conduct seemed reprehensible to you, you would certainly avoid speaking to me about him; I act the same with regard to certain questions and if I was clumsy enough to let you perceive the reason for my reticence, I took pleasure in imposing a constraint upon myself, no matter how insignificant it may have been, out of respect for your affections and even for your prejudices. In asking for your friendship, and in accepting it, I have sacrificed nothing to you. I keep my freedom of opinion, of expression and of action in complete integrity. Besides, it is only on this condition that I could have any merit in your eyes. On the other hand, I don't ask to be spared by you at all. When you speak to me "of the cold, cutting passion of my reasoning, of my animosities of race and faith, of my reasoned hatred," and so forth, I do not stop you, because I love and deeply value the rude frankness of your manner. I shall not even try to justify myself, so sure am I that sooner or later you yourself will realize how mistaken you are and that you will tell me so then without my having to ask you. It seems to me that I possess as much as any other person that inner sense which makes a distinction between frank and lasting relationships and those which are artificially imposed in a moment of impulse, out of duty or compassion. I also believe I know you well enough to realize what you might feel in any given circumstance, and yet I cannot see that you could consider yourself to have sufficient reason to withdraw from me the right to rely upon your friendship with an absolute confidence. I say this to you in complete frankness, upon my soul and conscience, setting aside all personal interest, as if it were a matter involving a third party.

It must nevertheless be understood that it is up to you to make the final reply to the question which you have put to yourself. Certainly you owe me nothing, but so that you may be completely free to understand what footing we are on with one another, I am going to relieve you of the last scruple which might still be bothering you. Please understand that, even if you found it advisable to break the relationship between us, I would not give up your friendship, and that later, the day when you came to recognize that you misjudged me, you would need say only a word to find me again exactly where you left me. In return for this frankness, you must also know that I am going to use my liberty of action freely. I am about to deliver to a publisher in Moscow the continuation of the *Okrainy Rossii*[75] (just between us).

Now you may judge for yourself, and you may rest

assured that whatever decision you may come to, the man with the cold emotions and the reasoned hatred, whom you mistakenly honoured with a brief friendship, will be eternally grateful to you for the good that you have done to him. Yours truly.

BARONESS RAHDEN TO IU. SAMARIN

April 23, (1869).

I did not deserve the cruel words which ended your letter today. If you meant to hurt me, you did so deeply. Your last lines also contain an accusation to which I shall not reply: there are certain things from which I shall never try to protect myself.

The bitterness with which you go back over the harsh expressions I used with regard to you proved to me only too clearly that they must have wounded you. I fully realize that I acted badly. I forget too easily that sincerity, before being transfigured by charity, is not truth, and I follow an egotistical instinct which satisfies only me. Please God that I not try to gloss over my faults! Nevertheless, whatever they may be I do not think that you were right in making them analogous with your hostile acts towards the Baltic Provinces. By a generous-minded effort you could unreservedly pardon me my personal offences, while your way of acting towards my countrymen inspires in me the duties of solidarity and revolt. Permit me to make use of the comparison which you yourself employ. If one of your family acted in a reprehensible way and my conscience should oblige me, for the sake of something which was higher than my personal friendship, to unveil the guilty acts of this individual, to judge them, to punish them, it seems to me that I should do as you have done

[75] Published in the *Russki Arkhiv* in 1869, pp. 1224-1361, under the title "Pravoslavnii Latyshy, 1841-42. Istoricheski Ocherk." (D. S.)

without hesitating. But I should proceed with a scrupulous care in weighing all of the proofs, and a zealous impartiality in highlighting all attenuating circumstances, I should find it difficult to accept dubious evidence, I should interpret nothing to the detriment of the act of the accused, I should not impute to him any possible crimes, I should not ignite the flames of defiance and of hatred about him; finally, if it were necessary, I should be a severe judge but I should ask God to keep me from being a prejudiced judge. And then you could without malice and without doubt hold out your hand to me despite my sentence and submit yourself freely to it. Would that be possible for you if I had passionately insisted upon finding your brother guilty? You leave me no way to come to you and say faithfully to you, "You are right!" even if I should be persuaded of it one day. Do you not feel that there are certain unjust exaggerations which cause the responsibility of good and of evil to be accepted uncritically for him who is being judged iniquitously? Regarding the sacrificing of one's conviction, and so forth, you make reservations which I don't understand. I prefer not to examine the sense of them too closely. The only thing that I have ardently desired for the future bears upon yourself infinitely more than upon the objects of your attacks. I still should have wanted to find in you the politician with broad views, the conscientious historian, and never either the party-man or the pamphletarian.

I repeat, if you were only the political antagonist of the provinces! But in your writings you show yourself to be the enemy and the detractor of a nationality which I possess, of the Church which is mine. From the moment you do so, I have no choice; the more precious my relationship with you is, the more compelled I am to sacrifice it. It is in that respect that I have been able, that I have desired to deceive myself for some time. My friendship is out of the question, whatever you may say about it. In renouncing the personal joys that it offers me, I acquire a further right to keep it whole, true, such as I understand it, such as I shall be happy to show it to you if ever you want proof of it. Your doubts do not affect it—in reality you have none about it—but you exercise the sad privilege of being able to wound with impunity feelings which you know to be faithful.

And now another very minor request. In a short time we shall be in Moscow; let us not go back over these painful disagreements any more. Let me enjoy, without mental reservations and without anticipating the morrow, that time of rest which I am looking forward to among friends who are dear to me. I have your advice to ask on several things. Your preface is also keeping me very busy, and finally I have a sincere pleasure in thinking that I shall be listening to you as before. Farewell, until we meet.

IU. SAMARIN TO BARONESS RAHDEN

Moscow, April 27, 1869.

Two words more, the last. I hasten to take back anything which displeased you in my letter and joyfully acknowledge that you have over me that immense superiority of a moral sense which is never disturbed by emotion. The blunt frankness of your language has never hurt me and I beg you to go on using the same tone; even if an accusation should be wrong, I am able to recognize and appreciate the motivation behind it. There are possibly matters which I have gone into more deeply than you and upon which you will be able to question me; as for me, I need a conscience which is more rigorous and more enlightened than mine, which will take me up from time to time. Concerning the local question, don't forget one thing; we are at the height of the *struggle*; we are facing the adversary, not the accused. It is a matter of combatting and not of judging. If I were to live until judgment day, my style would change. I think I know myself well enough to be able to state that, once the struggle is finished, if it could ever be a question of reprisals, my adversaries today, whether they wish it or not, would find in me a devoted advocate whom no one would have to coach in the arguments to be adduced in their favour.

I have only one further thing to say to you: that is that I shall be happy to see you again and to clasp your hand strongly enough to break it. Yours truly.

IU. SAMARIN TO BARONESS RAHDEN

Moscow, May 31, 1869.

I leafed through all of my papers without managing to come across the sheet with the religious review (*Repertorium*) which I quote in my preface. However it is impossible for it to have gone astray and I hope to find it among the papers which I have left in the country. I have also written to Bock for him to try to find the German translations of the brochures of Khomiakov. They will be sent to you directly from Berlin, if the book dealer can manage to discover them. It wasn't Leipzig where they were published, and the edition that I quote from in my translation is the French original.

Tomorrow evening I am leaving for my estate in Samara and with all my heart I wish you a good summer. A thousand thanks for the two evenings which I spent with you. All of my doubts have been dispelled; I no longer feel uneasy with you, I accept all from you and for my part I shall face up to you with impunity. I hope that this time we are on the right track and that we shall look at one another straight in the face quite openly.

My first article on the conversions of 1841 has just been published in the *Russki Arkhiv* of Bartenev, but to my great regret I cannot send it to you before I leave because the copies which I was to receive have not yet been bound.

When your travelling plans are set write me a word to say where I can find you in July. Yours truly.

BARONESS RAHDEN TO IU. SAMARIN

Oranienbaum, June 18, (1869).

The date and direction of our trip seem to be set for good; we are leaving July 1/13 and, instead of going to Carlsbad and Ragatz as usual, the Grand Duchess will take the baths at Gastein. She is going there by way of Berlin (where we shall remain a couple of days) and Salzburg, where her brothers, the Princes of Würtemburg, are coming to see her. The cure at Gastein is to last almost four weeks and what we are doing afterwards—I have no idea, but I have a feeling it will be the lakes of Italy. Since you did not give me your address in Samara, I shall take the chance of sending these lines to Moscow.

The severe, serious style of your last article pleases me *infinitely.* Nothing in this historical argument could hurt me—a few details do displease me—the whole thing distresses me and bothers me more than I can tell.

I hope wholeheartedly that your stay abroad will do you good; we are following such remote paths that we will probably not meet; goodbye then until the autumn, possibly even until winter. Farewell, and let me thank you once again for the good friendship which you have shown me.

I have not had the patience to wait for either your reply or Mr. Bock's, and your German preface has gone on to Leipzig. Don't trouble yourself any more to look for the *Repertorium* Article.

IU. SAMARIN TO BARONESS RAHDEN

Samara Government, Schloss
Vassilevski, June 15, 1869.

Gnädiges Fräulein!

As I estimate the colossal distance which at present lies

between us, I cannot get rid of one scruple which inevitably comes to my mind: that is, whether perhaps I expect too much from the mail when I express the hope that this letter may reach you. It is impossible to try to guess the time it will take.[76]

After having dug deeply among my papers, I finally found not only the piece of the critique which is dealt with in my introduction, but the German translation too of the three brochures of Khomiakov which I did not believe I owned. Everything will be sent to you this very day by registered mail. If you can find a free moment, send me a word in Moscow; I shall be there at the end of the month or at the very beginning of July, and I should like very much to know where I shall have the chance of meeting you abroad, supposing your plans for travel and for taking the cure are definitely set.

These last days all I have done is leaf through German newspapers, having brought an ample supply of them with me. I have found in them a great many curious revelations about the value of the protestation of the Livonian nobiliary body with regard to Mr. de Bock and company; I have even learned many details of which I was completely ignorant about the person of that notorious gentleman Iuri Samarin.[77] What happens, as soon as it is a matter of Russia and its interests, to the unquestionable good faith and literary conscience which are never deficient just so long as one is dealing with the Greeks, Romans, Chinese, the English or the Iroquois? I have not yet seen the book of Mr. Schirren (ex-professor of Dorpat), but I have heard, to my very great satisfaction, that the censor was letting it circulate freely. It is, then, only my brochures which will be prohibited in an absolute way. My Berlin editor will suffer from it, but the fact, however insignificant it may be, rounds out the present situation quite well as far as relations are concerned between

[76]The paragraph is in German. (Trans.)

[77]*Des berüchtigten H. Juri Samarin.* (Trans.)

those who call themselves oppressed and those who are called the oppressors. I hear too that censorship of a Lettic magazine has just been transferred from Petersburg to Riga; that's one way of stifling it quietly without seeming to, and at the same time invoking for oneself the right of free discussion. All that bodes no good for the future. People are too shortsighted and do not make good enough use of the advantages of the present, when everything could still be straightened out before Judgment Day.[78]

In the meantime, we have a tropical heat and clouds of gnats from which there is no escape. After cold waves of 30 degrees and blizzards which cover entire towns, now we have the calamities of the torrid zone. Extremes in everything, and woe unto those like me who have the poor taste to like what is temperate by nature or by good sense. Yours truly.

BARONESS RAHDEN TO IU. SAMARIN[79]

June 26, 1869.

I have just returned from a party at the Grand Duchess Catherine's and found your letter. It is kind of you to write to me in my beloved German. I joyfully accept the change of language and make use of it at once by thanking you for the happy moment which you have just given me. I read with a heavy heart the first pages of your letter: that was no longer the mild, conciliatory, almost serene tone of the last few times that we spoke together. Instinctively I asked myself: My God! What has happened? But when I read on and learn-

[78]The sentence is in German. (Trans.)

[79]Except for the postscript, the whole letter is in German. (Trans.)

ed on the last page that for the last fourteen days you had a most intimate relationship with German newspaper men and Samara gnats, while living under a tropical heat, and that it is probably as a result of this that you are unexpectedly attracted to moderate views and feelings, then all my worries gradually disappeared and became hearty laughter. I can't help laughing while I'm writing and seeing all the tragedy of your situation. Please do not count me among the Baltic correspondents who are irritating you. I, at least, have a certain, even if nebulous, understanding of your fierce goodwill and provident hatred for us. But because such a view demands a personal acquaintance with you, and even then a lot of faith, and because my countrymen have so far enjoyed only your books and not a conversation with you, you must not take it too much amiss if they are in doubt about the peculiar form of your attempts at rescue and on occasion call you "the notorious Iu. S." As for Schirren's book, it is forbidden, just as yours is, whereas before it was available upon signature in every book store, just as yours was. This was truly the saddest disservice they have done to the Baltic Provinces. I don't even want to speak about this book. It is in many ways a counterpart to yours, only much more dangerous for the provinces, because it confirms them in the worst of all errors, in their presumption. I too regard the dark future with fear. I foresee the coming of pain, sorrow, injustice and guilt, but these will not fill the abyss of hatred which has been torn wide open between people who should actually belong to each other. I had better stop here: my short moment of joy is long past. But I still have to thank you for your parcel, which, by the way, I haven't received yet. Yesterday I also received notice regarding the brochures from Berlin. Everything is too late for my impatience. Although the hard truth is that one can not undo anything in this world! So I hope to be able to remove the consequences of my hurry at least to the extent that I can send along the exact title of the brochure and the note in good time. But matters are perhaps different as regards a more important question. Your foreword is not proceeding in the way in which it was first begun. After initially accepting very courageously the new suggestions of Pastor Dalton, I am now worried about my independent behaviour towards you, and you would set my mind considerably at rest if you were at once to let me know if it is all right with you that the foreword appear *as a brochure.* I could still prevent this by means of a telegram. For, you see, Pastor Dalton says that the foreword is too long to appear in *one* number, would suffer if divided, would be read in a theological periodical only by exclusively theological readers, even though it properly belongs before the public at large, and as a brochure could be reviewed just as well by the theologians in their professional journals, etc. Pastor Dalton himself wanted the proof-sheets in order to publish in the Messner Evangelical Newspaper an article on the brochure which would appear almost at the same time as the brochure itself. These grounds appeared so justifiable to me that I gladly agreed to them, but now I am seized by all kinds of scruples. If only I had shown you the translation! I even allowed myself a few introductory words without asking you. Please, do not say "yes" to everything out of politeness. We are staying here until the 5th of July; otherwise nothing is changed regarding the trip about which I wrote you at length a few days ago. Farewell, may God protect you.

June 27, in the evening.

P.S. I open my letter again to tell you that I received the notification of your shipment, thanks again. Prince Obolenski is taking care of this letter, together with my kindest regards.

IU. SAMARIN TO BARONESS RAHDEN

Moscow, July 19, (1869).

My agent in Moscow was expecting me by the middle of June and did not send a single one of your letters. I found them on my table yesterday when I arrived in Moscow. Even though you slight me occasionally in supposing me capable of addressing compliments to you, it is impossible for me not to tell you that I read your letters with unspeakable pleasure. You are even more kind and more ironical in German than in French.[80] Continue to write in German, whenever you are in good humour, and let me add that I have no intention of later using this generous concession against you in order to force my own mother tongue upon you. You need not fear any *language pressure* on my part. My national pride will already be satisfied by the way in which I use your beloved German in my letters. The present reassuring remark is called for by your pangs of conscience. You want to know whether you have perhaps overstepped your authority, whether my introduction may appear as a brochure, etc. etc. But then you add to the question that I should not say "yes" to everything out of politeness. Alright! That my introduction should appear as a separate brochure I gladly agree to under the following conditions: (1) format, paper and print are to be equivalent to the luxury edition of the life of Caesar (by the emperor Napoleon); (2) the public is also to be provided with a faithful picture of my worthy person so that abroad one may impress upon one's memory the features of the "raging *strelets*." Are you now satisfied with the conditions, and may I too now break out into ringing laughter about your scruples?

I have finally received Schirren's brochure. If I had ordered and paid for it, I could not have wanted a more brilliant confirmation of what I had put forward about the provinces. The situation is changing: I feel myself so right

[80] The remainder of this paragraph is in German. (Trans.)

and so sure of my position that from today on the greatest moderation is becoming for me an obligatory rule of conduct. With God and the memory of you helping me, I hope to adhere to it. If, however, that should not happen, rap me on my fingers.

I am addressing this letter on the off-chance that it can find you through general delivery at Gastein. In ten days or so, I shall be at Ragatz and from there I shall write you to find out where and when I shall be able to see you before you return to Russia. Yours truly. P. S. The Emperor and the Empress were charming toward Cherkasski.

IU. SAMARIN TO BARONESS RAHDEN[81]

Ragatz, August 7, 1869.

Gnädiges Fräulein, and my strict and highly esteemed friend!

Allow me to write to you once again and to ask how you are. I don't know whether you have received my delayed letter from Moscow. Since that time I have been, as it were, following your footsteps and arrived in Berlin one day after your departure; then I stayed for two days in Wildbad at Miliutin's, two days at Duke Shcherbatov's in Lucerne, and now I am sitting quite alone in Ragatz, where I feel real nostalgia for the good old times of my first stay at this place, the beautiful days at Aranjuez.

Have you received any detailed news about the arrival of the imperial couple in Moscow, mainly about relations with Cherkasski? He has probably not said anything about it himself. This first meeting was awaited with the utmost tension, both by the whole of the bourgeoisie as well as by the Governor General, since the latter was hoping to find in the imperial attitude and mood a sign for his own relationship

[81]The entire letter is in German. (Trans.)

towards V. Cherkasski. Everything actually went as well as one could possibly have wished. The most unambiguous goodwill was shown in a way that has surpassed the most optimistic expectations. A friendly glance, a gracious address, a handshake, later an invitation to Illinski for dinner—nothing was missing, and now personal respect for the mayor, who was the spokesman, has risen 50%. The impression was especially striking because about less than five minutes before the arrival of the train the local authorities tried everything to push V. C. and the city delegates accompanying him back from the position which he had taken up in the waiting-room.

Miliutin's[82] mental condition has definitely improved. He understands everything, without any effort, and speaks much better than a few years ago; sometimes he still forgets the correct expression (especially proper names), but he seldom uses one word instead of another, and if it happens, then he notices it at once himself and stops talking. However, the doctor who visits him does not seem to have great hopes for further improvement.

I have finished reading Schirren's brochure here. The paper can not remain unanswered and I shall have to write a few short notes, in which I shall certainly try not to descend to the tone of my adversary. By carrying the antithesis between the local views and the interests and principles of the state to the extreme he has certainly done a service, for a solution has to be found for the misunderstanding between province and state, which unfortunately exists, is known, even though it is half disguised, and is becoming more acute every day. A clarification is now becoming an urgent necessity, no matter how painful it may turn out to be at present, for only thus can one avert for the future something which will be worse and sadder. I should also like to tell you something about some other papers of a very different type which

[82]N. Miliutin suffered a stroke in 1866, which compelled his retirement. See note on p. 17. (Ed.)

I want to work on, but I shall leave that for the time being. You can imagine how much I am looking forward to the appearance of the German translation and that I am mostly interested in the few lines which form the introduction. For the moment I only beg you to be so kind as to tell me something definite about your plans for Gastein and elsewhere abroad so that I can use that as a guide in paying a visit to you somewhere. Unfortunately, I cannot say as yet when that will be. You have probably heard that Princess Vassilchikov (nee Shcherbatov) has died recently; when her brother received the news he hurried from Lucerne to Kiev in order to be present at the funeral, and as he left he entrusted to me his family, who were staying in the neighbourhood of Lucerne. Now I have to visit them a few times from Ragatz and I'm thinking of going there for a day tomorrow; then I'll go on to take the baths myself. Allow me to express my deepest respect and my most heartfelt friendship. Your devoted.

BARONESS RAHDEN TO IU. SAMARIN

Gastein, July 29/August 10, (1869).

I received both of your letters the same day, that is to say, the day before yesterday; the one from Moscow was dated the seventh and postmarked the twenty-second of July. We are staying here some fifteen days more and the future is completely uncertain. It seems to me that the Grand Duchess will split her time between Salzburg and Zurich until the end of September in our calendar, and that we shall return home early. I shall say nothing to you about Schirren's brochure except that you are right, and besides haven't I already exhausted this painful subject? In general, I cannot write to you now except to give you the information you want. I beg of you not to write to me any more in German. If you have any friendship for me, be patient with me and continue to send me news of yourself. As soon as I have settled down again and recovered some of the gaiety which is proper for you, I shall be less laconic. Goodbye, I clasp your hand.

I must nevertheless add something that might interest you with regard to Cherkasski. I knew the details about the dinner and the reception by Lise Miliutin; before we left, at a little dinner at Oranienbaum, the Emperor spoke about Prince Cherkasski "with pleasure,"[83] as the Grand Duchess says, to express the most favourable sentiment[84] in these parts—and particularly stressed the very fair provisions that the prince made with regard to the affairs of the Polish clergy. The Grand Duchess is doing very well here, the baths are marvellous for her in spite of the bad weather.

BARONESS RAHDEN TO IU. SAMARIN

Gastein, August 10/22, (1869).

I don't know what your solitude at Ragatz is like but that which surrounds us here is complete; even the weather is joining in and is becoming another isolating principle, because it rains every day from morning to evening. The monotonous beauty of this gigantic split in the rocks ends up overwhelming with its charmless grandeur, while the incessant noise of our magnificent cascade produces upon the majority of those who are condemned to hear it the depressing effect of a dull irritation. Only seriously sick people come to Gastein—a real Miracle-Court!—or older people whose nerves are very weak. This indicates the extent of the social resources. And finally, any walk that is more than a brief stroll is quite tiring because you find that you have to go up or down real chamois trails, and to come back home with feet bruised by the sharp stones of the track. The picture has a

[83] *Avec gout.* (Trans.)

[84] *Stimmung.* (Trans.)

few dark spots, hasn't it? Well, except for the rain, I haven't got on too badly during this poor sojourn. That surprises you, I can see, for my last letter (of which I am somewhat ashamed, let it be said between us) must not have constituted convincing proof for you of what I am saying. But fifteen days have passed since then and who knows whether patience hasn't come to me while sleeping after one of those long walks; the utter, absorbing fatigue they produce in me is so very satisfying. The fact is that I can write to you in complete freedom. I have come once again to my decision about many irremediable things, which I was wrong to let my bad temper complicate and. . . . When we meet again I shall tell you the rest—it is so difficult to write about certain things. I hope that your cure helped you. Is it the "supernatural" which concerns you at the moment, or your inevitable reply? As I had a great deal of free time here, I have translated—with a thousand mental reservations—the *Tserkov' odna*[85] of Khomiakov, possibly to follow through from your preface. Speaking of your preface, I could in turn give it a rather curious historical introduction—but I shall resist. By the first week in September, you will be able to read yourself in German I am told. If you prefer to write to me in that language, do so. A word from you in any language whatsoever would have made me happy this last while.

A week from today we are leaving for Salzburg, where the Grand Duchess wants to rest from a cure which was otherwise admirably successful. The Grand Duchess Catherine and her husband will probably come too. If the weather stays bad in Austria, it is possible we shall go on to Switzerland; in any case we shall be back home earlier than usual, at the beginning of October. If we don't meet abroad, goodbye until Petersburg. May God keep you.

Anton Bliudov wrote to me from the Gallagans; with an extraordinary devotion and strength of soul these unhappy parents find, if not consolation, at least sustenance in inces-

[85]"The Church is One." (Trans.)

sant labour for the public weal, for the country. Madame Gallagan encourages her husband; she is the one who with true heroism animates him in his work.[86] Pobedonostsev[87] tells me that the trip of the Grand Duke's heir has been marvellously successful and that the Czarevna is forming a real, warm sympathy for that country which is receiving her with so much enthusiasm. The Emperor was too sick en route to inspect the guards of honour announced for Kiev. Right now he is fine.

IU. SAMARIN TO BARONESS RAHDEN

Geneva, September 7, (1869).

On my return from Chamonix and Martigny I found your letter of the twenty-second of August in the mail. The sight of your writing caused me a great deal of joy, but even without that encouragement I should have written you from here in any case. You can see that I don't let myself be intimidated easily. I do not know if this courage comes to me from the perilous leaps and the painful climbs which I have just carried out, or whether it is the effect of a conscience which, this time at least, doesn't have anything to reproach itself with;[88] but what I'm certain has a great deal to do with it is the absolute confidence which your sense of justice in-

[86] G. P. Gallagan had decided to found a college in Kiev, in memory of his late son. (D. S.)

[87] K. P. Pobedonostsev (1827-1907) began his career as a Professor of Civil Law at the University of Moscow. He tutored both Alexander III and Nicholas II in their formative years. He became a Senator in 1860, a member of the State Council in 1872 and Procurator-General of the Holy Synod in 1880. An outstanding reactionary statesman, he was a determined opponent of the reforms of the sixties and a stalwart defender of unlimited autocracy. (Ed.)

[88] Up to here the paragraph is in German. (Trans.)

spires in me.

I see according to your letter that we have led almost the same life, the only difference being that necessarily implied by the relative thickness of the soles we use. I pressed on as far as the Grand Mulet, which is the last stopping point before reaching the summit of Mont Blanc; I did not feel strong enough to reach it, in spite of the sidelong glances which the Americans who were following the same route shot at me in passing. What I saw goes beyond the wildest and strangest of anything that my imagination could have dreamed of. With the scene which I had before me at the summit of Montanvert, of Mauvais Pas, of Tete Noire, etc. the pictures of Calame, which I had admired some years ago, came back in my memory and this recollection doubled my enjoyment. It must be that art seizes hold of nature and translates it, so to speak, so that we can understand it properly and appreciate it completely. This is just another of the infinite variations on the triumph of mind over matter. Even without knowing how to hold a brush, you still need, in order to enjoy a landscape, to be able to see it as a picture.

After a week I was even more overcome by awe than footsore. Here I found to my very great joy a newly-built church, a faultless service, an intelligent young priest, and for compatriots, the Karamzin couple and Dmitri Obolenski who doesn't quite know how to explain the fate that brought him to Geneva. Tomorrow I am leaving for Lucerne, from there to Baden-Baden, where I shall spend a week with the Miliutins, then to Paris, London, and about the 12th or 15th of October I shall be in Petersburg where I shall hope to find you.

I am delighted at your fine idea of translating Khomiakov's piece on the Church, but frankly I have difficulty in understanding how this work could have stirred any protest within you or any mental reservations. Isn't the Church, such as he conceives it, a unity which has not affected liberty at all, but, such as results from the agreement of individual aspirations? Isn't that the ideal which the first, the real Protestants dreamed about while they were doing away with the circumstances which alone render its realization possible? This sort of Protestant is not found anymore today, in Germany at least . . . .

But I must stop before I go too far, and also because the clock which is ringing in my ears tells me that dinner won't wait. Goodbye then until Petersburg. Yours truly.

IU. SAMARIN TO BARONESS RAHDEN

(Berlin, October, 1869).

Permit me to take six copies of my introduction,[89] which I should like to send to those of my friends in Prague who do not read Russian. Yesterday evening I finished reading the translation, and I can only repeat to you what I said after having leafed through it. It seems faultless to me, and it's the passages about which I was most particular that have turned out the best. There are even two or three in which the translation renders my thought better than the Russian text. To see oneself completely understood is certainly the greatest satisfaction that can be given to an author. I hope that you may experience it some day.

[89]The German translation of the preface written by Iu. Samarin for the theological works of A. S. Khomiakov appeared in Berlin in 1869 in the form of a separate brochure entitled: *Juri Samarin über Chomäkoff. Ein Beitrag zur Kenntniss der neuesten theologischen Bestrebungen in Russland.—Aus dem Russischen.* The translation is preceded by the translator's preface: "Translator's introduction. The following translation of the preface to the second volume of A. S. Khomiakov's complete works is intended to acquaint the German public, but especially the theologians, with the position which the so-called Slavophil party is taking in Russia towards the Church. Khomiakov's name is little known outside of his native land. This preface to his theological works tells us better than anything else who he was, of his excellent gift, and of his ardent love for Church and

On publishing my brochures on the Baltic Provinces I risked irritating only declared enemies of mine and those whose hostility had been apparent long before anything of mine was in print. In rejecting "the accusations that have been circulated against him that he entertains a barbarically destructive racial prejudice," you have run headlong into your friends' prejudices and, even though you have told me nothing about it, I think I am right in guessing that the act of justice which you have courageously performed on my behalf must have cost you a great deal of anguish. I have only one way to show you my gratitude, and that is in never departing, in any of my future work, from a determined, consistent spirit of moderation. Yours truly.

native land.

"The author of the preface himself, Samarin, a close friend of Khomiakov, is at the moment regarded to be the head and the standard-bearer of the national movement. As one of the most zealous promoters of the emancipation of the serfs, he played both in word as well as in deed a most active role in the organizational work which preceded this great event in the years 1858-1861. Iu. Samarin is known as the most decisive enemy of the oligarchical-privileged constitution of the Baltic Provinces of Russia and their exclusive German-Protestant position in the empire. But the spirit of freedom and tolerance which fills the following paper and the high level of culture of the author, which has German sources, are a sufficient refutation of the accusations that have been circulated against him, namely that he entertains a barbarically destructive racial prejudice.

"In most recent times an unusual interest in Russian affairs has sprung up in Germany; political, social, literary questions are being examined closely, discussed in detail, an opinion is formed of them; but it is the first time that the German public meets with a religious creed and one which is not something formal, theological, but something living, something that has outgrown the scholastic control of a school and yet has a scientific foundation. May the Protestant theological world make use of its most noble privilege and meet this new phenomenon with objectivity and justice!" [The text in quotation marks is in German. (Trans.)]

At the end of the brochure are found the table of contents of the second volume of the works of Khomiakov and a few comments by the translator. (D. S.)

BARONESS RAHDEN TO IU. SAMARIN

(December, 1869).

Will you do me a great favour of patience and severe criticism by reading and correcting the enclosed translation? You will see that I have left enough margin for all the observations you may care to make. I rather hope you will be happier with the style—at least I have tried to be as German as possible. Professors Engelhardt and Kotliarevski of Dorpat were good enough to check the correctness of the translation and of the theological terms; in these two respects they have been really helpful. The rest is up to you. I hope you won't too much mind the tiresome task I am giving you and which really I should have spared you, busy as you are; but it is here the work of your friend, and so I am more scrupulous than I would be for you. Now that my little job is finished I realize the pleasure it has given me, and I am very grateful to you. The men and the things which are around me, the common and utterly frivolous interests which I can feel endlessly bustling, make any occupation doubly precious which sets one's thought in another system of ideas and removes it far from everything which is transient. Very best wishes.

IU. SAMARIN TO BARONESS RAHDEN

Moscow, December 20, (1869).

Your letter antedated mine by several days. I had begun to write to you to get news of you and to ask how the work, that I now have in front of me, was coming. Work is really the word for it; I speak whereof I know, thinking about the time and the effort which my very imperfect translation of the three French brochures of Khomiakov cost me. So far I have only glanced through yours and, from what I can judge of it, it seems admirable. You possess in every language inexhaustible stylistic resources and such a real talent to render effortlessly the most delicate nuances of thought that in reading you one wonders how it happened that you did not go right into a literary career. You must surely at some time have thought of it, and I believe that your abstention was rather an exercise of will or an act of intellectual maceration.

Ever since I perceived, partially at least, the sphere of ideas in which the solitary part of your existence is spent, I have more than once mentally compared you with the author whom you have just been studying by translating him. No one more than he could appreciate you. How many times I have heard him lament on the dearth of lives which are completely healthy in heart and soul, on the lack of a skeletal framework in people's character, on the worthlessness of this insipid geniality which springs from the debility of nerves and the flaccidity of intelligence, which is too lazy to feel the need to judge and consequently loses all merit by condemning nothing. Possibly at first sight these externals may have shocked you; to consider him properly from a moral point of view, you would perhaps have had to re-examine some biases, but all that would have been done automatically and you would eventually have come to esteem him deeply, and even become close friends with him. You will understand my retrospective regrets that chance did not bring you two together.

There is much else to write of, but I don't have the time here. We are just about to close our session of the *zemstvo*, and dossiers and reports are raining on us from every direction and a great majority of the members are not even taking the trouble of leafing through them. On the other hand, Prince Cherkasski is functioning at the Duma like a pump that sucks and blows, drawing to him and sending off business with a rapidity which disconcerts his colleagues. I am looking forward impatiently to the respite the Christmas holidays will bring us and then I shall take the pleasure of sifting through your translation and quibbling with you at my leisure. On the fifteenth of January, Aksakov is to come to Petersburg for his trial,[90] and he is the one who will be bringing your manuscript to you. You must admit, though, that you are not at all seriously expecting any corrections from me.

Let me thank you once again and clasp your hand. Yours truly.

IU. SAMARIN TO BARONESS RAHDEN

Moscow, January 2, 1870.

May this new year be good to you; and may I join to this wish my thanks which are no less sincere. I have studied and sifted through your translation with a pleasure which you can well understand without my having to explain it to you. I have, so to speak, sat you down in front of the man whom I venerate most in all the world,[91] and I have been happy to see that you have readily grasped the essence of his thought. It is precisely those passages which seem to me most significant that you have rendered the best. I have quibbled with you quite freely on every point which I found at all debatable; but I did it, of course, only in the firm belief that my observations would not bother you in the slightest. If you were to accord them a value they don't have and accept them in trust, I should be truly pained.

What type of publication do you intend?

There is nothing new here, if I overlook railroads, which are almost becoming a mania. While waiting for them to be built, you can manage on Orel's to do less than ten versts an hour. We have just received the statutes for the new congregation of missionaries patronized by Her Majesty the Empress. I

[90]The question of the suppression of the newspaper *Moskva* was to be resolved definitively at the State Council. (D. S.) See pp. 13 fn. and 80.

[91]A. S. Khomiakov. (D. S.)

wonder whether people are voluntarily satisfied with delusions, or whether they have come to the point of losing all notion of what constitutes life. Man is always so easily satisfied with mere *appearance* and one's demands are so humble in this respect that it is even impossible to object.[92] Yours truly.

The few lines placed at the head of the Essay in the second volume of the works of Khomiakov do not seem to me suitable as an introduction to this same Essay published separately. I suppose that you will have your translation preceded by a few words directed to the German public. I strongly encourage it for the very interest of the subject. If, however, this was not your intention, this is what I would propose, if I were in your shoes. I shall express myself in Russian because quite certainly you will have less difficulty translating me than in correcting my German.[93] Those of the German public who are even the slightest interested in the development of religious ideas in Russia will perhaps not refuse to take this "essay" into consideration which is translated literally from the Russian original which, itself, was published recently, for the second time, in the collection of the theological works of A. Khomiakov. In a concise, but scrupulous, study the author has primarily illuminated those points of doctrine which distinguish the Greek confession on the one hand and the Roman and Protestant confessions on the other. He has aimed at showing that the apparent contradiction among a good number of conceptions which have been colliding for a long while in Western religious polemics (such as justification by faith and justification by works, scripture and tradition, individual freedom and ecclesiastical authority, etc.) disappears before a full self-consciousness of

[92]The sentence is in German. (Trans.)

[93]From here to the middle of p. 133 the text is in Russian. (Trans.)

the Church which he confesses. This voice from the East seems to me worthy of some attention, particularly at a time, on the one hand, when the Roman Church, impelled by some sort of fate or by the law of logical necessity embodied in events, is ready to censor itself by carrying its claims to the final extreme, or, on the other hand, when the cornerstone of Protestantism, Scripture (insofar as it consists of strict historical fact), seems to be broken apart and pulverized beneath the sledge of a relentless historical criticism. It is now, above all, in view of the effects of the movement which has developed in the West in the realm of faith, that a propitious occasion seems to have arisen to pay serious attention to a Church, which, up to now, has been the object of reproach, perhaps ill-founded, for its so-called immobility and inertia.

The "Essay" of Khomiakov first appeared in Russia in a theological review published under the strict preventive censorship of the religious authorities; it may therefore be deemed to have received the approval of the Russian Church administration.

The corresponding numbers are written in pencil in the text.

1. *Tserkov' odna*—as a general thesis, is far from indicating the contents of the whole Essay; I have kept it at the head of the work out of a possibly exaggerated feeling of piety, even though finding it out of place. If need be, it ought to be placed at the beginning of the first section, and I do not think I am far from the author's intention in recommending this slight shift to you. 1. *Die Kirche ist eine. Ihre Einheit ist eine*, etc.

2. Instead of "*theilhaftiger*" (*pokariaiushchikhsia*) could one not say "*sich willig fügender*"?

3. "*Gegeben*" gives the literal sense of "*daetsia*" properly, but I believe that "*geboten*" would be more in keeping

with the thought, if indeed "*geboten*" really means "offered."

4. "*Um des Menschen willen*"—here let me contradict you. The text says "*dlia*" and not "*radi*." "*In den Augen des Menschen*" gives the thought exactly, but I wonder why "*für den Menschen*" shocks you? People do say: *für mich haben die Volksgesänge einen Sinn, für einen Ausländer sind sie sinnlos.* You yourself translate later "*dlia Nego*" by "*für Ihn (Gott).*"

5. I have no criticism to make of "*Selbstoffenbarung*," but consider whether "*Erscheinung*" would not be more exact in the sense which Kant gave the word "*Erscheinung*," in opposing it to the idea of essence (*das Ding an sich*).

6. It seems to me that the particle "*nur*" is not in the proper place, which slightly changes the author's thought. It (the Church) repulses *only those* who voluntarily refuse to enter its bosom—that is the sense of your translation. However, this is what the author means: the Church does not judge or condemn those who voluntarily refuse to enter its bosom; it, so to speak, *only* recognizes their refusal or, in other terms, *only* spurns them. "*Priznavat*'" means here not only "*betrachten*" but also "*seine Erkenntniss aussprechen.*" I will not pretend to correct your translation and I offer you my poor German only to convey the author's thought: *hinsichtlich derjenigen die sich selbst willig von ihr ausschliessen, thut sie nur die geschehene Scheidung erkennen und aussprechen, indem sie sie, als ihr nicht zugehörige, von sich ausschliesst.*—The problem is to express clearly the difference that exists between "*ausscheiden*" (which is the Greek sense of anathema) and "*verdammen*" (which is the Latin sense of the same word).

7. "*Nur sich selbst*" is not exact. A judicial sentence passed on oneself always presupposes a split within an individual, something that can be reconciled with the concept of the Church (as defined by Khomiakov) as something pervaded by Divine Grace.[94] Professor Engelhardt has understood the thought quite well, but his paraphrase is wordy. If

"*sie richtet nur für sich selbst*" is not German, I would have said: "*nur auf ihrem eigenen Gebiete hat sie zu richten.*"

8. Could you not keep the "*cherez*" *Khrista* (*durch Christus*) instead of *in Christo*? The idea is this: human imperfection has reasonably been able to furnish material for judgment and condemnation only from the day in which the possibility of perfection in the condition of human existence was established *by* the fact of the man-God. He alone has control over man because he himself is really a man. He alone is judge, therefore the Church is so in his name, as by delegation. I do not know whether it is "*durch Christus*" or rather "*von Christo*," etc.?

9. "*Ne khitrit*," *geht nicht auf krummen Wegen*—it is not exactly that. The verb "to finesse" would render the thought properly. Could one not sav: "*Sucht sich nicht durch Kunstgriffe zu helfen*"?

10. The adjective "*apostolisch*" should modify "*Schrift*" as well as *Lehre: in der apostolichen Schrift und Lehre.*

11. I would have added: "*jedoch.*"

12. I would prefer "*zu fügen.*"

13. *Edinstvo ikh—die Einheit ihrer Aeusserungen in Schrift, Tradition und Werken*, etc.

14. "*Aufheben*" would perhaps be better than "*zerstören.*"

15. "*Weisheit*" or "*Erkenntnis*" (*mudrost'*).

16. "*Ansehen*"—is that not rather "*den Anschein*"?

17. I would propose: "*die Kirche . . . ist sich, kraft einer inneren Erkenntnis, die ihr nie fehlen kann, alles dessen worin sich ihr Wesen offenbart (oder gestaltet) vollkommen bewusst.*"

18. Instead of "*denn*" (for), I would prefer "*so*" (thus).

19. Here I think that "*Werke*" (work, *opus*) would be better than "*Thun*," all the more so since this term, which is broader, was used before to render the word "*deistvie.*"

20. "*Werk*"?

[94]The sentence is in German. (Trans.)

21. "*Die*"—I would prefer "*alle*."

22. "*Vechnomu*"—why not "*Ewiges*"?

23. "*Vlast'*"—might, "*Macht*," rather than "*Gewalt*"—*sila, nasilie.*

24. "*Dogadka*"—supposition, hypothesis: "*Vermuthung*"?

25. *Pered Bogom i sviatoiu Tserkov'iu: vor Gott und vor der heiligen Kirche.*

26. "*Begnügt sich*"—contents itself; I would prefer the equivalent of: finds itself reduced to, etc.

27. I would prefer: "Indem *die Kirche ihren Glauben an die dreieinige Gottheit bekennt, bekennt sie* zugleich *ihren Glauben*" etc. . . .

28. *Wesen und Dasein für sushchestvovanie*—correct, rendering the meaning completely, the word chosen is much closer to the original than the text itself.[95]

29. "*Zeugniss*"—does not exactly give the sense of "*oblichenie*." This word is taken from a definition of faith borrowed from the Scripture and very commonly used in the teaching of our Church: "*Vera est' chaemykh izveshchenie veshchei 'oblichenie' nevidimykh.*" Faith is the assurance (or the confirmation) of what one hopes for and the "manifestation" (or the incarnation) of invisible things. The root of the word "*oblichenie*" is "*lik*" (image, form). "*Oblichenie*" —noun, formed from the verb, makes the process organic by which what is invisible by its essence acquires for human intelligence the certitude of a visible object, becomes accessible to contemplation. I cannot find the equivalent in German.

30. It would be better, I think, to link the sentence beginning with "*Die*" to the preceding sentence with a particle. This is the sense: the invisible alone is the object of faith, for what is visible is perceived by the intelligence by means of the senses. However, we say: we have faith in the Church and we are right in saying so, considering that the Church is not a congregation of Christians, but rather, in its

[95]The comment is in German. (Trans.)

essence, something invisible—the spirit of God, etc. . . .

31. The "*auch*" should be located between "*ist*" and "*die*" not after "*Kirche.*"

32. Instead of "*sichtbar,*" to better express the thought, I would have said here "*erkennbar.*"

33. "*Zu finden*"—quite correct!![96]

34. "*Izsiakli*" means exhausted; *Izsiakshi istochnik*—a spring which has been dried out.

35. It is not "by" the Church but "to" the Church: *der alttestamentlichen Kirche vorgeschrieben.*

36. Why not say "*Thier*"? Here the author is alluding to the question raised and discussed in the Latin Church, that is whether a rat which has eaten consecrated bread has taken Holy Communion.

37. "*Ne slykhavshago*" does not mean: who would not listen (accept), but rather who has not heard, to whom it has not been preached: *dem das Gesetz Christi nicht verkündet worden ist.*

38. I find that "*Gerede*" is perfectly fitting for the idle and indecent questions with which the scholastics have burdened Latin doctrine and which are not even attempts at explanation.

39. "*Elementaren Kräften*"—lacks precision; I would have preferred "*Natur-Kräften*" to render "*Stikhii.*"

40. I do not know whether "*zwiespältig*" really means "of two species." In rejecting the idea of "*dvoiakost' very*" the author alludes to the different modes that the Latins distinguished in faith, to prove that at least in several degrees it was powerless to effect salvation without works. I believe that "*zwiefach*" would be more exact.

41. It would be, I think, more proper instead of "*er thut Werke*" to say "*thätig, also wirkend; ist er aber einmal wirkend, was für Werke werden da noch gefordert?*" So that faith may possess the power of salvation, it is necessary that it act virtually, without action, as a *fait accompli*, being

[96] Quite right. (Trans.)

required of it—seeing that becoming a *fait accompli* is not always within its power.—That is what the author means.

42. Instead of: "*der ohne Werke ist*," say rather: "*der nicht wirkend ist (oder der sich nicht bethätigt).*"

43. I see, according to this passage, that the Lutherans differ from us in rendering the text of the Epistle to the Hebrews. "*Nevidimykh oblichenie*" seems to me deeper in thought and more energetic in expression. The invisible world forms itself (takes on form) within a belief.[97] In any case, whether I am right or wrong, it seems to me beyond doubt that one should stick to the translation accepted by the Lutherans.

44. The word "*ist*" should come between "*Gott*" and "*in*."[98]

45. Rather than "*allein*," wouldn't "*durch sich selbst*" be better?

46. Add: "*des todten Glaubens.*"

47. "*Vollendet werden*"—do these words properly give the idea of "*sovershenstvuiutsia*"? I should like something along the line of: "*im fortwährenden Steigen begriffen.*"

48. "*Gabe*"—seems useless to me—"*Alles Gute*," etc.

49. "*Vse tvorit blagodat'*"—*in allem ist die Gnade das Wirkende.* (I do not know whether one can say in German: "*alles wirkt die Gnade*").

50. Wouldn't "*aufgehen*" be better?

BARONESS RAHDEN TO IU. SAMARIN

St. Petersburg, January 8, (1870).[99]

How good you are! Your comments must have cost you a precious amount of time; I could not accept such a sacrifice

[97]The sentence is in German. (Trans.)

[98]The sentence is in German. (Trans.)

[99]The text reads "8 Juin (1870)." (Trans.)

were I not to associate it with the memory of your friend, whom it is as important to you as to me to interpret with clarity and fairness. It is not with confidence but with conviction that I accept your remarks. You may imagine my satisfaction as I noted that in many places you substituted for a correction of Professor Engelhardt the term that I had used at first. So I triumphantly re-established to their original rights my four exiled words: "*Selbstoffenbarung*" has again become "*Erscheinung*" and "*Thun*" become "*Werk.*"[100]

There are other inexcusable errors of the copyist, oversights, inversions, even misinterpretations which I should never have given you the trouble of correcting. On a few points, however, I should like as translator to explain my reasoning to you, as if to ask you once again for your final sanction.

Sec. 2. . . . "*So wirkt und erkennt sie nur innerhalb ihrer eigenen Gränzen, ohne die übrige Menschheit zu richten* (in the words of the Apostle Paul to the Corinthians[101]) *und begnügt sich damit diejenigen als ausgeschlossen, d. h. als ihr nicht zugehörig, anzuerkennen, die sich freiwillig von ihr ausschliessen.*"[102] The sense is much more stressed in this way. If I did not emphasize it any more, it is because I was aiming at as literal a translation as possible.

I really must tell you how perfect that passage of yours is: "*Denn Christus kennt das Seine, und die Kirche in der Er lebt ist sich, Kraft einer inneren Erkenntniss u.s.w.*" I am completely charmed by it. Elsewhere the nuance is so delicate and accurate when you put "*geboten*" instead of "*gegeben,*" "*durch Christus*" instead of "*in Christo,*" "*Anschein*" for "*Ansehen,*" "*erkennbar*" instead of "*sichtbar*": it is incredible that a person can have such sensi-

[100]Following the colon the sentence is in German. (Trans.)

[101]The phrase is in German. (Trans.)

[102]From the close of the parentheses the original is in italics. (Trans.)

tivity for a language other than his maternal one!

Sec. 7, page 10. Is this better: *Wer sich von dem Geiste der Liebe lossagt, u. s. w.* "*muss sich auf äusserliches Wissen beschränken*"?

Sec. 8, page 10. I had translated: "*Ist nicht der Glaube ein Zeugniss des Unsichtbaren*?" This definition, borrowed from the Epistle to the Hebrews (ch. XI, v. 1), is rendered, as you know, by the Lutheran translation which I use when I quote. Here I had more liberty and wondered about another expression for "*oblichenie*." Modern German translations of the Scriptures say: "*Ein Nichtzweifeln an dem Unsichtbaren*," or "*eine Ueberzeugung*." The Russian translation says: "*Uverennost' v nevidimom*." Lemaistre de Sacy: "that which convinces us about the things that we do not see." Martin: "a showing forth of things," etc. Döllinger says in his work, *Christenthum und Kirche:* "*Der Glaube ist der Seelenzustand der das Unsichtbare versichtbaret*." Luthardt in his *Apology for Christianity* translates: "*Der Glaube ist eine Ueberzeugung von dem das man nicht siehet*" and defines: "*Der Glaube ist eine innere Erfahrung des Unsichtbaren*." Finally the English translation says: "Faith is the evidence of things not seen." None of these expressions seems to me completely suitable for the admirable word *oblichenie* and I allowed myself the following reasoning: If I experience within my being that which cannot be seen in such a way that it becomes for me an irrefutable certainty, as my existence itself is, then this inner experience is a representation, that is, a witness of that which cannot be seen.[103] The English word "evidence," which in a particular sense means "*Zeugniss*," further confirmed my choice of this term, which Professor Engelhardt understood since he let it stand. Nevertheless I feel fairly sure that it is not "*erschöpfend*," possibly even ambiguous—and so I would propose to you: "*Ist nicht der Glaube ein inneres*

[103]Following the colon, the sentence is in German. (Trans.)

Wahrnehmen or *Veranschaulichen* or *Versichtbaren*[104] *des Unsichtbaren*?" You also want a particle to underscore the sense of the sentence which follows; what do you think of this: "*Ist nicht der Glaube eine innere Veranschaulichung des Unsichtbaren? gleichwie die sichtbare Kirche nicht eine sichtbare Gemeinschaft von Christen ist, sondern der Geist Gottes u.s.w.*"

Do you insist upon "*Thier*" instead of "*unvernünftige Creatur*"?—I cannot understand how I could have written "*verlästet*" for *izsiakli*; I have put back the right word: "*versiegt.*"—I had said "*zwiefach*"; Professor Engelhardt put "*zwiefältig*" and "*einfältig*"; I suppose that is the consecrated theological term, but I shall look into it a little more.

Sec. 9, page 15. Will you approve of this—it is a slightly different version from yours: "*Ist er (der Glaube) wahr, (Galat. V, 6) so ist er lebendig, d. h. in der thätigen Liebe wirksam; ist er aber wirksam, welcher Werke bedarf er dann noch*?" I still have qualms of not translating literally enough. Your slight expansion is quite a bit better for the real sense, while I had held myself strictly to the terms of the original and to the words of the Lutheran translation of the Epistle of St. James. It is also according to St. James that I had written: "*Alle gute Gabe*," but "*Alles Gute*" goes quite well.

There are two passages in which I do not entirely share your opinion. In sec. 1 you reject "*theilhaftig*," substituting for it "*sich der Gnade willig fügende Creaturen.*" "*Sich fügen*" contains a nuance of concession which I cannot admit concerning grace. Grace casts you on your knees like St. Paul, or else it penetrates your heart little by little as with the man who was blind from birth: it always subdues or it reigns, one submits to it or shares in it, one does not resign oneself to it.[105] Could one not say: "*welche (die Gnade) lebendig*

[104] I do not like this expression, which bears the earmark of too forced an invention, but it is supported by the authority of Döllinger and that is something.

[105] The last phrase is in German. (Trans.)

wohnt in einer Vielheit vernünftiger Creaturen, die sich der Gnade unterwerfen"?

The other expression is "*vollendet*"—I do not know what better could be found, because "*vollenden*," much better than "*vervollkommen*" or "*fördern*," means to bring to perfection, to accomplish, to achieve, in ascending order. See the Epistle to the Hebrews concerning those witnesses of the faith who died before the coming of Christ.

In closing let me repeat to you that I am infinitely grateful to you for your corrections. You understood afterwards how earnestly I wanted them—how could you possibly have thought otherwise?

There is something else which bothers me. Everything you tell me about a possible *entente* between Khomiakov and myself cannot but be extremely precious to me; I see also in that a proof of your friendship, but are you not deluding yourself about me? In believing me capable however imperfectly of understanding the thought of Khomiakov, are you not assuming that I must share it to some extent. The idea of usurping a confidence or an opinion is so abhorrent to me that I should not want to leave the shadow of a doubt in your mind about the freedom of conscience and action which I fully retain, because it is my privilege to do so, I would almost say my Christian obligation: everything that is *Christian* has a right to my most ardent sympathy. What, then, when it is a matter of the Church of the country to which I belong, a Church which I venerate because I have learned to know it, and whose strength I value because of its gentleness! It is misunderstood, it is judged wrongly out of ignorance; how eagerly would I not seize upon every chance to show it in its true light! How gratifying it would be for me to bring my grain of sand to a work of truth, which, in enlightening minds, must necessarily spark fraternal charity in men's hearts. What does the divergence of dogmas, which do not bring about salvation, matter to me. What does it matter to me that you should consider me outside of the Church—I experience none the less a great joy in being able to say to many other Christians: you think them dead—they are living! But all this does not imply any solidarity of doctrine, any tacit acceptance of any teaching whatsoever that is contrary to Protestantism. What I think, what I say, what I do is strictly Protestant. Do you think after that that Khomiakov, the son and champion of a visible and infallible Church, could really have come to an understanding with me? I do not think so, however much I may regret it.

You would do me a real favour by writing a little introduction to the Catechism from your point of view. I would translate it conscientiously, and we would put "*Vorwort des Herausgebers*" at the head of it, with a footnote number, which would remind the forgetful reader in a footnote that you are the one who edited the theological works of Khomiakov, and in that way each one of us will keep the place which belongs to him. Farewell. If I have not wished you a happy New Year in writing, I hope that you know, that you believe, that this wish is hearty and cordial.

IU. SAMARIN TO BARONESS RAHDEN

Moscow, January 21, (1870).

One of these days you will have my reply about all the passages of your translation which still cause you some doubts, but for the moment let me make my profession of faith to you on a personal question which is very vital to me. I hasten to reassure you completely, not about my intentions—that would be useless—but about any ulterior motive, even about any expectations on my part.

You are a Protestant through and through[106]—I know, and for you Protestantism is not merely a doctrine, it is above all a moral principle, it is freedom in matters of faith, and it is also an ensemble of memories and traditions, which

[106]In German. (Trans.)

it would be impossible to divorce from yourself. The typical Christian man, such as Protestantism conceives him, is more attractive to you than all of the saints of the calendar, and in this I share your predilections on many points. You judge doctrine according to its fruits and you never inquire whether it is the product of the Christian element or of the particularly Protestant element. It is neither out of indifference nor out of weariness that you do not grapple with this question. It is perhaps because you are reluctant to put your most cherished convictions and affections upon the point of a syllogism (*postavit' na ostrye sillogizma*—to use an expression of the late Kireevski).[107] In that again you are right.

I recognize for my part that, according to the admirable definition of Khomiakov, the individual is always a Protestant, because he is constantly striving for the truth and for the good,[108] and that the Church alone is Catholic. I even believe that, to be consistent about it, whoever feels himself to be a Protestant ought necessarily to admit the Catholicity of the Church, for the inner justification of one's striving actually rests upon the recognition that truth and good constitute an objective reality lying outside of ourselves.[109] Will you ever come around some day to the same conviction? I do not know, and I shall forbear even from wondering about it, for here we are touching the limit of debatable and verifiable things. To be completely comfortable with you I need only have full and complete confidence in your good faith and not to feel in myself any desire to influence you in any matter whatsoever. Will you then please remain straightforwardly what you are and let me continue with you an exchange of ideas which, I believe, cannot but be profitable to the both of us.

There is a passage in your last letter to which I should like to draw your attention: "Do you think that Khomiakov,

[107]See note on p. 6. (Ed.)

[108]This phrase is in German. (Trans.)

[109]Following the last comma the sentence is in German. (Trans.)

the son and champion of a *visible* and *infallible* Church, could really . . ." etc.—I am not going to offer you a refutation, but rather an analysis of the two underlined terms. Do you know why you reject them as the antithesis of your profession of faith? The reason is that you and all Protestants establish between them a relationship which doesn't exist. Nothing of what is visible in the Church is infallible in itself (*an sich*) and nothing of what in the Church is infallible can be seen by sight. To be more clear about it I shall try to explain myself in another way: what quite properly revolts your instinct of Christian freedom is the exterior sign, whatever it may be, used as an everlasting tag on every manifestation of infallibility or as a criterion for truth. You have the feeling (and to my way of thinking this is the great merit of Protestantism) that every exterior sign can be confiscated or falsified in favour of error. Your conscience tells you that our Lord asks not only more of us, but something quite different from an act of submission or a token adherence to a flag, to a chief, a congregation or even a book. Once again, in this you are in the right, and you are of the Church without realizing it. Apart from the sign, to which it is supposedly chained, what is infallibility? It is the intimate sense of truth, always identical to itself, as a permanent virtue in a latent or active state. To deny this virtue would be to recognize that the gates of Hell could prevail against the Church of God, or, in other words, to hand over to chance the future of Christian humanity.

The word "active" here implies the faculty of showing itself in any way whatsoever, and I doubt that it could in this sense prejudice freedom. These words of the Scripture: "the Spirit of God blows where it wills"[110] do not mean that it is itself only on condition that it not show itself; nor do they mean that everything which is accessible to the senses is to the same degree a direct manifestation of the Spirit; they

[110]St. John 3:8. Samarin wrote, "L'Esprit de Dieu souffle où il veut." (Trans.)

mean on the contrary that the Spirit does manifest itself, and that it does so in complete liberty—or, in other words, that every form, every action, every word can at his discretion be its organ. Why then, to come back to the Church, should we suppose that it cannot be but invisible, that is to say, deprived of the faculty of manifesting itself or bound in the exercise of this faculty to *one* palpable and visible form to the exclusion of all others? It is always these two terms, however, which keep coming into the question: the Church as an abstraction, or the Church as an authority recognizable by an exterior sign. And yet you do admit *one* manifestation of the Church as a moral being, always identical to itself, that is to say, infallible—one alone: a selection of chronicles, sermons, poems and epistles to which you give the name Scriptures. Why this sole manifestation to the exclusion of every single other one? Why should the author of the Scriptures, who is neither Moses, nor St. Luke, nor St. Paul, but rather the Church, why should the author have lost the power of speech—just as soon as the book was finished?

I am not going to insist upon this aspect of the question, which I believe is sufficiently clear, but I owe you an explanation of the reasons which lead me to reject the exterior sign in the name of the Church. The radicalism of my opinion on this point will probably not seem very consistent with the doctrine taught among us as being that of the Church. I realize this, and you may have no doubt that the great majority of our theologians, if they were called upon to judge me, would find me tainted with heresy. It is generally supposed that between the Latin Church and ours there is a divergence in that the one accepts the person of St. Peter's successor as a divinely inspired organ, while the other attributes the same virtue to the company of Bishops united in Ecumenical Council. There would be therefore, on both sides, an acceptance in principle of an exterior sign, and divergence in fact. I admit that I held this doctrine for a long time, but after considerable reflection I have abandoned it. What struck me at first was that on these grounds we have always been beaten by the papists. Once the principle is admitted, they alone are consistent, offering us as a sign a person whose visible nature is unquestionable. Looking more closely at it I observed that the Church had never recognized in advance the quality of ecumenicity (*vselenskost'*) in any Council. It has never said: such and such a doctrine is true because it was proclaimed by an Ecumenical Council; quite the contrary, it is only after having recognized the doctrine as true that it has attributed to the assembly which formulated it the title of Ecumenical Council. If need be, I would undertake to prove that there exists no juridical evidence by which an Ecumenical Council, as an organ of infallibility, can be distinguished from any other assembly of bishops. This evidence has not even been sought by anyone, and in this respect it is impossible not to recognize the immense importance of the Council of Florence. We reject it, and yet the solemnity of the convocation, the number of bishops present, the immense majority of those who accepted its decisions, the negligible number who protested, everything would seem to justify its rights to an absolute authority. Providence seems to have willed that in that memorable assembly all of the exterior signs which human weakness could have clutched at should have been wanting in truth and should have put themselves in the service of error.

The Spirit of God is not an abstraction: it exists and manifests itself, it speaks and acts—seek it in good faith, seek it always and you will be able to perceive it; but if, wearying from your exertions, you hope by an act of exterior submission to still the cry of your conscience which yearns for the whole of your being to be impregnated with truth, the Spirit of God will escape you and you will find yourself face to face with an idol. That is what seems to me to be the lesson that comes out of the whole history of the Church . . . .

But enough of that—it has been quite a dissertation to impose upon you. I cannot help but smile thinking of the type of letter which will be coming for you at Michael Palace; it's almost an impropriety, or at least a sort of revolt against the milieu in which you make such a fine pretence of living. Yours truly.

BARONESS RAHDEN TO IU. SAMARIN

Sunday morning, (January, 1870).

For perhaps the first time since we have known one another I did not feel in your last letter the coldness of sharp steel beneath the apparent gentleness of the reasoning, and I cannot tell you how much good it did me. So that is what you are, that is what you really think! Why was I not long before able to discern that great depth of patient goodness and true liberty? And I who talked of biases and blind prejudices in others! From now on with you I shall have no more need for that vulgar tension of mind called courage. You have given me the security of confidence in spite of your disapproval of what I believe in. I am profoundly grateful to you for the trouble you are taking in elucidating for me certain questions which are transfigured by your way of seeing; and since you are willing, I shall from time to time send you my ignorance and doubt. Once again let me thank you with all my heart. Farewell, I am leaving you to go off to mass.

IU. SAMARIN TO BARONESS RAHDEN

Moscow, January 24, 1870.

Since I am far from pushing modesty to the point of indifference, I cannot hide the fact from you that your approbation has given me the greatest pleasure. If my joy turns into pride you are the one who is responsible.

Here is what I would now propose to you, after having studied closely all of the passages in question, and always assuming you will have the last word.

Sec. 8, p. 10. The different versions of the passage of the Epistle to the Hebrews prove that the Greek word translated into Slavonic by "*oblichenie*" can be interpreted in a subjective sense (*Nichtzweifeln*, *Ueberzeugung*, *uverennost'*, etc.) as well as in an objective sense (*Zeugniss*, evidence, demonstration, etc.). It is the second alone which dominates in "*oblichenie*." The word is far from being common; it did not turn up by itself and certainly the translators searched for it, they may even have forged it for the occasion. If I were convinced that everyone would understand "*Veranschaulichung*" as you interpret, I should have no criticism, but being in doubt I would prefer "*Versichtbaren des Unsichtbaren*." Evidently Döllinger is the one among the moderns who in his way of understanding the Apostle comes closest to the Slavic translators. The expression is strained, you are right, but "*oblichenie*" is too.

Sec. 7, p. 10. "*. . . muss sich auf aüsserliches Wissen beschränken*" (for *ogranichivaet sebia*, etc.) is all that could be desired.

Sec. 8, p. 10. (the last lines of the page) "*gleichwie*" is precisely what I was looking for.

Sec. 8, p. 13. In requesting "*Thier*" instead of "*unvernünftige Creatur*" I am myself showing *Unvernunft* and bad taste; I am ashamed of it and recant.

Sec. 9, p. 15. The translation that you propose: "*Ist er (der Glaube) wahr, so ist er*, etc. . . ."—seems perfect to me. "*In der thätigen Liebe wirksam*"—gives the author's idea even better than the original text.

Sec. 1. "*Unterwerfen*" is quite properly the word for "*pokoriat'sia*" and renders the idea perfectly. I do not understand the sense of "*sich fügen*" very clearly. You are likewise right in retaining "*vollenden*," and I cannot understand how the root of the word did not make me realize how accurate your translation really was.

Did I not send you the draft of an introduction, just a few lines in Russian, if my memory serves me? I did not keep a copy of it. If it is convenient for you and if you have it at hand could you please send it back to me to look over again. I have one further question to put to you. In Berlin you promised me three or four copies of your translation; if it doesn't cause too much trouble could you get them to me by I. Aksakov or by any other means? Let me repeat to you that, even mentally, I have never allowed myself to wish to influence the liberty of your religious conscience. Yours truly.

P. S. We are having weather cold enough here to break paving stones, and the cholera is growing in a disquieting way.

BARONESS RAHDEN TO IU. SAMARIN

January 29, (1870).

Here is your introduction—whether you make any changes in it or not, would you please not forget that this sheet is mine and send it back to me just as it is. I am embarrassed at having forgotten a promise: the Aksakovs will bring you half a dozen copies of the preface. I am anxious too to see the catechism printed. Once again thanks with all my heart.

It has been horribly cold here—the two Grand Duchesses are sick.

IU. SAMARIN TO BARONESS RAHDEN

Moscow, February 12, (1870)

You certainly know, without my having to tell you, how happy your last letter made me. The ice is broken once and for all! I was sure of your esteem, but I felt that you were always on guard, if not to thrust at least to parry, and I was afraid that that pose, which is not natural, would eventually tire you. Now that fear is gone, I can breathe easy. That does not mean that I believe myself authorized to give free reign to my natural personality—on the contrary: your confidence imposes obligations upon me, I know that and I accept them.

Many thanks for the blotting paper. I am happy to have it still in front of me and I very frequently have recourse to the dictionary—so frequently that I am ashamed to admit it.

After having reread the few lines of introduction to the Essay on the Church, I think that if need be they could be left as they are. It is only a matter of setting the point of view and, if I were to let myself go on to develop anything, I do not know where I could stop.

Nothing new here, except the arrival of the inquiry commission concerning the proclamations affair. I shall spare you the absurd rumours which are going about in this respect.

Have you read or leafed through the book of Professor Oettingen of Dorpat: *Aphorismen aus dem Gebiete der Moralstatistik*? According to the excerpts and the book reports I have seen, it must be a serious book and of a sound, moral purpose even though profoundly hostile to Russia. Yours truly.

BARONESS RAHDEN TO IU. SAMARIN

(February, 1870).

(Translation of the preface. See pages 132-133).

Für denjenigen Theil des deutschen Publicums, der mit einiger Aufmerksamkeit die religiöse geïstige Bewegung in Russland verfolgt, dürfte es nicht ohne Interesse sein diesen Versuch kennen zu lernen, der, wörtlich aus dem Russichen übersetzt, zum zweiten Male in der Sammlung der theologischen Werke von A. Khomiakov abgedruckt worden ist. Der Verfasser beleuchtet in einer gedrängten, aber vollständigen(1) [111] Uebersicht der Lehre von der Kirche,

[111] The observations corresponding to these numbers are found in the following letter of Iu. Samarin. (Ed.)

hauptsächlich die trennenden Unterschiede zwischen dem orientalischen Glaubensbekenntnisse und dem Latinismus und Protestantismus. Er sucht darzulegen, wie vollkommen die scheinbaren Widersprüche, die sich von Alters her in der religiösen Polemik des Occidents bekämpfen, (als da sind: die Rechtfertigung durch den Glauben und die Rechtfertigung durch die Werke, die Schrift und die Tradition, die subjective Freiheit und die Autorität der Kirche u.s.w.) in der Fülle des Selbstbewusstseins (der Selbsterkenntniss)(2) *der*Kirche aufgehen, zu welcher er sich bekennt. Sollte diese Stimme aus Osten kein Gehör verdienen, in einem Augenblicke, wo die Lateinische Kirche, von Schiksalsmächten getrieben, oder kraft der logischen Nothwendigkeit die den Ereignissen innewohnt, sich selbst ihr Urtheil zu sprechen(3) droht, indem sie ihre Ansprüche bis auf schwindelnde Höhen schraubt,(4) während der Eckstein des Protestantismus die Schrift (im Sinne eines streng begränzten historischen Factums) scheinbar unter den gewaltigen Hammerschlägen der umbarmherzigen historischen Kritik in Splitter zerbstiebt.(5) Eben jetzt, im Angesichte der Resultate jener abendländischen religiösen Bewegung, wäre es wohl an der Zeit mit tieferem Ernste eine Kirche zu betrachten, die bisher den vielleicht unbegründeten(6) Vorwurf ihrer sogenannten Bewegungslosigkeit oder Verknöcherung(7) getragen hat.

Die nachfolgende Schrift von A. Khomiakov ist zum ersten Male in Russland, in einer unter strenger geistlichen Präventivcensur stehenden Zeitschrift erschienen—folglich darf man diesen "Versuch einer katechetischen Darstellung der Lehre von der Kirche" als von der russischen Kirchenverwaltung autorisirt erachten.

I am extremely sorry for bothering you again, but I need your disapproval of the awkward constructions or of the faulty expressions here before I can make up my mind to deliver this preface to the public, and I am so impatient to get it done. The translation is free, you will notice—the sense has remained exact, the arrangement of the words is a little different. Thanks for your tireless patience—now at last you can have some peace. Thursday[112] your friends will be thinking warmly of you. Yours truly.

IU. SAMARIN TO BARONESS RAHDEN

February 21, 1870.

You take the trouble to translate me and yet you are apologizing to me! That sounds almost ironical![113] I find nothing to criticize in the translation as such, but I beg you not to feel bound to the text. Possibly by being more free you yourself could make a few changes.

1) Would not "*bündigen*" give better the idea of "*gedrängten aber vollständigen*"?

2) You are perfectly right in preferring "*Selbsterkenntniss.*"

3) Instead of "*zu sprechen*" would it not be better to put "*auszusprechen*"?

4) "*Bis auf die Spitze treibt*" instead of "*bis auf schwindelnde Höhen schraubt*"?

5) Here the translation is irreproachable, but it seems to me that I am the one who hasn't expressed his idea properly. I meant to say that it was a matter of the material expression and not the spirit of the word of God. This is what I propose to you: "*der Eckstein des Protestantismus—Gottes Wort (als fest bestimmte historische Thatsache, als Buch) unter den Hammerschlägen einer geistlosen, wenn auch scharfen Kritik sich aufzulösen droht.*"

6) "*Unverdienten*" instead of "*unbegründeten.*"

[112]Probably with reference to the 19th of February, the anniversary of the emancipation of the peasants. (D. S.)

[113]The sentence is in German. (Trans.)

7) I do not know whether there is a noun from the verb "*erstarren*": "*Erstarrheit*"?

Many many thanks for all the trouble you are taking and for your kind thoughts. Yours truly.

BARONESS RAHDEN TO IU. SAMARIN

May 3, (1870).

I have just come back from a ceremony which made a very great impression upon me, and the memory of you superimposed itself so naturally upon what I was hearing that I cannot help but talk to you about it. Father Ianishev said mass in German this morning for the admission of Mr. Biering into the Orthodox Church. The young people of the academy sang in German, one of the students read the Apostle quite well in German—throughout the whole service. You Russians will never really be able to have an idea of the effect it creates! I know the mass by heart—well, when I heard those familiar prayers said in the language in which I think, which is the most intimate expression of my interior life, when the Creed, the Consecration, the Lord's Prayer were pronounced with the same words which have been familiar to me ever since I first prayed—I cannot tell you how I felt all the fibres of my heart vibrate!

I experienced a feeling of *true* catholicity—the oneness of the faith adapting itself to all human languages. And isn't one's maternal language, after faith, the dearest of all things? I had a sudden insight[114] into the profound miracle of the languages on the day of Pentecost. Oh! all those who had come together certainly had enough of a notion about the language of the Apostles to understand them; but to hear eternal truths, truths of fire, preached all of a sudden with the words you babbled in your childhood, words you

[114]The beginning of the sentence is in German. (Trans.)

thought in your youth—that's what penetrates you like the life of your life! For the human being it is a precious and inalienable privilege; it was one of the forces behind the Reformation and is one of the treasures of your Church. I was happy that no idea, apart from the Christian idea, threw any shadow across that religious act, whose thoroughly fraternal and charitable tone was set off with perfect simplicity by Father Ianishev in his brief address. From a superficial point of view, German sounds marvellous in the chants as well as in the prayers, in spite of the pronounced accent of the priest and chanters. There is even, with the necessity all of them were under to enunciate a foreign language slowly and distinctly, something grave and solemn which is quite appropriate. On the other hand, though, the numerous repetitions are all the more striking in German—I do not believe they are a Germanic trait—and then there are barbarisms in Raevski's translation which could easily be cut out. The congregation was very numerous, high society being represented by a small, attentive group. A Protestant pastor followed the service with interest, together with a crowd of ordinary people who fervently took part in this historic event without realizing its real significance! Farewell, kindest regards!

I reread my letter and am frightened at the political arguments which might be drawn from it, but which your kindness will not seek out.

IU. SAMARIN TO BARONESS RAHDEN

Moscow, May 11, 1870.

Many thanks for your kind letter and especially for the frankness with which you shared your impressions with me. I am incapable of reciprocating the pleasure I feel when I read you; I almost always find in your words the substance of my thought or feelings which I would never have been able to express in as simple and accurate a manner. Do not be afraid of my abusing your frankness by reading into your words deductions which might dismay you, and which in any case I reject as much as you do.

I think that I have finally understood, much too late I shamefully admit, the intellectual and moral difficulties in the utterly isolated position which you occupy in the no-man's land between two temperaments, two nationalities, two social spheres, where the mutual antagonism springs perhaps from a lack of mutual understanding. You are probably best of all and most keenly aware of the misunderstandings on the two sides; you are deeply hurt by the injustice of the judgments and appraisals on the two sides; but it is precisely because you do not unconditionally join either the one party or the other that you cannot satisfy either of them.[115]

I can even guess, even though you have never said a word of it to me, that the impatience, the ignorance and occasionally even the grossness of what is called *die altrussische Partei* make you suffer less than the irremediable biases, bred by pride, which you find in the opposing camp whenever you try to enlighten it. As for me, I am in the middle of the melee where I am both being stabbed and trying myself to stab in return; while I accept, as an obligatory rule of conduct, the most severe justice, I do not believe myself particularly apt for the role of judge; but, believe me, never will the turmoil of the struggle make me deaf to an appeal coming from above.

Cherkasski, scarcely back, has plunged again into business; he is still suffering a great deal, rarely sleeps, and his recovery is very slow. Without being a doctor, I can clearly see that a permanent intellectual tension, coupled with as complete a physical immobility as his, is not at all good for his state, but unfortunately he has the bad habit of turning

[115]The sentence is in German. (Trans.)

any advice you give him into a joke. What are you doing this summer? Yours truly.

IU. SAMARIN TO BARONESS RAHDEN

Moscow, June 11, (1870).

Mr. Grote passed on to me the parcel[116] from you which I have been waiting for impatiently. I have again reread the translation, which I think admirable, and I thank you from the bottom of my heart for all the trouble you have taken. I know enough about the art to have some idea of the difficulties which had to be overcome. Certain German publications have dealt with the first translation which I owe to this same pen. I recall one critic who was very hostile toward me but who did justice to the merit "*der eleganten Uebersetzung*."[117]

I recently sent a new brochure to my Berlin editor. It is a reply to Messrs. Bock and Schirren.[118] If you should happen to come across it and find it weak, colourless and devoid of vitality, you can blame all that on the person who more than any other made me blush about my excesses by teaching me, by her example, the charm of moderation. Yours truly.

[116]The reference is to the brochure edited by Baroness Rahden under the title: A. S. Chomäkoff, *Versuch einer katechetischen Darstellung der Lehre von der Kirche. Aus dem Russischen* (Berlin: Behrs Buchhandlung, 1870). The translation of Khomiakov's catechism is preceded by the preface reproduced previously. (D. S.)

[117]"Of the elegant translation." (Trans.)

[118]*Otvet gg. f. Bocku i Schirrenu po povodu Okrain Rossii Iu. Samarina* (Berlin, 1870). (D. S.)

BARONESS RAHDEN TO IU. SAMARIN

June 16, (1870).

If I were not hoping to see you very soon, I would write you a volume to thank you for your short note and to permit me to make a few observations on the art, of which you are a thorough master, of causing pain and pleasure at the same time. You will be coming soon, won't you? Prince Obolenski tells me that he is expecting you some time this month. We are staying on the Isles now only until the 24th and after that I shall have hardly any chance to see you. Oranienbaum is so far and my job so demanding! In what language did you write that brochure I have been yearning to see for so long? You can tell me all that yourself. Sometimes I think that I feel too happy to be seeing you again, so, inevitably, you will be thoroughly unpleasant while you *are* here, but at the same time I am willing to run that risk.

IU. SAMARIN TO BARONESS RAHDEN

Moscow, June 28, 1870.

I have put off my reply to the last moment while I still had a glimmer of hope of finding you in Petersburg. Now I must give up.

I am riveted to two committees from which it is impossible to get away—it would almost be an act of cowardice. You will have to take my word for it and I shall spare you an enumeration of what I have done and what remains for me to do. Your letter has given me courage. I love to see you in this mood.[119] If I had managed in your presence to contain myself enough not to kick up a fuss, you would have thanked me! Well, I would have braved your doubts, your distrust;

[119] *In dieser Stimmung.* (Trans.)

and, as there is nothing as brave as yesterday's coward, I would boldly have tackled all the most irritating subjects that I had made up my mind never to touch upon with you. I am quite serious: ever since that terrible reprimand I once received with regard to the *Okrainy Rossii* I have been a little afraid of you, and I cannot tell you just how happy I am to have this feeling. It is healthy and there is nothing painful about it. If I did not feel it, I would be missing something that is necessary. Ever since the death of Khomiakov I had lost all fear of anyone.

I remember an evening I spent at your house in conversation, a year and a half ago I believe, which left such a pleasant impression upon me that I like to go back over all of the incidents in my memory. With your arms crossed on your chest, you looked me up and down, always ready to parry the sword thrust you were expecting, and yet I could clearly see, I felt, that you were good and kindly disposed towards me. In short, all that I ask of you is to remain always what you are, and when you are unhappy with me to tell me so without trying to spare me. These are not just words that I am addressing you, I am speaking to you as an honest man and as a brother.

Since I do happen to be in a rather frank vein, I must confess to you an act of cowardice. I added to my manuscript when I sent it to Bock the list of persons to whom I asked him to send my brochure and I did not dare put your name on it. The reprimand was still fresh in my mind, and yet you will see how moderate I was. With regard to my manuscript, you put a very strange question to me: you ask me what language I used. How many then do you suppose I have at my command! And besides, how could I have abandoned the threat of revenge I hold over my adversaries, that of forcing the gentlemen to decipher what I am saying.[120] Sometimes I even amuse myself by using uncommon terms in order to make them run off to their dictionaries.

[120]The last phrase is in German. (Trans.)

Have you read, or have you at least heard of, No. 153 (July 1st) of the *Hamburgischer Correspondent*? I am sorry not to have been able to send it to you. In the Stuttgart column, it deals with an interview with a delegation of the *Evangelische Allianz*. It is very curious. According to the correspondent, the old regime and our Church *en bloc* are supposed to have been handed over to public contumely. It is the Church which allegedly raises an insurmountable barrier to the good intentions of the master who once again would be merely a fortunate accident among his own people. Poor Church! Now it is going to be reproached with being unbending and intractable. That is where it gets you to be obliging. As a matter of curiosity I must also point out to you in the last number of the *Russki Arkiv* an *ukaz* of the Holy Synod, which publishes a *Vysochaishee povelenie* of the Emperor Alexander I, *o tom, chtoby dukhovenstvo v propovediakh ne smelo pripisyvat' zaslugam Gosudaria Imperatora to, chto, est' delo milosti Bozhiei.*[121] The triumph of Christianity over the Roman persecutions is trumpeted very loudly; I find it far more significant that it should have withstood the baseness of its servants and the solicitude of its protectors. Shall we yet see the dawn of a better day? . . .

Pardon me for having rambled so much; I am writing you between two commissions, on the fire brigade and on taxes.[122] Around the 15th of next month I shall be in Samara; let me give you my address: Syzran, Government of Simbirsk. I embrace you and clasp your hands. Yours truly.

[121] An order from the Emperor forbidding members of the clergy to attribute, in their sermons, to His Majesty that which is the work of divine mercy. (D. S.)

[122] The last phrase is in Russian. (Trans.)

IU. SAMARIN TO BARONESS RAHDEN

Vassil'evski, July 26, (1870).

What is your opinion, my dear lady, about the great political storms that are rising on the horizon?[123] In spite of the lulling effect of the countryside, which is so pleasant and inviting, it is irritating in these times[124] to feel oneself in Asia. The newspapers take six days to get to us in Moscow.

It seems to me that the Great Mover, which the German school used to qualify as historic necessity, becoming embodied in events without the actors willing or knowing, had not for a very long time made itself felt in such a palpable way, against all probability, and in such direct opposition to the little autocrats who claim to manage the world.

Could a sufficient reason be found to explain what compels the papacy to cause a scandal in uttering its last pronouncement[125] which no one asked it for? And this war, whose proportions make even those who have nothing to lose by it shudder, did someone really will it? . . . I was about to quote you a famous Latin line, which conveys in an admirable way the action of what in human affairs constitutes the *element*, as an impersonal power without any awareness of itself. If we have really come to that point and if in the drama which is just beginning the favourable odds are to be in indirect proportion to the degree of *Bewusstsein*,[126] I am not anxious for my country. What do you think about it?

In the countryside I found several things which very much heartened me. First of all, the grains are fine and promise an abundant harvest if the weather holds. The village

[123]The sentence is in German. (Trans.)

[124]Allusion to the Franco-German War. (D. S.)

[125]An allusion to the proclamation of the dogma of papal infallibility by the Vatican Council, 1870. (D. S.)

[126]Consciousness. (Trans.)

school is working perfectly, without the master or the teaching method counting for very much in this, but thanks rather to the good will and the surprising intelligence of the pupils. Optimism is not one of my failings, yet in this younger generation with their bright, eager eyes, who guess what you are trying to say to them before you have pronounced a single word, I greet with confidence a race of men such as this country has not yet seen. Today's fathers, a sad end-product of serfdom, who are now powerless to effect either good or evil, will wind up in the tavern—that is inevitable—but between them and their children, who will know how to read, there will be a chasm.

Give me news of yourself, I beg you. Has the war upset your plans for the summer? Yours truly.

BARONESS RAHDEN TO IU. SAMARIN

Oranienbaum, August 3, (1870).

Where did you get the happy idea of writing to me without waiting for my reply to your last letter. I am stupefied at so much generosity and more grateful than I can say, for you have not spoiled me as far as correspondence goes, and more than once I have wondered if it would ever be possible for you to forget the *Soll und Haben* to the point of spending a thought before depositing the exact payment of past accounts. But we are living in a time of extraordinary events and I accept this morning's pleasant surprise like an historical event. Why aren't you here? I can see that you understand so well the real nature of what is going on! Yes, we are witnessing one of those great providential judgments, which occur in all their majesty only when the moral blindness of men is no longer capable of making short shrift of evil. There is in this direct action of God something which puts the most haughty on their knees, whether they be actors or spectators of the drama. It is futile for the German *school* to become lost in clouds of speculation when, at the news of a first decisive victory, fifty thousand persons, massed in front of the chateau and on the *Unter den Linden*, break with a common accord into "*Eine feste Burg ist unser Gott*"[127]—*there* is the secret of triumph, in this *living* faith which may wander, may go sadly astray, but which affirms its real existence by its very lapses and which maintains a wariness in every conscience which is avid for truth.

I should like to be able to tell you the amazing, the incredible details of the French disorganization. The complete inadequacy of the government and the absolute demoralization of its agents is frighteningly manifest in the simplest incidents; one wonders if the patriotism of the masses, who believe in nothing, will be effective for very long in withstanding these disasters, and whether misfortune can regenerate a nation as cynically greedy for material pleasure. The inability to believe in a noble sentiment, in any sort of disinterestedness, the habit of acting only with and on bad human passions has so clouded the judgment of Louis Napoleon that he has become the victim of the grossest mistakes, thanks to the erroneous reports of agents formed after his school. He was *perfectly* sure that the southern states and Hanover would rise up to a man against Prussia. He and his people were likewise incapable of understanding that a man can be discontent without becoming a traitor to his homeland. Do catastrophes which do not touch us directly ever profit us? Will our eyes be opened to today's evidence? Will we ever understand that *moral* victories must always and in everything precede any important exterior, and interior, conquests—that a man is really subject only to superior powers which enlighten and raise up. All of this is elementary and yet, except for you, there are so few people who believe it; you can repeat it as much as you like, but the pure and limpid well-spring of the idea drips on the marble of indifference and leaves so little trace of its passing!

[127] "A Mighty Fortress Is Our God." (Trans.)

The clash of arms is hurting the promulgation of papal infallibility. Count Khotek[128] who, in parenthesis, is going to Vienna to receive further instructions, was telling me yesterday what policy had been laid out by the German and Austrian bishops. They will *remain silent*[128a] on the new dogma. The opposition remains latent, there must not be any schism; in order to prevent this no word is to be said about the catechism, the infallibility question is not to be stressed —until the calling of a new Council, after the death of the Pope and when the time is propitious, in which the ancient principle of permitting new truths in dogma is to be reactivated throughout all Catholic Christianity in order that the inconvenient achievements of the last few years may be removed.[129] I thought I would never get to the end of my sentence! You should be happy with it—it is real German.

How many things of a general and personal nature I should still like to tell you. It is almost impossible to write about the first sort and I do not have the courage for the second. You need an average of two or three years to understand what I try to say—and you will agree that is a long time: only the stars have the right to pour forth their light that slowly! When in spite of myself I make practical observations about your nature as a fixed star—the sun moves much more quickly—I am a little overwhelmed by it. You are wasting your time making the most kindly talk with me, your confidence in me does not have the virtue of solidity, and hardly resembles the complete security which your way of feeling, of thinking and acting inspires in me. You have not sent me your reply to Schirren!! You have not yet understood that I accept beforehand any attack from your good sword because I *believe* that it has not been *dipped in the poison of the redskins*, and that one recovers or one dies without bitterness from clean, honest wounds.

[128]B. Khotek (1829-96), a representative of an ancient Bohemian noble family, was the Austrian Ambassador to St. Petersburg, 1869-71.

[129]The previous two sentences are in German. (Trans.)

What you tell me about your home truly charms me—I like, too, to hear the less sombre tone of your forecasts for the future. My heart always aches at your sadness; when your Moscow friends tell me that you are exhausted, I am very sorry, for me, for you, and for the country—nothing is created without joy, it is joy which fortifies, and I expect such fine works from you!

I can scarcely manage to end this letter; for two months I have been leading an impossible sort of existence, thoroughly outward and thoroughly dissipated—you can find in that the reason for my prolonged silence. Now that your kind thoughtfulness makes me blush for it, more than any reproach could have done, I have overcome all the obstacles, I have closed my door firmly, and this is the result. Thanks from my heart. Write soon, I beg you. We are staying peacefully here until further notice.

IU. SAMARIN TO BARONESS RAHDEN

Vassil'evski, August 23, (1870).

You have a thoroughly Prussian mind, my dear lady and your mood frightens me.[130] What do you think about Bismarck's schemes, offering Napoleon Belgium *sub rosa*; underwriting the Paris riot and furnishing it with revolvers, having a parley with an adventurer like General Turr, and so forth. Doesn't Prussian arrogance strike you at least as cutting as French boastfulness? I confess that my dignity as a moral being would have been deeply bruised if France had had the upper hand, but it is impossible for me not to recognize in the jubilation of the Prussian triumph certain wrong notes which grate on the ear. The worship of force is beginning to prevail over the cult of liberty—that is a symptom we recognize, a new despotism in seed. I speak about it as an

[130]The sentence is in German. (Trans.)

observer, allowance being made for any preoccupation with national interest, without nevertheless having any illusions in this respect. It is evident that the impetus given to the Prussian nation will not stop at Paris. You have probably read the famous article in the *Kreuz-Zeitung* on the reprisals awaiting any neutrals. It is significant only as an indication of the prevailing mood,[131] and without having to be warned we know anyway that a concentration of forces such as has been brought about in Prussia *produces* war and does not wait for it. Clashes between races, as in the fifth century, with railroads, telegraph and machine guns—that is what the future seems to hold for us. This present-day Prussia, which is astounding the world and which has a network of schools as its basis of operation, music-gymnastics co-operatives—and other clubs,[132] is still the product of a group of men who were called Stein, Hardenberg, Scharnhorst, Schönlein and Stegemann. When I think of the moral elasticity demonstrated in the humiliated and broken nation which these men have rebuilt, and when I compare this age (the object of early studies of mine) with what I have right here before my eyes, I tell myself that you have to believe in the future as the patriarchs did, and to know like them how to resign yourself to your own affairs.

I still have no news about my brochure. My friend Bock (I mean the book dealer) has said nothing to me and at this point it would be almost improper to remind him of his obligations. As soon as my reply is published you will receive a copy of it; if I had a moment of indecision, which I did confess to you, you have punished me for it and I have suffered the punishment, but I protest against your supposition that I lacked confidence in you. No, positively not, it wasn't that. One day while we were speaking on the political colour of those from the Baltic Provinces in the service of the state, I objected to their always having supported the cause

[131]The last words are in German. (Trans.)

[132]*Musik-Turn-Consum—et autres Vereine.* (Trans.)

which was contrary to liberty, and you answered me: I must recognize that the criticism is well founded. With that, I said no more, but I felt sorry. It is not always a happy thing to have been right, and an extorted confession can be just as painful for the person who receives it as for the person who, in making it, renders homage to truth in the face of his personal sympathies.

Let me come back again to Prussia and France. It seems to me impossible that a land which acclaimed Voltaire as the most brilliant incarnation of its national genius could produce a new Jeanne d'Arc; but I wonder whether another country, whose moral spring has reacted so nobly against the trials of adversity, would not weaken under the weight of triumphs. The temptation is quite a bit more severe. Surely this triumph would be the beginning of the end for the Germany we love! It seems to me quite possible that when all is said and done there will be only two Germans of the old stock left: yourself, to begin with, and then maybe your very humble servant, who cordially clasps your hand.

P. S. How does it happen that I have never heard you utter a word of Russian. I know full well that you are a thorough master of the language and I wonder why I might not make use of it writing to you. Quite certainly my French must often shock you, and by dint of having to read it, you will end up unlearning all your spelling. I warn you, be prepared.

BARONESS RAHDEN TO IU. SAMARIN

Oranienbaum, September 6, (1870).

Will you kindly do me a favour. When I wonder with satisfaction at the unimpeachable triumph of moral forces over the illusory power of a deceitful regime, please stop saying: *sie sind durch und durch preussisch gesinnt*![133] That

[133]You have a thoroughly Prussian mind. (Trans.)

reminds me too much of the peremptory affirmation of a few pietist Swiss acquaintances of mine who used to repeat with horror that I had become a Catholic because I wanted a church to be beautiful, and because I was fervently giving myself over to study, as well as to the contemplation of Rome. Coming from them, such interpretations have just made me shrug my shoulders; coming from you, I lose patience, not to say I am almost pained. Why can you never fully see how I mean it?[134] I love so much to talk to you without the need for commentaries, with the firm confidence that you will make up for any laxness in my expression or reasoning. It is above all in the presence of the great cataclysms of the moment that I need to discern with you God's plan and to leave aside human affairs which are always miserable in at least some respect. How can you pay any attention to trivial little details, peddled and distorted by the Moscow *Gazette*, such as the underhanded intrigues of Bismarck, or his talks with an intriguer, and so forth. Does all that really matter when a world is crumbling down? Can that influence me in my judgments and disenchant me with the national movement which is uplifting Germany? After having afforded yourself the enjoyment of these two or three stabs you become yourself again all of a sudden and the remainder of your letter echoes my soul.[135] I, too, fear to see the erring ways of a united Germany and their fatal consequences making an appearance just at the very time when the future promises, with the king's death and the country's exhaustion, to bring a little order back for a while to the bellicose and despotic tendencies of the present. Imperialism transplanted into Germany—that makes you shudder! So many simple, male virtues put to the service of a conquering power—that is not what the great men you admire wanted, men who were courageous regenerators of a fallen country! But it would seem that an immutable law is

[134]The last phrase is in German. (Trans.)

[135]The last phrase is in German. (Trans.)

making individuals as well as nations continually stray away from the worship of one sole true God towards idolatry, and that no one will escape the death which is its inevitable consequence.

The Germanic races will have their turn; the Slavic element, the impatient heir of their great role, is already dawning on the horizon—may it understand in time that the challenge is to bring serious, loyal and persevering force to the struggle. . . . When I dare to express this wish I am looked at with suspicion: possibly it is a piece of Baltic treachery; at the same time the opposing camp considers any moderate opinion like a desertion. Gentleness being, alas! the least of my qualities, it is sometimes a great effort to remain fair-minded and serene. So how grateful I am, how moved and full of joy, when delicately benevolent behaviour like yours catches me unawares! I thank you from the bottom of my heart.

We are leaving Oranienbaum the day after tomorrow; it is on the Isles that we shall finish out our autumn. Would that we were not going abroad after the conclusion of the peace. I must still tell you of a discovery which I made with the help of Mr. Semenov and of a strange experience connected with it. The discovery is a very gifted, very distinguished, very original and very proud (thank God) compatriot, who is already recognized in the learned world abroad for his scientific works in the realm of zoology and comparative anatomy. He is a Ukrainian, is called Miklukho-Maklai,[136] is only twenty-four years old, has travelled in Abyssinia, on the Red Sea, to the Canary Islands, and so forth, and is preparing to leave for *New Guinea*, an almost unknown land which he wants to explore thoroughly. That is enough to arouse the

[136] N. N. Miklukho-Maklai (1846-88) was a naturalist, ethnographer and explorer. He was one of the early scientific investigators of New Guinea and travelled extensively in Micro- and Melanesia. While he produced no major work, he left ethnographic and anthropological collections of significant value. (Ed.)

interest of the most apathetic person, isn't it. Even if he were a Turk, wouldn't as bold, as radically dangerous an enterprise receive some attention? Well, apart from Mr. Semenov who obtained for him, through the aegis of the Geographical Society, a free passage as far as Batavia on board a state-owned ship which is going to sail around the world, I was able to get him only an invitation to Oranienbaum where he spent a few days. The most zealous patriots, the wildest Slavophils, our sailors and protectors of the Geographical Society showed only an apathetic indifference when faced with such a rare thing as an independent man, who asks nothing of them, not even moral encouragement, but who craves a bit of respect for his science. Mr. Maklai on the other hand is struck at having found in Morocco the most spontaneous and the most generous Prussian hospitality on board a frigate, while in his own country he feels himself to be completely ignored.[137] What sort of patriotism is it then that does not accept even the solidarity of great things? If you had been here, there would have been at least three of us to clasp his hand as compatriots.

Farewell, think kindly of me—again, very sincere thanks.

IU. SAMARIN TO BARONESS RAHDEN

Vassil'evski, September 15, (1870).

In three days I am leaving the country, earlier than I should have wanted, and about the 1st of October I hope to be able to go to Petersburg, provided I can be sure of finding you there. I can also put off my trip if your stay at Oranienbaum is to be prolonged. Since ultimately it is you who will settle my plans, will you please have the kindness to write a word to me as soon as you receive this letter.

[137] The last word is in German. (Trans.)

Since I wrote you the last time, how much has happened, one thing after the other.

I hope soon to be able to chat with you about them. Yours.

BARONESS RAHDEN TO IU. SAMARIN

Kamennyi-Ostrov, September 25, (1870).

We shall be staying here indefinitely, for it seems that travel plans have been put off, if not abandoned, and Michael Palace is undergoing interior repairs which make it uninhabitable right now.

Until we meet on the Isles, then; it will be a great pleasure to grasp your hand and to hear you speak of what is going on around us in Europe and in the country. I have still to thank you for the brochure[138] which you sent me—it is written with a nobility and a moderation which make the truths it contains all the more powerful. With sincere friendship.

BARONESS RAHDEN TO IU. SAMARIN

November 7, (1870).

Here is a word from Mr. Naville[139] which I have just received; I am passing it on to you immediately. If I were not in such a glum mood I should have taken the pleasure of writing to you. But even though I am not being articulate

[138]Iu. Samarin's brochure: "Otvet gg. f. Bokku i Schirrenu po povodu Okrain Rossii." (D. S.)

[139]Evidently in connection with the deputation of the Evangelical Alliance which in 1870 appeared before the Emperor Alexander II near Stuttgart. (D. S.)

with my tongue or my pen, you know that I am thinking of you with sincere, kind thoughts.

BARONESS RAHDEN TO IU. SAMARIN

November 11, (1870).

Here is another article on the question you are interested in. It seems rather vague to me and is not supported by the authority of a signature like that of Mr. de Pressensé! I have to give it back when I am through with it. It is with a faint sense of anxiety that I send this account to you. What are you going to do about it? Please do not interpret this anxiety as a lack of confidence—no, I am perfectly sure that you do not and that you cannot but wish the advancement of liberty of conscience in every form—and yet I tremble that in raising this question a new source of irritation might be added to all the others!

Whatever the case may be—here is what you asked me for! I clasp your hand, and am yours truly.

IU. SAMARIN TO BARONESS RAHDEN

November 17, 1870.

I am eagerly seizing a convenient chance I have to send you these lines. A thousand thanks for the information that you were kind enough to ask of Naville. I was awaiting it with some anxiety for if the testimony of Mr. de Pressensé had turned out to be identical with J. Eckhardt's version, I should have had to redo the whole introduction to a piece of work[140] which I shall be sending to Berlin one of these days.

[140]The third fascicle of the *Okrainy Rossii*, published in Berlin in 1871. (D. S.)

Happily for me there is no problem.

Enclosed you will find an exact copy of the address[141]

[141] A translation of the copy of the address, which was attached to the letter, follows here. (Trans.)

"Sire! For fifteen years Russia has patiently put up with unexampled humiliation, in the firm hope that growing incessantly beneath your supreme aegis it would opportunely recover liberty, strength and the respect which is due it in its external relations. Inspired by Your kingly conscience You decided, Sire, that the moment had come, that the hour had sounded for Russia to throw off the illegitimate bonds which had been imposed on it by its enemies. It was not secretly, but openly, that You denounced certain articles of the Treaty of Paris, that treaty long since torn up and trampled beneath the feet of those very people who had created it to the detriment of Russia. The word which You pronounced solemnly in the name of the Russian people and country shall not remain fruitless. It shall become an everlasting fact. Whatever may be the perils which threaten us today, we are certain that they shall not take Russia unprepared; they shall certainly find it drawn up in serried ranks about Your throne.

"It is with greater confidence than formerly that Russia now envisages the future, for it is aware of an incessant moral regeneration taking place in it. Each of the great reforms which You have already brought about or which are now in process, each of those which are still expected from You, is for Russia, as at the same time for Your Majesty, a new source of strength. No one more than You, Sire, has acquired rights to the gratitude of the people and no one has been paid this by the people more ardently. It is from You that it has received all these gifts, and it is in You that it continues to see the most certain guardian of the liberties it has received and which have become for it as necessary as daily bread. It is from You alone that it awaits the crowning of the beneficent reforms which You have undertaken, and, above all, the granting of freedom of thought and freedom of the press, without which the soul of the people will wilt, without which its relations with authority are stripped of sincerity and truth,—freedom of the Church, without which even preaching remains ineffectual; finally, freedom of conscience—the most precious of treasures for the human soul.

"Sire! External and internal affairs are intimately bound together. The measure of success in the realm of external relations lies in the strength of the national feeling and the self-respect which the State infused into all of the functions of its vital organism. It is only in remaining faithfully bound to the principle of nationality that the organism of the State is strengthened, that the borderlands of the State are secured to it, and that that unity is founded which is an immutable historic legacy from Your forebears and ours, and which has served as an ensign for Moscow since its foundation. And even today it is beneath that banner that all classes of the people will rally to Your first call, Sire, and this time irrespective of conditions—like an immovable phalanx—filled with utter confidence in the goodness of God, in the justice of their cause, and in You. The sovereign's confidence in his people, a wise reserve in liberty and honesty in submission on the part of the people, the reciprocal and indissoluble union between the sovereign and the people, founded upon the community of national spirit, upon the accord between their aspirations, and their beliefs—that is our strength, that is what will help Russia to fulfill its high historic mission.

"Yes, Sire, You have only to command—we shall say in closing, repeating the words spoken by our forefathers in 1642 in reply to that ancestor of Yours who was the first Sovereign of Your dynasty—You have only to express Your will and we shall be ready to put to Your service our possessions and our blood; but as for our opinion—we have spoken it."

which the whole Duma of Moscow signed just an hour ago this evening. The original, directed to H. M. the Emperor, will be put in the mail tomorrow morning and will arrive in Petersburg Thursday, at the same time as this letter. However, as it will not be presented to the Emperor until Friday by the Minister of the Interior, I must ask you to keep this copy to yourself for four or five days. The address was written by Prince Cherkasski and touched up by Aksakov. What is remarkable as a symptom is the fact that it was accepted unanimously by all the members of the Duma, almost 150 in number. The thing was done in full consciousness.[142] Yester-

[142] The last three words are in German. (Trans.)

day we had a preparatory meeting of forty people, in large part merchants and bourgeois. The address was read and reread, commented upon and discussed *en bloc* and in detail. These gentlemen consequently had twenty-four hours in which to reflect. I will admit to you that at first I was strongly opposed to any sort of address—I do not have the time to give you the reasons for this; but once the question was decided in principle I supported with all my strength that passage which you can guess without my needing to point it out, and when I saw the whole assembly accept it in full consciousness and with conviction, I signed along with the others. I do not believe I was wrong, silencing every political consideration in linking myself to a resolution in favour of religious liberty.

The year which is about to begin will perhaps bring us some painful ordeals but it will also give us civil equality in matters of taxation and military service. I hope, too, that it will prepare for a freeing of consciences. Perhaps I shall see the achievement of these three goals—that is all that I desire for myself.

And with that let me clasp your hands. Yours truly.

BARONESS RAHDEN TO IU. SAMARIN

November 21, (1870).

I received your November 17 letter an hour ago. You must have realized in writing it what joy you were providing for me in it, so I should not like to put off for even a single day expressing my gratitude to you. Sentiments, principles, fine language—everything went straight to my heart. I was greatly moved in imagining you—and all the more so because of my awareness of the wrongs which I have done you recently and of which you have no inkling. There is one area with regard to you in which I have not completely been able to overcome a gnawing distrust, and that is the matter of religious tolerance. I have been tormented by misgivings; I sent you the promised reports[143] only with extreme reluctance—in short, I suffered a lapse of faith, which I am now expiating by confessing to you. I fully realize it is more difficult to pardon a doubt than any other offence—but I cannot do otherwise than be completely sincere with you, at my own risk. What consoles me a little—even a great deal—is to feel once again that you are infinitely more worthy a person than I.

IU. SAMARIN TO BARONESS RAHDEN

Tuesday, (December 1, 1870).

Pierre Vassil'chikov is taking care of this letter for me; in the present circumstances I prefer to avoid the mails. Your last letter touched me deeply and made me smile at the same time. You are good-natured enough to imagine yourself at fault with respect to me, and you even claim to be in a moral sense worth less than I! I shall leave you with these illusions only on the condition that you will not change when you have lost them. That is all I ask. But, frankly, tell me what is bothering you. I am concerned because of the good which you have done me and which you can still do me, and I shall promise for my part to reply to your doubts with the same frankness. As far as liberty of conscience is concerned, I can state, in all truth, that I wish it to be absolute, for everyone and without any restriction whatsoever. In this respect, my opinion has never changed and between you and me there could have been a divergence only upon questions of fact. You believe in captious promises with a view to bringing about conversions, which I take exception to, and you refuse to believe about real persecutions in the opposite sense which

[143] A reference to the deputation of the Evangelical Alliance, which had an audience with the Emperor near Stuttgart. (D. S.)

I have seen and verified with my own eyes. But whether the facts are true or false, we are in agreement in deploring them and thoroughly condemning them—that is what counts.

Right now you certainly know more than I do about the fate of our address. It seems that it is causing a bit of embarrassment. Prince Cherkasski was given to understand in a couple of words that were slipped to him (keep this between ourselves) that certain people would like to see it *corrected*, but I must acknowledge, to the honour of Prince Dolgoruki, that he did not insist! Evidently it was only to fulfill an order to take the lay of the land. I could tell you at great length about the qualms of *conscience* around here, and I say *conscience* and not solely of calculated interest. It is a fact: every sign of approval or disapproval which comes from above raises for us a question of conscience. In the eyes of the bulk of the third estate, power is still authority of a moral order. I do not know whether that is a good thing or bad, but it is still an immense lever which will soon break. If only one knew how to use it! I am sending the note back to you with a thousand thanks. Yours truly.

BARONESS RAHDEN TO IU. SAMARIN

December 5, (1870).

I have just this very moment been told that there is a chance to have something go to Moscow—I have only ten minutes before me, but I must thank you for your last letter and tell you in a couple of words what is going on.

The animosity and the vicious joy of the adversaries of Prince Ch. are continuing. It seems that he was much more advanced in the favour of the Master than was generally thought. As much as I admire the address, as much as I love eternal principles, I do not regret that your wise and faithful counsel did not win out. What are the occult powers which at any given hour blind the most astute minds and make them miss the goal they have almost hit. Well, whatever the explanation may be, I am convinced that in a few years from now the ideas in the address will have gained ground, possibly more rapidly than if a minister had championed them—and isn't that the important thing?

There is quite a flurry here over a raid upon the Forestry Institute where professors and students were arrested in quite large numbers. The most mindless nonsense and the most immoral conduct were linked together there; the cult of Karakozov[144] and the crudest atheism was professed. The story goes that a certain Mr. N., a professor, whose wife played a role in the student troubles of 1860, is the heart and soul of this conspiracy. The Emperor seems very much overwhelmed by all these underground intrigues which he considers so much base ingratitude. I beg your pardon for naming you in this company—but recently, in an expansive moment, the Emperor, who was speaking with a close friend about all these painful experiences, said with a certain tenderness: Well, anyway, Samarin whom my father had put in the fortress[145] speaks of him only with a sort of worshipful respect and gives him his due! How does one explain such analogies? At the ministry of public education secret libraries of materialistic and socialistic books have been found, in the schools of the interior, especially in the land of the Cossacks of the Don; students of the Academy of Medicine were exchanging correspondence with the young boys and girls of secondary schools and were furnishing them with book catalogues, and were offering too to serve as purchasing agents!! And people think they can overcome these destructive elements with an enslaved Church!! Finally the priest of

[144] D. V. Karakozov (1840-66), a revolutionary-terrorist and student at the University of Moscow, tried to shoot Alexander II in 1866, thereby initiating a social and political revolution. (Ed.)

[145] That is, in the Peter-Paul Fortress, where Samarin was imprisoned in 1848. (Ed.)

N. University, who occasioned much merriment among the students and exposed religion to every type of derision, has been dismissed for incapacity, will you believe it? Oh, surely not! He made stupid political jokes at the beginning of one of his lectures, and the secret police obtained what good sense and conscience had been calling for vainly for *twelve years*!

Farewell, my thoughts are with you more often than ordinarily. Since you wish well of me, wish me a great deal of patience. There is a sort of person who makes my blood boil in my veins. They are the friends of Job. . . . With all my heart.

IU. SAMARIN TO BARONESS RAHDEN

Moscow, December 30, 1870.

You are worn out with letters to read and write, with business of every sort—I know all about it, so I shall be brief and discreet.

I cannot end the year which is running out without saying a word to you—it's an old-fashioned custom I have followed since my childhood—and without thanking you once again for all the good moments and all the salutary feelings for which I have become obligated to you in 1870. Nothing will change between us; I say it with a joy and confidence which make me feel proud and happy. As much as I am horrified by what the Catholics call direction of conscience, I do experience the need for a communion of consciences. A word, a shrug of the shoulders, a simple glance is often enough when it comes to us from a person in whom we have absolute confidence, in order to cut short any indecision and to shore up a tottering good intention. You can do a great deal of good in this way—if you did not realize it, you may take my word for it.

Receive my felicitations, my best wishes and the clasp of my hand. Yours truly.

IU. SAMARIN TO BARONESS RAHDEN

(Petersburg, the beginning of 1871.)

I am making restitution to you of the two books, with many thanks. After having looked carefully through them, I am finally convinced that what I was looking for is not to be found for the simple reason that it never existed. My anonymous correspondent was simply making fun of me. I wanted to go knocking on your door yesterday evening, but I learned that you would be engaged in the exercise of your functions and I put off my visit to today at around 8 o'clock. If you do not send me any word I shall consider myself as good as received. Yours truly.

IU. SAMARIN TO BARONESS RAHDEN

April 13, 1871.

Every day recently I have been on the lookout for a chance to send you the third volume of the works of Khomiakov[146] and a long letter which was to serve to present it. Just this evening I learned that Dmitriev was leaving for Petersburg tomorrow morning. It is impossible to let such a good chance escape, and likewise impossible to finish my letter by the time he leaves. I have only time to write you a few lines. Let me make two requests of you. First, please keep for yourself alone the volume I am sending you. It is a contraband copy. I obtained it before all the legal formalities were completed and, if it became known, the censor could give the printing house a bad time. The other thing I ask of you is that you abstain from any final judgment about the work I am giving you before considering all I have to tell you

[146]*Zapiski o Vsemirnoi Istorii,* to which Gogol applied the surname of "Semiramide." (D. S.)

so as to explain its origin and to show you the author's plan and goal.

If you have the patience to leaf through the volume you will see right away that it is something quite undigestible and that it is impossible to connect it to any genre of literary production whatsoever. It is not even a sketch; it is a heap of material which lies beneath the gaze of the mind which is later to co-ordinate it all. Never did the author dream of publishing his work, he never hoped even to finish it. I must stop so as not to let myself drag on.

There is a great variety of things I could write you about. If only you knew how much I miss you and how many times I think of you. Let me warmly clasp your dear, faithful hand.[147] Yours truly.

P. S. If you have the chance would you please pay my respects to the Grand Duchess, and explain to her how happy I was to learn that she had been kind enough to remember me in speaking about Moscow to the Baron of Mengden.

BARONESS RAHDEN TO IU. SAMARIN

April 23, (1871).

You told me one day that I expressed myself better in German than in French; let me return the compliment—or the truth. You are decidedly more amiable in German than in any other language! You take on an air of kindliness[148] which suits you marvellously. Really, you are reverting to your original nature when you surrender yourself to German virtues—the old Scandinavian blood is claiming its rights and you are coming back to goodness, your heart's real homeland.

I am extremely grateful for your parcel; it is so well

[147] The sentence is in German. (Trans.)

[148] The phrase is in German. (Trans.)

hidden from everyone's eyes that I myself have not even leafed through it. Anyway, Mr. Dmitriev will tell you whether I could have had the time to open a book these last days. Thanks to the Prince of Orange, Michael Palace has become as mundane as ten years ago. A *Thursday* has been revived with a show and supper . . . a runtish affair, the degenerate descendant of a royal race! Apart from the form of it, everything was missing: the surge of ideas, the breadth of scope, the glitter of wit, former friends . . . . This contrast made me a little sad and certainly neither Mr. Valuev's conversation nor Count Peter Shuvalov's urbanity did much to put these impressions out of my mind. Mr. Dmitriev will bring you up on the news of the day. We shall not be leaving Russia until July. The Grand Duchess, to whom I delivered your message, wants to take the baths of Gastein around then. Is this your birthday today? In any case I hope it is a happy one and I am going off to mass where one always thinks of one's friends better than anywhere else. Yours cordially.

IU. SAMARIN TO BARONESS RAHDEN

Franzensbad, July 22/10, (1871).

I shall take the chance of addressing this letter to Petersburg, fully realizing that you are possibly only a day away from here. Unfortunately neither my research in the guest lists,[149] nor the questions I have been asking right and left have told me anything about your present whereabouts. On leaving Moscow I had intended not to go beyond Berlin, to stay there only three or four days and come back by Petersburg where I was counting upon still finding you. But everything has changed: the doctors I consulted strongly advised me to take a cure at Franzensbad and here I am settled in for two more weeks. I am far from complaining,

[149]The words are in German. (Trans.)

for nowhere else do you feel yourself as free, temporally and physically, as at the waters, if, that is, you do not feel caught up by the music and the casino.[150] As far as acquaintances go, I have come across only Princess Vorontsov and the Countess of Hauterive (Hélène Stahl) whose husband, although a cavalry officer of the ex-army of the North, stands apart from his compatriots by being very modest and is willing to recognize that in the last analysis it was the Prussians who had the upper hand over the French.

My book dealer in Berlin has provided me with a whole crate of newly published material for my perusal. After having set aside all the brochures on the war, I held on to the philosophic and religious works. Judging by the bulk of the publications, what now dominates in Germany is nothing other than *positivism*, inaugurated by Auguste Comte, popularized by Stuart Mill and expounded upon by Carus, Voght and many others. It is hard to believe. Germany, after having crushed France and constituted itself as a political body, Germany, whose industrial progress offends England, by an incredible after-effect is undergoing the intellectual influence of these two countries in the domain of thought, in that very same realm in which Germany was most at home.[151] And there it is back at the starting point of Locke, Condillac and the whole French eighteenth-century school which admitted as reality only what was perceived by the senses. That nature as an external manifestation can only be absorbed and not thought, that in the field of thought one is working exclusively with concepts, that whatever occurs in the spiritual realm can be grasped *directly* only by the human being—all this people seem to have forgotten.[152] What good then were Kant, Schelling, Hegel and the whole great philosophical school, this magnificent intellectual bouquet whose crumbs

[150]Cursaal. (Trans.)

[151]Following the comma the text is in German. (Trans.)

[152]The sentence is in German. (Trans.)

have fed us for more than half a century. I do not need to add that this pronounced tendency towards what is wrongly called positivism implies an absolute negation of any religious data. That is a view that is now out of date.[153] It is no longer even a question which has the advantage of stirring people's minds as it used to. We are beyond that.[154] There has even recently been a public course, I forget where, to show that in the last analysis Darwin did not forbid his disciples to believe in God, with the condition, though, that this belief not be considered other than a matter of personal taste and of intellectual comfort. The Protestant press has protested loudly but it has been jeered at. I observed so often in my youth that once he got to a certain age every man became incapable of understanding any change in ideas which were destined to go beyond his intellectual level, that I distrust my own impressions now. In what seems to me only to be a deplorable end, there may possibly be a beginning. This sort of atrophy of thought, when it is folded back on itself, is possibly only a transformation which I can no longer even sense. God grant it, but I will frankly admit that I do not understand anything about it any more.

I share your pain on reading the newspaper account of the trial of Nechaev,[155] Ustinov, Priev, etc. A strange bunch of people![156] Judging by the candor of their confessions and by the childish self-assurance with which they delight in ex-

[153]The sentence is in German. (Trans.)

[154]The sentence is in German. (Trans.)

[155]S. G. Nechaev (1847-82) was a revolutionary and theorist. In 1869 he established a tightly disciplined conspiratorial group as a step towards achieving revolution. Suspecting one of his comrades of treachery he had him murdered and was subsequently arrested and sentenced in a trial which stirred great interest. Sentenced to twenty years' imprisonment in the Peter-Paul fortress, he died there. Ustinov and Priev were fellow conspirators. (Ed.)

[156]The sentence is in German. (Trans.)

posing the grossest of absurdities down to the last detail, you would be tempted to see in this whole affair nothing but a youthful straying; but suddenly this youthfulness, which should by its very readiness to let itself be swept along towards an ideal, keep an instinctive check on itself against anything improper—you see it coldly carrying out a murder in which cowardice goes even beyond the cruelty of it. What an omen, and what a sad lesson to be drawn from this pathetic trial! Will people at least be able to learn from it by getting back to the source of the trouble. I have seen a very remarkable change come about before my eyes, a change which I do not think has been fully perceived yet. In my school days, the generation which was studying underwent the influence of the teaching body directly. You became impassioned for or against what the teacher said; you had among your professors certain preferred ones; there were too, some who were frankly hated—but, all in all you lived in the same circle of ideas, the teachers, as it were, held the thought and the will of their pupils in their hands. Today, all that has changed. There is something of a gap between those who are teaching and those who are listening. The number of students has gone up, the courses are being taken with perhaps even greater assiduity than before. Exams are being prepared for because they have to be, but the spirit of the younger generation is no longer there. What dominates them and fashions them is no longer the University but rather influences, books, personalities on the outside. The teaching body has no longer any grip on its listeners. It no longer even holds the secret of their worries, it is a word which rings out in the void. To fully understand the causes which have brought about this change you must first be aware of the general laws which regulate movement in the world of ideas; now the men who in our country are called to direct public education have a great deal of experience especially in matters of passion and personal interests, but I doubt very much whether their childhood memories have put them in a position to understand what the phrase "to be dominated by an idea" means. It is a type of mental sickness from which these gentlemen have generally been preserved by their sound constitution.

You have probably heard that the Moscow provincial assembly, like many others, had pronounced itself unanimously in favour of the abrogation of every privilege with respect to direct taxation and of an absolute equality in taxation. This completely voluntary sacrifice, which the government did not provoke, which it even tried to avoid, would have filled me with joy and aroused great hopes in me ten or so years ago. Today, I see things differently, I should have preferred a more stubborn and more prolonged resistance. The capacity for abnegation is certainly a negative virtue and a condition for any progress, but when it springs from an absolute incapacity for any sort of resistance it betrays at the same time a social laxness, which explains why, once the negative work is completed, the vital forces and the spontaneous initiative to fill in the void are lacking. We sacrifice everything with prodigious ease, which astonishes the world because we are horrified at the efforts which any sustained struggle would require. If these lines should happen to come to the attention of Messrs. Bock, Schirren and Eckhardt, can you imagine what would happen! Apropos of Bock, have you seen his latest brochure? There is rather a curious account of the audience the Emperor accorded last year to the deputies of the Evangelical Society; there is also a long deduction (more than 10 pages) to prove that I am in effect merely an agent of Count Shuvalov, advised and inspired by him.

You have certainly seen in the German newspapers that the great Protestant delegation expected from America has gone to Stuttgart and was received by the Emperor. These gentlemen have based their request on Count Bebrinski's famous report. The newspapers are not saying yet what reply was given them. And so that liberty of conscience which our sectarians have been vainly demanding for almost 200 years, and which is refused the municipality of Moscow, we shall possibly owe it to a pressure from outside, if indeed they do not prefer to make it into a new privilege for the exclusive use of the Baltic Provinces—which I think more likely. You can easily imagine how I feel . . . .[157] But enough of that. I shall not apologize for my interminable verbiage—I have left you in peace for so long. If you have a spare moment to write me, I shall be in Moscow in two weeks. I should like to beg you to break, even just for once, your absolute, thorough silence about everything to do with you personally, but I am very much afraid that it would only be so much wasted effort. Yours truly.

BARONESS RAHDEN TO IU. SAMARIN

Oranienbaum, July 30, (1871).

Fifteen days ago today I received your letter from Franzensbad. Thanks to your utter silence and a fanciful bit of information from Prince Obolenski I thought you were at Samara, where I really had a little hope that the solitude, silence and boredom would react upon your correspondence faculties. Franzensbad having fulfilled the desired conditions, I am extremely grateful to you for having obeyed and had it not been for the arbitrary time limit you yourself set, I should have replied immediately to your letter which gave me such very great pleasure. I would be even more disgruntled at your long silence—which I realize is quite natural though—if I were not getting my share of the epistles which you are sending off to the whole of Russia. I should tell you that I have read and re-read your work on taxation.[158]—Through the mist of a thousand mysterious details the general ideas were

[157]The sentence is in German. (Trans.)

[158]The "Sovremennaia Letopis'," a weekly supplement of the *Moscow Gazette*, had published in its number for June 16, 1871, the Report of the Zemstvo Commission of the Moscow government on the reform of the poll tax (capitation). Iu. Samarin was the president of this Commission and it was he who had drafted this Report. (D. S.)

even to me so clear, so great, and so generous that they covered all the rest with their light and that I felt an unalloyed delight, quite above the almost painful interest which I cannot help but feel for your other literary work.

How much I regret not having seen you this summer! Who knows when we shall meet again. The Grand Duchess's trip is put off from week to week because of a sharp knock she gave her arm getting into a carriage. The contusion brought about a swelling which has not completely gone down. They are unwilling to set out until she recovers completely and I am afraid our return will be set back by the same amount. I followed the Nechaev trial very closely; the interrogations and the hearing make up an entire volume. I waited in vain to hear anyone, whether judges, lawyers or the accused, pronounce the words God, or duty, or evil, or good, or repentance! We can overlook the great criminals but the so-called honest people, the real guardians of public morality, what about them? Yes, and I can go even further and state I have yet to meet a single person in the multifarious public I get to see who has considered the actions and opinions of these unfortunate young people from the point of view of sin, of evil, of the manifest infraction of an inner law. The *complete* absence of the Church, in its *indirect* expression, struck me very strongly. And how many magnificent elements it could have spiritualized. There is an abundance of disinterested devotion, brotherly feelings, simpleness at the very bottom of that pit of horrors which moves me in spite of myself . . . . I would rather not speak about it, for a heart which becomes too sentimental loses its sense of proportion, and mine is crying out to heaven.[159] What a fine expression! When you have vainly called for justice or man's compassion, there comes a time when facts cry out to heaven—and never in vain!

I still have not thanked you for your different parcels; I am taking Khomiakov away with me so as the better to study

[159]The last phrase is in German. (Trans.)

him in the silence of some lost valley. Here Oranienbaum's ordinary sociableness takes up a lot of my time, and then too I often go into town, where the community Dinners engross me as much by their theory, which requires some elucidation, as by their somewhat tiring practice. There, too, I have a chance to observe the physiognomy of unknown classes, which I am understanding better to the extent that I am able to overcome the primitive distaste I used to feel in the midst of that rather dirty mob. You want me to tell you about myself—well I am going to confess to a feeling which I know will greatly displease you. To be for six hours on end in the midst of hundreds of individuals who wipe their faces with their napkins, who eat—ah, I would sooner not think about it! who exude vulgarity—it is a sacrifice whose difficulty shames me for it provides me with the exact measure of how little true charity I have. Nevertheless, those at the community Dinners and myself have finally managed to become good friends and I have not given up hope of some day overcoming, to the extent of complete submission, my exclusivism—which is German—in its outer impressions.—But why all this personal trivia? You asked for it and it's solely to obey you that I have just filled an entire page with myself. Besides, you yourself never do it—and although I am sometimes very much pained to hear from others that you are sad or sick, I am hardly ever irritated because I can understand the inner process which makes you keep silent. I shall explain it to you in the words of a young friend of mine whom you also know, Mr. Miklukha-Maklai. He was writing recently to his sister from one of the ports of Patagonia: "You reproach me with not giving you fuller details about myself and you are partly right. But the more and more apparent the grandeur of my enterprise and the extent of the scientific results I expect from it become to me, the more the *idea* possesses me, the more myself as an individual recedes into the middle, into the distant background, and I simply *forget* to talk about him." Isn't that it? What the *idea* is for men, is it not possible that its counterpart for women is the concern for other people, in all its ramifications? And those moments of introspection, of inward contemplation of one's struggles, one's weaknesses, one's intimate joys, should they not be reserved for those close talks where there is no reticence, no mental reservations, and in which the entire soul is given, with its most exalted aspirations together with its meanest human weaknesses? For that, the living word is needed, the affectionate influence of the friend who listens, the help of a thousand little incidental things . . . a sort of thoughtlessness which eludes the written word.

Farewell, may God keep you! Think kindly of me. Yours truly.

IU. SAMARIN TO BARONESS RAHDEN

(1871).

Between the writer of this letter[160] and M. de Bock there is a divergence of opinion, not upon the moral legitimacy of the means set in motion, but solely on their opportuneness. To transform a question of interior policy into an international question, to stir up Germany against Russia, which in official idiom is still called the *common homeland*—why not, if this system is to bring about the intended goal, but doesn't one make a mistake in counting too much upon the support of Prussia? The whole problem is there. I will gladly admit that it is debatable, there are arguments both for and against, although personally I am inclined rather to the opinion of Mr. von Bock—but that is not the problem. Let me put another question. If present-day Prussia were to learn that in one of the newly annexed provinces there exists a party which is attempting to provoke an intervention by the French, in order to protect the local interests of this province against the action of the Prussian government, and if, to

[160]We do not know what letter is referred to here. (D. S.)

reassure Mr. von Bismarck, one were to say to him that on the other hand another party is condemning this mode of action because it doubts the efficacity of a French intervention—would Mr. von Bismarck declare himself to be satisfied? Would he accept *this sort* of condemnation as a sufficient proof of devotion to Prussia? Would he recognize that that is all that can be required of good citizens? Would he not take a second look before putting the men of this second party (of the party of the wise and the moderate) at the head of the administration, the tribunals, the Prussian armies?

BARONESS RAHDEN TO IU. SAMARIN

April 11, (1872).

I am on the point of leaving for Courland, where I shall spend a few weeks, possibly two months. If I have a great deal of courage, I shall write from Libau, it will even be a special pleasure for me to tell you from there, as from anywhere else, how the thought of you is always in my memory and dear to me. May God keep you. Yours truly.

Is this the book you wanted? I am enclosing with it a very well done and very brave brochure—from the materialistic and grossly nihilistic point of view held by our medical academy.

BARONESS RAHDEN TO IU. SAMARIN

Libau, April 23, 1872.

I am not too certain whether it is your birthday today, or not, but it does not matter: I shall take it as an excuse to wish you once again all the best. Really the November St. George would suit you better as a patron saint and director of conscience with his warlike temperament and his vigorous lance. And there I am right in the midst of the dragons you are trying to slay. Good God, how harmless they are! And what a burning desire it would take to unsheath a sword against someone or something and to attack them! I instinctively foretold this winter what I have found here. Alas! I was only too right. The intelligence level, the capacity for creative action are so mediocre! The overwhelming incentives of industry, commerce, and common interests would so readily furnish the solution for a problem, which itself cannot be resolved by force, without degrading its object. Provincialism, such as we have it at home, is capable after all only of a passive sort of courage: resistance is its favourite weapon, but this becomes powerless in the long run when it is not kept sharp by the cruel devices brought to bear against it. If I were the Sovereign, how I would congratulate myself for having in one corner of my empire at least a handful of subjects capable of this blind tenacity which prefers what it believes to be *its right* to the finest innovations. In certain cases, when stubbornness becomes too irrational, and particularistic egotism too flagrant, in the last extremity doesn't one still have the recourse of walking resolutely over them! But in general, for ordinary life, what a blessing in a traditionless empire are these tiresome elements of resistance which are so useful elsewhere, in the affairs of state as in the imaginative moves of social doctrines.

I have landed here in the smallest and least attractive town of Courland. Half a dozen various societies, though all of them exclusive, exist side by side. The aristocracy is represented only by ruined families who are obliged to fall back on public schools for the education of their children, and by a legion of noble old maids, who live on pennies with the decorum which is due to their birth. Among them I have found a cousin of my mother, a Miss de Medem, already very old, who embroiders and knits wonderfully well and works endlessly on all the trousseaux of her young relatives with an irascibility of character and a haughtiness worthy of her old name. She earns her living this way, never asks anything of anyone, and still finds the means to give to those who are poorer than herself. Could this proud independence be compatible with a more flexible and more amiable nature? Must not our virtues always be bought with faults which take root in the same generous earth as they—just like that tare which the great Sower in the Scriptures talks of and which unconcernedly he lets grow alongside the grain. The merchants, real Téniers figures, and typically vulgar, still form a coterie determined by wealth. The teaching body too lives apart; it shuns the uncultivated company of the greater part of the businessmen, and is hardly ever admitted into the company of the squires of the land.

The Russian society, composed of customs employees, a few officers and engineers, enjoys an unflattering reputation in the matter of morality. Its meeting place is the open house of N., whose wife makes her old husband play the most foolish of roles. There is drinking and gaming in their house and you find that free sort of debt-ridden life there which the provincials hold in horror and which for them is synonymous with dissoluteness . . . . From this has emerged a mute, rancorous antagonism to which it would be wrong to apply the term national opposition, but which seems very much like it and which is exploited in this sense by both sides. The arch priest of the Orthodox Church, Fassanov, is highly esteemed; people are grateful to him for his honourable bearing and no one thinks of slandering him. On the other hand, the second priest is a source of scandal with his bacchanalian parties. I couldn't begin to list the defects of a different sort of clergy and the German community, particularly its egotistical narrowness—ridiculous and stupid as individuals, disgusting in the mass.

In spite of all that, though, just look at the results of the united work of these very same unattractive people. Libau has two very well kept orphanages, three elementary schools (I am speaking only of the establishments which depend upon the town), a navigation school, a shelter for young children, a hospital, a gymnasium,[161] a theatre, two parks, another one which was reclaimed from the seashore, and so much else! The public pence are counted and administered with an unvarying slowness and probity. The revolutionaries among the council members[162]—and there are reds even among them—work, it is true, for fifteen years to obtain some improvement, however useful it may be—but once voted the sums are never withdrawn, surveillance is constant and each man considers it a question of honour to face up to his commitments, today as yesterday, tomorrow and always. How wisely and liberally this country could be governed and could be made a gold mine for the common homeland! For as long as I have really known you, you know that it has been my wish to see the Baltic Provinces in your hands. This ingenious combination would bear the best fruit. This Russia, which is feared and despised, you would at last make it respected; the Provinces, at first rightly terrified, would quickly submit to a real force which was incapable of abusing its rights and which richly blessed those entrusted to it . . . . All this seems like so much childishness, doesn't it? And yet how much truth there is in the feelings which engender these dreams!

Farewell, I clasp your hand and am yours truly.

IU. SAMARIN TO BARONESS RAHDEN

Moscow, May 15, (1872).

Your last two letters, the one that came with a book and especially the last one written from Libau, gave me a great deal of pleasure. After leaving Petersburg, I felt very badly about having spoken to you of that book which you could not have felt any delight in sending me. It was a mistake

[161]The word is in German. (Trans.)

[162]The word is in German. (Trans.)

which I shall not make again. You do not like people to talk to you about your letters, I know, yet I shall face up to your displeasure. You have only to cross your arms and to assume a coldly resigned air, which has cut me short more than once. The fact is that I feel rather sprightly in your presence, without being in the least humiliated. No one has made me turn in upon myself and reflect as much as you. I have already told you: there are passages in your letters, words formed by you and forgotten, which often come to my mind and which I know by heart. You must have a good dose of pride (for fundamentally that's what it is) never to have seriously felt the quite legitimate temptation of public literary activity. If I knew how to render, as you do, what I see and feel with the same precision, the same lack of effort, without ever groping, with a perfect sense of proportion, I would write volumes. Your picture of Libau is a little masterpiece—I am a fair judge for I know the social milieu—and what you say about the general state of the country is quite accurate. You need only to finish off what you have said without changing anything. No one recognizes more than I do the moral value and political necessity of a spirit of resistance, which is determined by sincere convictions, even though they may be rather narrow-minded. Among those who possess it and make use of it, it is the hallmark of every *character* in the English sense of the word; for those against whom it acts, it is a most efficacious pedagogical procedure. But when you make use of moderate, legal resistance for your own end, you must recognize that it is legitimate for everyone. Unfortunately it is the contrary which happens. In order to be completely certain of being able to offer resistance at home with impunity, people make it their business to condemn on principle any resistance at Petersburg, and it is vigorously checked wherever it seems about to spring up beyond the Provinces. Do you think, for example, that, the day on which the Third Section would seriously consider setting the punishment for a look of greed, Count N. would refuse to be involved, he who is so adept at dragging out the Livonian tribunal reform? Scores of boys from Orthodox families attend the Protestant Peter-Schule in Moscow, and all's fine! In Livonia, the Protestant consistory was recently declaring that it would no longer institute a charge against the pastors of the province for having administered Sacraments to members of the Greek Church; it was right, and the whole German press applauded this courageous act. However, it now happens that this same consistory is launching a coercive warning to the *Petropavlovskoe Bratstvo* of Riga for having dared accept Protestant pupils who were attracted to the school, which is run by the Brotherhood, by the teaching of Russian. I have the paper in my hand. It ends with the demand for an exact list of the guilty parents in order to take action against them. Naturally enough, the German newspapers will not talk about all this. They will prefer to reproduce Dr. Wurstemberger's report and a good number of similar bits of information on the sad state of Russian schools and upon how they are absolutely incapable of competing with German schools. In Petersburg steps are being taken which have as their avowed goal to gag the Russian press, and these very same newspapers are endorsing them in advance, every paper without exception, and the most liberal ones right at the forefront. No one is ignorant of the fact that they merely reproduce the ready-made dispatches which come in to them from Riga, Dorpat and Petersburg. All of that is perhaps fair war, but in any case it is war.

I am happy to see you say that you were accepting my intentions and that you have even consented to let me get to work. Since it is a dream which we are both having, let me tell you that if the absence of any hostile feeling and of any disposition to take up the past and to recriminate could suffice, I should perhaps have been foolish enough to undergo the test, God and yourself helping me. It was deep down a labour of peace I had in mind as I began publishing, and if my tone was bitter and harsh the reason is that at the point things had reached, it was necessary to raise a scandal in order to be listened to. Besides, a peace is not lasting unless the two subscribing parties are thoroughly conscious of what is rightfully theirs. And yet it was much more a matter of making the government realize that it was giving way too much, than of making the Provinces reconsider exaggerated claims. Unfortunately I began too late.

In a short story which the *Russki Vestnik* is publishing, the author brings Princess Dashkova[163] on the scene in her twilight days. He has her reply to a visitor who wants to make her express hope for the coming of a time when a fraternal *entente* would be established between the Russians and the Poles: "That time will not come, because it has passed; we have let it escape without availing ourselves of it." The same could be said of the Baltic Provinces. The fusing of the local German element with the main German body has, in the realm of ideas and sentiments, been brought about under our very eyes. It is a question now only of conflict between a province and the State of which it is a part; this conflict has been transformed into a struggle between two races and now forms only an episode, a vanguard skirmish which precedes the great battle day. That is what poisons the simplest and most trifling questions and makes them insoluble. The same thing is happening in Bohemia, in the Military districts, and in other areas. Germany as a whole recognizes it and is preparing for it, we alone seem to foresee nothing. We attach a ridiculous importance to individuals' attitudes, to such and such a word attributed to the Emperor, to Prince Frederick, or to Count Bismarck, and we forget all too easily that in Germany there is a power which is called public opinion, and which sooner or later brings itself to bear on the government. To fully understand the situation, it would be good, it seems

[163]C. R. Dashkova (1743-1810) was a friend and confidante of Catherine II. She was Director of the St. Petersburg Academy of Science and the Russian Academy, the latter organization being established at her instigation to improve the Russian language. As Director of the Russian Academy she was responsible for a number of publishing ventures of scientific and cultural importance. (Ed.)

to me, to find out something of what is being taught in the primary schools, what is being said in the non-commissioned officers' clubs, what is being printed and read in the very small newspapers which you can scorn but which in spite of that remain influential in the countryside and suburbs. Just recently I was reading in one of these broadsheets a conversation between a Prussian and a man from the Baltic Provinces: "When will our turn come?" asked the Livonian. "Have a little more patience," replied the Prussian. All that is nothing, it is said, just as a penny is nothing either, and yet it is these little pennies which, as they accumulate, form great capital funds before which people bow down.

When I try to understand what is awaiting my country, carrying in its own entrails that same element which is arming against it on the outside, many things make me shudder, but there is one which reassures me about the outcome of the struggle which I shall not live to see. Those of our people who are aware of the attitudes of our neighbours and a segment of our fellow citizens with regard to Russia retain nonetheless their intellectual and moral lucidity with regard to Germany. They readily appreciate the genius of a race which is hostile to them and would blush at being unfair to an individual as to the nation as a whole. If it were otherwise, the enlightened part of the public would become indignant and silence them. Wherever the German element dominates, the contrary is the case. As soon as it is a question of Russia, or of a Russian, intelligence seems to become clouded and conscience dumb. The most honest people accept deliberate lies as a means of action; men who are honourable in any other matter cast themselves headlong into calumny, and the public shrugs: no one objects, no one censures. This makes me hope, that, whatever may be the disappointments and the humiliations through which we shall have to pass, if a day of revenge should ever come, we shall not give way to temptations of vengeance.

Have you read or glanced through in the *Vestnik Evropy* a series of articles by our friend Kavelin[164] on the psychological questions of the day? It is very dry, very hard to read, but there is a great deal of conscientious work, a great deal of substance and the style is remarkably precise. The author feels himself to be at an impasse and would like very much to be able to get out of it, without having to resign himself to bow down before what he thought was shattered! From the shipwreck he hopes to save moral freedom and conscience, while he is throwing overboard the idea of a God who is not only creator and legislator with regard to general matter but who at the same time exercises a providential control over the individual and inspires in him the strength which the fulfillment of every moral law requires. There is nothing new in this, but what is really remarkable about it is the good faith, the honesty with which Kavelin stamps this singular compromise. I promised him a few comments in writing and I have not done anything yet. I am wondering whether pushing him to a more logical solution, which he might balk at even more, would be doing him a favour. Would it not be better to let him become converted by himself? What do you think?

I am taking a chance in addressing this letter simply to Libau. You did not give me a more detailed address. Let me make a proposition to you: write to me at length only when you feel fully disposed to do so, without ever saddling yourself with it—that is a thought which bothers me and I want us to be quite clear about it—but please keep me informed about your stay there, if only with a line or two. My brother's sickness, *Duma* business, the examinations in my school and so on will keep me in Moscow probably until the middle of June.

Everyone has left Moscow, but there will soon be a

[164]These articles appeared in book form in 1871 under the title of *Zadachi Psikhologii K. Kavelina.* (D. S.) K. D. Kavelin (1831-85) was a prominent historian and jurist who began his career as a Westernizer along with Belinski and Herzen. He developed into a vigorous exponent of reform on Liberal constitutional lines. See *Sobranie sochinenii K. D. Kavelina* (4 vols.; St. Petersburg, 1897-1900). (Ed.)

reflux for the exhibition. I do not know whether I told you that the Moscow *Duma* had asked, on a motion I made a few months ago, that the compulsory subsidy required of the town for the upkeep of theatres be reduced proportionately to the subsidy paid by Petersburg for the same purpose. At the same time the *Duma* undertook to divide the balance remaining into two equal parts, turning one part over to the Conservatory, as an annual subsidy and dedicating the other to the primary schools of the town. This subsidy would have ensured the future of the Conservatory. Just recently we received from the Ministry of the Court a formal refusal, of which I shall give you a copy, sending it to Petersburg. Instead of Gluck and Mozart we shall have, as in the past, vaudeville couplets, fabric waves, cardboard rocks, and so on. Yours truly.

IU. SAMARIN TO BARONESS RAHDEN

Moscow, May 28, (1872).

Here is the business of the theatre subsidy I spoke to you about in my last letter. The delay in sending it to you was due to our recently having had family troubles which have prevented me from thinking of anything else. Yours truly.

BARONESS RAHDEN TO IU. SAMARIN

June 1, (1872).

I heard through the Obolenskis of the grievous blow you have received; it seems useless for me to tell you that I share it very intensely with you. Even if the death of a loved one is imminent for a long time, the moment when he no longer is, when his place in the family circle remains empty, is always a moment of great pain, whose keen bitterness no one can really know before having passed through this destruction of what is for all of us the fundamental unity of the heart—the family. Thank you very much for having thought to send me the paper about the Conservatory. The Grand Duchess was very much touched by this concern, for the fate of the Moscow Conservatory is one of her remaining interests. Thanks again for your letter which was sent to me from Libau—I shall answer it some other time soon, for I am always glad to write you and I shall be a great deal more so when I can tell you what causes a last bit of constraint in my correspondence.

Farewell. The Pentecost season is approaching; of all the manifestations of God, this one touches my soul most closely. Ever since childhood, the idea of the Holy Spirit descending upon men of goodwill gave me shudders of religious expectation. May the Lord be with you that day and always! Yours sincerely.

BARONESS RAHDEN TO IU. SAMARIN

Kamennyi Ostrov, June 16, (1872).

Your cousin is leaving tomorrow; he is taking my letter, and yet I am very sorry in a selfish way to see him go. With him gone, there will be nothing left but a friendless desert, nothing but a population of tiresome, indifferent people and statesmen triumphing in a vacuum. Nature is quite right in being horrified at it all. I am therefore going to create a silent world for myself, set apart, a world of books and sincere correspondences; you are the first to inaugurate it. Suffer me nevertheless to set at the head of it an introductory chapter which will be especially dedicated to you: "On serious flattery and on the childish and mortal consequences of it." Serious flattery—you are the personification of it. Do you really think you can with impunity say to me, with a tone full of conviction, that my last letter was a little *chef-d'oeuvre*? Do you forget who you are, and that consequently every word of encouragement or praise from you carries weight in the consciousness[165] of those to whom you are speaking. Consider moreover just who I am, that I have a great friendship for you and the habit of believing you—well, to put it bluntly, simplemindedly! And now imagine the consequences of the *chef-d'oeuvre*! What is most vital in me is the clear conscience of my moral silhouette, cut out in black. I hold fast to it, I have always defended it victoriously in myself against the pink, or green, or blue clouds, with which people have tried so hard to colour it! I have set around it a good broad plain which is arid and barren; it would be impossible to approach it along covered or flowery paths, for the slightest enemy stands out on the horizon. But when *you* march right up as a friend and straight out tell me without any circumlocutions: "Why do you resist the pleasures of literature? You are full of talent, you have only to wish . . . ." Pardon me, either I am not following you too well or else it is simply a matter of a murder. My disturbed, frightened self-awareness[166] forgets about the enemy, it drinks from the cup you hold out to it—it is sick, it is dead. That is the tragic side of the matter; the ridiculous side is there too. Suppose I should embark one fine day on the surging sea of public life. What should I launch on it? A book? Oh, certainly not! It is a serious matter to confront a somewhat interesting subject and to want to exhaust it in depth; to do that arduous studies and long meditations are needed, along with a capacity for analysis and an aptitude for synthesis which are rarely found together in the mind of a woman. First of all, while my self-awareness[167] still has a breath of life in it, I shall forego that, and you too, for I consult you of necessity and you are beginning to get a little frightened at having succeeded so well. No book—a brochure on a subject of current interest—a narrative which is not too

[165]The word is in German. (Trans.)

[166]The word is in German. (Trans.)

long, not too learned, witty rather than reflective, racy, full of verve, escape literature which amuses. Good God! Alright, here I have pulled out all those adjectives—I take your bait and I try to measure up to your expectations. I write, I rub out, I scratch, I am not in the slightest gay, nor racy either, nor the least learned in the world—oh! as far as that goes, I remain faithful to the programme! Well finally the work is finished. I submit it to your clairvoyant criticism and you in your turn are very much embarrassed. You are surprised, you rub your eyes—is that really it? How woolly and pallid and doctrinarian it is! Alas! it is pure German tediousness! You tell me your opinion; I think you are very fickle in your assessments. You must have been out of sorts that day. A talent like mine does not produce exceptionally bad stuff! And there I am, then, really taking myself seriously. There is a second piece, if you are upset with the first. Or even what do you think of a third try? Facility is no longer what I am lacking. How right you were—now I recognize myself! Why did I not begin trying in my youth to speak out loud to an attentive public? Time is necessary for real masterpieces to become accepted—I shall no longer see my glory! . . . And the tracts trail along one after another and the brochures rain down—I play with the idea of a great book, I quickly jot down memoirs! And there you are satisfied, my fine friend, the world owes these masterpieces to your persuasive eloquence! And our friendship? What has become of it in this literary whirlwind? Let me keep it, I beg you! Do not flatter me, because I believe you. I have put my hand to the plough—humble work suits me, because I believe in the resurrection of the slightest seed which I cast into my furrow. If from time to time you care to encourage me to persevere in spite of the brambles on the rocky ground, please do so, for you know that your tokens of friendship mean a great deal to me, but don't delude yourself about me and don't try to make me share your illusions.

[167] The word is in German. (Trans.)

After the calm, charming freedom of my country life, I feel very tied down with the thousand little obligations of my court existence; I scarcely have time to read during the day, to try to follow the religious discussions which are shaking the moral world. Everywhere the same hurricane swirls around the same problems. I have in front of me the voluminous sermons of Mr. Beecher, the great American preacher, the "Essays" of Rev. Fowle—Switzerland, Germany, Italy are echoing the same concerns. All of that is full of boldness, of license, if you will, of blind temerity; but out of it all must come some sort of perfection, for the powerful breath of religious life, which can no longer draw any satisfaction from a prescribed faith or even from submission, is rumbling behind these tempests. Those who are most advanced, who might be thought impious, still have a fervent and unfulfilled yearning toward God which is very moving. It could be said that the people of Israel have set out towards another Thabor on which they seek with anguish a new transfiguration of their faith. People have drawn so far away from Christ, they have so obstinately buried his glorious face beneath thick veils—yet look how they all come back to him, though, to seek in his pure doctrine, in his holy individuality, the solution for the mysteries which terrify them. Man or God, downwards or upwards, he is the sole end. The history of the passion is repeated throughout all its phases with a poignant presentness, and the unconscious hands of the executioners fasten once again on the top of that cross, on which the Saviour of the world seems to die, the prophetic words of Pilate: This is the King of the Jews. Up until now I can see only *one* sure thing in these violent struggles, and that is that scientific arms serve the cause of religion badly and that it can henceforth overcome resistance or the attacks of incredulity only on some other more positive ground than that of abstract speculation. Dogmatic subtleties no longer arouse anyone, but what still remains, beyond appeal and beyond refutation, is the example of a spotless life, of straightforward truth, and of the disinterested devotion of an eternal charity. Human motives can surprise you with their arid selfishness, and will generally disillusion sincere souls in the long run; the flaw in their impure drives inevitably forces them to make compromises—each generation will have to drop lower and lower in its capacity for perfect action—while the silent argument of the *real fact* of Christian life, from the evidence of which no man can escape, will prepare the base for the general rebuilding of Christianity.

Prince Obolenski will talk to you of more current matters than my hopes for a religious future. He will bring you up to date on our political and social life. Nevertheless, I still want to reply to a passage in your letter which seems unfair to me. You say that there are many Orthodox young people who attend the Peter-Schule without the Synod seeing anything objectionable in this; I can add that priests' sons abound there, because they are able, along with other good studies, to learn their mother tongue there and receive the teaching of their Church. Against this you set the unjust and intolerant Livonian Consistory which becomes upset at seeing Protestant children go to the schools of the *Bratstvo* (Brotherhood). Do not overlook, if possible, the real basis of the question. The *Bratstvo* makes no secret of proselytism (to my knowledge Protestant teaching is not allowed there) and it is perfectly fair to let them assert themselves in their effort to expand. But then the Consistory is quite within its right and duty, too, in warning its flock of the bad influences lurking around. Convert! Look, there is a whole volume in embryo in this single word! I shall spare you it today so that I can come back to it another time. Tell me where you are going and I shall gladly write you—that will be my escape from a great many troubles. May God keep you.

IU. SAMARIN TO BARONESS RAHDEN

Vassil'evski, August 1/13, (1872).

Glancing through the newspapers recently, I learned of the death of a young naturalist (I cannot recall his name) in whose fate you took a lively interest. What a sad death: in the space of a couple of months, two men victims of their devotion to science! You can doubtless guess that I am thinking of Hilferding.[168] How does it happen that you never met him? He did not have a broad intelligence but he was a fountain of knowledge, an indefatigable and fundamentally honest worker whose unpretentiousness[169] would disarm even those who were the most hostile to the general principles he espoused. He was also a disciple of Khomiakov. Outstanding men have always been less rare than persevering honest workers who can content themselves with the modest role which befits them, and yet it is they who give excellence to the social order.

You disagreed with me[170] in your last letter, but I still maintain all I was saying to you. Certainly, if you had ever consulted me on my opinion I would have told you so frankly and bluntly. I would even have pushed criticism to the point of quibbling. If you doubt it, try me. Yours truly.

[168]A. F. Hilferding (1831-72) was a slavist, philologist and historian of stature. He was a Moscow Slavophil and was strongly influenced by Khomiakov. He made a special contribution as a folklorist, see *Onezhskie byliny* (1873). (Ed.)

[169]The word is in German. (Trans.)

[170]The phrase is in German. (Trans.)

BARONESS RAHDEN TO IU. SAMARIN

Petersburg, September 7, 1872.

We are on the eve of going abroad where the Grand Duchess will seek, under a more temperate sky, a prolongation of our fine summer just ended. At present the weather is frightful: it is raining torrents; a cold wind, a gray sky, indescribably heavy and sad, which is peculiar to Petersburg, brings us back to reality after the charming dreams of three months of light and warmth. I am a little like the weather this morning. What I wouldn't give for an hour of conversation with a friend! For want of mutual conversation, I shall have recourse to a written monologue. Perhaps that is better than anything else! Do I not have the presentiment that the *entente cordiale* is already a political illusion between us, and that the circle of our common ideas is closing tighter and tighter, to the point of becoming an almost imperceptible dot. Can our friendship not suffer from it in the long run! You can see that I *have* taken on the colour of the weather. I am going to re-read your letter to calm me and then make a suitable reply to it. What do I find in it? Two obituary notices—one about an individual who is not dead, for, thank God, that poor Miklukha-Maklai is very much alive in his desert isle—and the other about a man I never knew. Then there is a paragraph with a terse, slightly bitter stubbornness, and then your name written out in full. Apart from that, there is not a word about yourself; there is not even a reply to what I might have written you! I fold up the letter again; it does little to cheer me up.

It would be better for me to give you some news of the world. Petersburg is completely deserted. Prince Urussov and Princess Dolly Obolenski alone animate this gray wasteland. No minister has come back yet to the fold; the members of the Imperial family are almost without exception all away travelling. There is some talk of a marriage of the Grand Duke Vladimir with Princess Mary of Mecklenburg-Schwerin.

You know of the mourning of the Orlov-Davidovs and the Panins. Semenov is resting up in Dresden and in Venice from his statistical work; Pobedonostsev and his wife are in Remplin with the Grand Duchess Catherine; the Abazas are sojourning on their land at Kiev. The Grand Duchess Helen wants to spend a few days in Berlin with her brother, then go on to Florence, and then come back to Russia by the beginning of November. This forced trip and this return in the worst season worry me very much.

Farewell, take care of yourself; may God be with you and bless you.

IU. SAMARIN TO BARONESS RAHDEN

Vassil'evski, October 22, (1872).

Do not be alarmed at the thickness of the package! I take up only the smallest part of it. You will find in it a long letter, or rather the draft of a letter, which I have just received from Ivan Aksakov. He writes me that he did not have enough time to finish it off. It is a study on the Orlov-Davidov family; it seemed remarkable to me from a couple of angles, and after having read it you will understand why I wanted to pass it along to you (quite confidentially) and to have you share the impression it made on me.

You will admit, will you not, that it is impossible to be a Protestant through religious temperament without being one out of conviction. As far as I am concerned, I prefer a hymn to a picture, and I understand the philosophic formula better than the legendary tale, and so I have always wanted for the Church to which I belong not a violent rupture with its past but rather a spontaneous awakening of the spirit which created Protestant life. I mean that sober belief as it manifests itself in the moral practice of a household and in daily life.[171]

[171] The sentence is in German. (Trans.)

Now it so happens that that is almost what Aksakov discovered with his Otrada neighbours as the product of a Protestant slip grafted upon an Orthodox stem.[172] I could go on at length with you about this but I am having incredible difficulty in expressing myself in French. This language which was familiar to me in my childhood and youth is slipping completely away from me. When I write to you it is always *in order to tell you something* and I will admit to you that I find it very hard to resign myself to giving you my thoughts in an incorrect or vague form. Please don't suppose that this is due to an author's vanity; a well-written letter is a homage as much as any other. And so one fine day I shall take my courage in both hands to ask your permission to write you in Russian, at least to have recourse to Russian when I do not have the French.—Why are you scowling at me? Although I have never heard you pronounce a word in my tongue, I know you have a sound knowledge of it and that you understand all of its nuances. Don't forget that I have printed proof of this.

Now let me say a word to you about what is keeping me busy in the country: it is my schools. I have two, and about the 15th of November I shall open a third. My first school, divided into two classes, is composed only of children who are, unfortunately, very much too young. Ordinarily I give only two lessons a day there, solely in order to obtain a good understanding of the procedures to follow and to let my schoolmaster understand thoroughly what I require of him. In my innocent ignorance I thought that primary teaching was an easy thing. I did not suspect that it was a science. The book by Baron Korff[173] (may thanks be rendered to him) was a revelation for me as it has been for others. Following his directions I ground at the business a little, I opened the

[172]In the letter in question, I. S. Aksakov was sketching the portrait of Countess O. I. Orlov-Davidov, a woman strict in her Orthodox convictions but whose morality showed the influence of a Protestant mother. (D. S.)

books which he cited and when I perceived all that I had been ignorant of and had neglected up to that point, I felt ashamed for having so long failed to recognize not only the necessity of the moment but even my own personal vocation. Don't laugh too hard, and give me the chance to pride myself on my success as a schoolmaster. All modesty aside, the results which I am obtaining prove to me that I possess the required qualities for the profession: a boundless patience and calm, the children's taste, and the art of getting the attention of a whole band of eight- and nine-year-old brats. I am able to guess the character, temperament and intellectual limits I am dealing with quite well and it gives me a very great pleasure to determine the method of teaching which is most appropriate for them. All that would be more than enough to settle me down here forever, but I am neither able nor willing to abandon my mother and sister for six months of the winter, and unfortunately to run back and forth between Moscow and Samara, as my sister does between Moscow and Serpukhov, is quite impossible. My second school is of a different sort: the eldest of the pupils who attend it is forty years old. For several years the parishioners of the village had been gathering on Sundays, after matins and before mass, in the communal hall to listen to a reading by an old peasant. As his voice would often fail him, I offered him my services. At first so as not to scare off my listeners, I had to continue the reading of the legends they were used to, then I led them little by little around to asking me to explain to them our Slavonic liturgical books, and now I am giving them quite an organized catechism course. Today the hall was full. I do not need to tell you that in these lectures I am learning more than I am teaching. What a mystery there is in the religious life of a people which like ours has been left to itself and is illiterate! You wonder where it all springs from, and, when you try to get back to the source, you find nothing. Our

[173] *Russkaia nachal'nia shkola. Rukovodstvo dlia zemskikh glasnikh i uchitelei sel'skikh shkol*, ed. Baron N. A. Korff. (D. S.)

clergy does not teach, it officiates and it administers the sacraments. For people who cannot read, the Bible does not exist; the divine service alone is left, together with some prayers which are transmitted from father to son, as the only links between the Church and the individual. But it does happen (I am quite convinced of this) that the people definitely do not understand anything, around our parts at least, about the liturgical language nor even about the "Our Father"[174] which they often recite with omissions or additions which make nonsense of it. And yet in each of these untutored minds, there is, as in Athens, an altar raised by some unknown hand to an unknown God; in each, the real presence of a providential will in every event of life is such an unquestionable fact and one that is so thoroughly acquired that, when death appears, these men to whom no one has ever spoken of God, open their door to him as to a familiar and long-expected visitor. They render their soul to God[175] in the literal sense of the word.

Your last letter is sad—you are feeling the effect of the weather. That is a weakness I did not know you had and which I am glad to find out. If I too were to let myself go to the point of listening to the voices of autumn, I would get carried far away, but, in my capacity as a hunter, I face up to them and I do the same with regard to your forebodings. You will never persuade me to share them. To cure you of them and to pass my assurance on to you, I shall say only one thing: you have done me good, you can do a great deal of this to me, and that would not be the case if we were mistaken in thinking that we understood one another. If this letter precedes you to Petersburg by only a few days, you could still send me back Aksakov's, mailing it to Syzran, for I shall not leave the country before the first sleighs around the middle of November, but if your sojourn abroad should be

[174]The two words are in German. (Trans.)

[175]This first part of the sentence is in Russian (Trans.)

prolonged, mail it to my sister's house in Moscow just to be on the safe side.

You know how I value your letters, so you can imagine the joy which the sight of your hand-writing would give me here where I am living in complete isolation. Unreservedly yours truly.

BARONESS RAHDEN TO IU. SAMARIN

December 30, 1872.

I hope this letter will reach you on New Year's day—may it let you know what I am asking God for you by way of happiness, peace, and joy! Please do not secretly reproach me for not having replied to you—I did it a thousand times in my thoughts, and with what gratefulness! It was at a time of the greatest sadness in Florence, during the sickness of the Grand Duchess. I felt very much alone, overwhelmed with many responsibilities and left completely to myself to take care of everything. Your letter came to me as if heaven had dictated it to you to console me and to take the place of the support of your strong, gentle friendship in my loneliness. I ought to have written you about how good this was for me—I should have right away, I know. I have often reproached myself for not having said anything to you about it—please pardon this outward silence. You are going to be arriving in Petersburg, so I shall not send you back the letter, or rather the little masterpiece, of Mr. Aksakov, which I must restore safely to you. If you want to get it back before coming here, tell me in Russian, I beg you, even though your modesty with regard to French is unheard of. Farewell, may God bless you and keep you.

IU. SAMARIN TO BARONESS RAHDEN

Moscow, February 28, (1873).

Prince Shcherbatov is going to Petersburg to visit hospitals. He is counting upon your protection and I did not want to let him go without sending you a warm greeting. The rather sketchy news reaching me from time to time concerning what is going on around you bothers me very deeply, and is making me rather anxious about you. I am always afraid that you will turn your back on Petersburg and that you will be lost to us. It seems to me that I know you well enough to have some reason to fear the effect upon you of the charm of renunciation. You may tell yourself then that whatever your existence at Petersburg may be, you are the one who will set the goal for yourself, and that you will certainly have plenty of chances to work and to dedicate yourself. I am writing to you as the ideas come to me, faced with all sorts of suppositions that keep going through my head; if it is nonsense, please do not hold it against me.

I have learned something today that has touched me deeply. Some years ago, one morning, at Prince Odoevski's, I saw a photograph which you possibly remember: the Odoevski couple and you around a tea table. It is the only photograph of you I have ever seen. While I was studying it, Odoevski must have noticed that I had some pleasure in seeing you again, but he did not say anything to me about it. After his death, the photograph and the frame have frequently been moved and it was only yesterday that his niece, Madame Perfil'ev, finding it again, noticed a few words written on the back by our excellent friend: "After my death, to be given as a souvenir to Iu. F. Samarin."[176] I am to receive it tomorrow. I hope that you will allow me to keep it.

If I do not ask how you are, you should be grateful for

[176] These words are in Russian. (Trans.)

my discretion. It is also a sacrifice, the best proof of devotion which I can give you at this moment. Yours truly.

BARONESS RAHDEN TO IU. SAMARIN

Petersburg, March 17, (1873).

Prince Shcherbatov disappointed me very much by leaving without warning me; I wanted to write you at some length, to mention a thousand little things which today I shall merely indicate to you in a summary fashion. Why are you not coming to Petersburg before I leave! I should have been happy to destroy a bit the wretched impression I must have made upon you without realizing it, and, too, your counsel is very dear to me. It is with great distaste that I am forced to think about myself, to speak about myself, and my future, which really is so very inconsequential! You seem to believe that I am shaping lofty plans and that I am going to adopt fierce resolutions. It would be painful for me to risk being censured by you and that is why I shall explain to you, *and to you alone*, what my present position is, begging you to give me your sincere opinion about my intentions.

Since the death of the Grand Duchess has given me back a sad sort of freedom, I have had only one real desire—that of consecrating the rest of my life to looking after the charitable works, and to maintaining the ideas, with which for twenty years my existence has been associated . . . . In the meantime, the organizing Commission is deliberating upon the form and composition of the future Administrative Council for the Grand Duchess' foundation; it is a question of strongly establishing a principle, and no personal motives must enter into consideration, before the most important thing is settled; my friends, my work, my explanations and any possible influence I may have, everything is bent to realizing the only ideal monument, worthy of the memory of the Grand Duchess, in its most complete form. Once the new government has come into power, I shall quietly withdraw. I could again establish myself in independent fashion in Petersburg, where I would certainly not lack for activity, and live there on the pension the Emperor assures me. Here we are touching on an intimate part of my life which it is difficult for me to discuss even with you. I should never want to put the *comfort* of my existence above natural duties, which I could henceforth fulfill only with the help of a certain economy, in a milieu in which this would be possible.

You have possibly heard of a proposition which the Queen of Würtemburg made to me to come and replace Sister Gagarin in Stuttgart. The Emperor has rather pressed me to comply with this desire of the Queen and if he goes on, I shall see myself in the position of paying my debt of gratitude with a year of exile. But it would be impossible for me to expatriate myself for longer, to abandon, for the mundane cares of a German court, both the concerns of the land to which I should like right up to the end to consecrate the whole strength of my soul and the friendships which are my life's joy. You will accuse me of being ambitious when I say this—the concerns of the land—and yet I mean it in a very humble sense. From the remote corner of a hostile province, I shall try to promote, by means of charity, ideas which have become sentiments for me, and I shall honour the memory of the Grand Duchess by putting into practice in obscurity what she taught me in a more extensive and more brilliant sphere. That is how I intend to reconcile the demands of my position, my nature, and my duties. Tell me that I am not wrong—I need this to sustain me in my isolation and in my future plans. Their cost will be too heavy for me to risk adding your disapproval. Yours, as always, with my heart and soul.

IU. SAMARIN TO BARONESS RAHDEN

Moscow, March 20, (1873).

Why did you not have me come if you wanted to speak with me—I would have come at a sign. What can I say to you now that I see you resigned, with your mind made up. Nothing in your plans will change no matter what I may say to you, and you are having me speak to you only so as to taste even more bitterness, so that you can fully realize the sort of suicide which you have taken it into your head to commit. I was right ten times over in my presentiments. Well, so be it! I shall be frank. To begin with, I cannot understand anything whatsoever about your intention of renouncing an activity for which you were suited, for which you are made . . . .

I do not understand either why it is absolutely necessary for you to go to Stuttgart . . . . That part of your programme (I mean the trip to Stuttgart) has, however, a good side to it—and that is that it is a matter of only one year, but what bothers me very deeply is your ending. I shall set aside my personal regrets; I shall not speak to you either of the moral torture which you would undergo, with your eye fixed only on the final goal. Never will you again become what you would possibly have been had you never left your province, and given the person you are you can gain no control whatever over the *entourage* you would have to deal with in Courland. Among us, you may have been wounded by people's sharp tongues, but when you have spoken you have been listened to with respect, and people have improved! Over there you would be faced with immutable, irremediable hostility and with a contempt (*einer Geringschätzung*) which is exalted into a national conviction. Between, on the one hand, an administration which cannot even garner esteem for itself, and on the other the constant goading coming from abroad, there is no longer any possibility of mediation.[177]

[177]The word is in German. (Trans.)

No one would listen to you. Things have been pushed too far; a catastrophe must happen.

I cannot tell you how pained I am when I think of what is going to happen to you. May my forebodings prove groundless. I do not have enough details; I see your position only in very general terms; maybe my reasoning is faulty, for want of a close enough perspective, but I am simply telling you quite frankly what I think and feel.

Tell me at least when you are intending to leave so that I can clasp your hand once again. Yours truly.

BARONESS RAHDEN TO IU. SAMARIN

March 25, (1873).

I thank you from my heart for your letter—whose friendliness I feel in spite of its unfairness . . . . It seems to me that you do not fully realize my present position. My activity up until now had no other basis than the will and confidence of the Grand Duchess; one single official nomination, but coming *solely from her*, that of trustee[178] of St. Helen's School, gave me a sort of outside base. I am using it to remain where I am, until the new organization is definitely settled, and to watch, in fact if not by right, over what seems useful to me in the way things are run . . . .

If you give any thought to the real state of affairs,[179] you cannot accuse me of any haste, nor, I believe, of any lack of moral courage. I have not *decided* anything—I told you what I believed I must do, while standing ready to alter course if need be . . . . What *is* true is that I am too desirous of dedicating my life to the service of a venerated memory not to have certain reservations about working for it—personal motives do so much to screen objective truth.

[178] *Popechitel'nitsa.* (Trans.)

[179] *Sachlage.* (Trans.)

The question of an obscure existence in the Baltic Provinces seems more natural there than anywhere else because I come from there and, all things considered, Libau is preferable to Toropets or Kolomna, were it only because of the sea. But, again—I set so little store by my plans that I ask only to scrap them if you can advise me of anything better. Please do not hold it against me; if nothing changes, I shall be very happy to see you.

IU. SAMARIN TO BARONESS RAHDEN

March 24, (1873).

I wrote you the other day under the influence of the pain your letter gave me. If, because I did not see clearly what your position is, my reasoning is faulty, if my frankness came out as rudeness, please do not be angry with me but rather attribute my tone only to the fear of losing you. It is Dmitriev who will be bringing you this letter. You have known him for a long time. Let me add too that he is sincerely devoted to you. Yours truly.

BARONESS RAHDEN TO IU. SAMARIN

Petersburg, April 18, 1873.

Grand Duchess Catherine asked me yesterday in a formal and insistent way to continue to look after the foundations which the Grand Duchess had *especially* charged me with. This makes it possible for me to remain in Petersburg and to devote myself to a service which to me is sacred. By dint of quiet attention and modest work, I may possibly be able to make myself a bit useful in the general area of that glorious heritage of intelligent good works; in any case, St. Helen's School will continue, Elizabeth Hospital will develop, the community Dinners will not be closed, as long as I am there. This upturn in my fate is a blessing from God; I accept it with trembling because the responsibility is great and my courage is always on the point of weakening. You are one of the first persons to whom I have spoken in a *positive* way of my intentions—I should not like to declare them yet, for several delicate and very painful questions are involved which I must settle in an amicable fashion. Independence is smiling upon me—it may afford me great benefits in view of my life's goal . . . .

Have you pardoned me yet? Pass all of this on to Dmitriev. Yours from my heart and forever.

IU. SAMARIN TO BARONESS RAHDEN

April 22, 1873.

I do not need to tell you how happy your letter made me; please believe me when I say that my ego, content at having been right about you, has nothing to do with this. What I shall miss a little is your *salon*, which had a character of cloistered serenity all its own.

I passed on the contents of your letter to Dmitriev; he is sick, gravely according to his doctor, although at the moment there is no danger. Yours truly.

BARONESS RAHDEN TO IU. SAMARIN

Siedlec, July 9/21, (1873).

How long it has been since I have had any word from you! Why did you not reply to my last letter? I am taking my courage in both hands to put this indiscreet question to you for it seems to me that you have been angry with me for some time and I don't know why. You surely cannot still harbour any bad feeling about the way in which, at our last meeting, my great sorrow was absorbing me. I do not know how to do anything in half measures, and even less how to love in a lukewarm and cautious way—and I held for the Grand Duchess a passionate affection! All the grief I suffered was doubled by the ideal aspirations I held for her intelligence, her glory, her moral perfection. Now that she no longer is, I remember nothing but the grandeur of that rich nature and of the tender gratitude which I owe her for having initiated me in feelings and inclinations which are my best support in my extreme isolation. Has my friendship for you become any less vital because, in the first pangs of grief, I could express only my sorrow? I have regained my equilibrium now, I do not bother anyone with my mourning. If I were to have the joy of seeing you again, I would not let myself go again as I did then; but could that possibly be the reason for your silence at a time when any friendly word from you would have consoled and bolstered my heart? You misread my first letter too, attributing intentions and fantasies to me which I did not have—events have proved this to you. You may be assured that I never hesitate to admit a real fault—even an unconscious one—that I am stricken by anything that can harm a friend; but I guard and defend my feelings as my most sacred property—those which I have towards you as much as any others. We touch eternal things by means of our feelings, much more than by our ideas which are necessarily restricted, faulty and often so self-centred! Could I possibly have been wrong? Was I wrong in letting Madam X make me uneasy about your discontentment at the way I received you in Petersburg? How I do want to think so! No, you simply have not had the time to write me, you have not felt like doing it . . . but this evening *I* felt such a great need to speak openly to you that I could not resist it, and here is my letter!

I am in Poland at my sister's; her husband is commanding a regiment of grenadiers stationed at Siedlec, the most desolate spot in the world if it were not for the joys of a happy family I can share in and many phases of human life to observe and to understand. The common activity of your good triumvirate[180] of former days has also provided me with an unexpected pleasure; in this sad administration it is the commissaries charged with overseeing the business of the peasants who, virtually all alone, enjoy any real respect. The peasants' welfare seems quite real, the influence of the nobility, which has never been able to become an aristocracy, no longer exists and I am proud to report to you that the institution is founded. There is something revolting in observing the apparent contrast between the vestiges of princely existences which were lived here in former days and the total absence now of institutions which are useful to the masses.

In three weeks I am returning to Petersburg where I left a number of practical jobs which I am gradually learning about. My burning desire to see the last wishes of the Grand Duchess realized in the founding of a clinical institute, which would have been complementary to her other work, will not be realized, I am afraid.

Shall I see you again this winter, my dear friend? I shall not be going to either Stuttgart or Libau—will you be staying the whole year in Samara? Are you busy with the evangelization of your peasants as last year? How I should like to manage to arrange for myself a hermit's existence in Petersburg without any worldly obligations, without conventional duplicities, without selfish preoccupations—in a word the existence of someone who feels herself on the point of death and, without any regret, sees everything that is not eternal slip quickly into the shadows of the past.

You would give me immense pleasure by writing to me soon, telling me all about yourself. May God be with you. He has promised those of pure heart that he will.

[180]An allusion to the mission to Poland, carried out together in 1864 by N. A. Miliutin, Prince V. A. Cherkasski and Iu. Samarin, to study the peasant question. (D. S.)

IU. SAMARIN TO BARONESS RAHDEN

Vassil'evski, July 19, (1873).

There is no need for me to tell you how happy I felt in recognizing your writing on the envelope of your letter of the 9th. It was a long time in coming; I have just received it and the bearer is leaving for Syzran in a quarter of an hour. I shall have only just enough time to reply to you, putting off for the next mail the great many things I could have written of, and a request I intend to address to you.

Seriously, could you possibly imagine that I could be angry with you? And, good God, why? Just for having found you deeply stricken by a loss which rocked your personal life! Again, how could you have formed such a queer notion, even for a moment? I shall not complain, since I did get a page from you which was very touching; but I shall never be able to pardon myself for having, without realizing it, given rise to anxiety, suspicion, which must have been painful for you. After our last meeting in Petersburg, I left you with a feeling of deep disquiet. Knowing your promptness in answering, I felt that writing you would be, on my part, an unpardonable lack of delicacy, and yet since I did want to hear from you, I could think of nothing better than to speak to Madam X. She generously accepted my commission and acquitted herself of it as best she could, but it seems that I must have expressed myself badly if she thought she could see anything in my attitude resembling personal displeasure. Since that time, I have always followed you from a distance, and just recently, having received a letter from Prince Cherkasski telling me that you were asking after me, I was about to write to you when your letter forestalled me. That is the pure truth.

Again, this is only a reply. I did not want to put off for a single moment the chance to justify myself for a wrong for which you had already pardoned me! As for my letter which is already begun, it will follow this one in a few days. Yours truly.

P. S. Pardon my spelling mistakes. I have not had the time to consult the dictionary you gave me and which I never part with.

IU. SAMARIN TO BARONESS RAHDEN

Vassil'evski, July 26, (1873).

Let me first of all address two requests to you, but only on one condition: if they embarrass you in the slightest, or if you feel the shadow of a scruple, please do not bother yourself at all about them and consider them as not having been made.

You have probably heard of a certain Mr. Richter (possibly you know him personally): Ph.D., a Russian imperial Councillor of State and knight of several orders, author of a history of the Baltic Provinces which are incorporated into the Empire[181] etc. etc. and of a brochure entitled: *Ocherk istorii khrestianskago sosloviia v prisoedinennykh k Rossii pribaltiiskikh guberniakh,*[182] 1858. I should like to write him on my own to ask for some historical information. Could you let me know his address, his Christian name and patronymic?

Then my second request. I am currently working on a history of the emancipation of the peasants of Livonia from 1796 until 1819. Among the unedited material which I have been gathering for a long time, there are some memoirs on the agrarian question and a series of letters written to Count Kochubei (later Prince), minister of the interior, from two Sivers counts belonging to two radically opposed parties. One of them, opposed to emancipation, very hostile to the college

[181] From the colon the text is in German. (Trans.)

[182] Outline of the History of the Peasant Class in the Baltic Provinces of Russia. (Trans.)

of provincial counsellors (*Landraths Collegium*) and a strong partisan of the administrative institutions of Empress Catherine, was, I believe, in 1803, a *Landrichter* and signed himself simply: Count Sivers *at Bauenhof*; the other was a *Landrath*, and signed himself Frederick *at Ranzen*. During the same period, around 1804-1807, there was in Livonia a third Count Sivers who ended his days in retirement, Empress Catherine's confidential agent whose memoirs were published several years ago. Of these three Sivers the one which interests me most is the second one, who became very well known for an eloquent discourse he gave at the *Landtag* of 1803, at the time of his break with the nobiliary body. Samson, who does not resemble him in any way and did not like him at all, calls him a man of the old school.[183] He was at the beginning of the century the great advocate of emancipation, although he remained an aristocrat through and through, and uncompromising where the privileges of the provincial college of which he was a member were concerned. His memoirs, his letters and speeches have stirred the greatest admiration in me for his intelligence and particularly for his character; I should like very much to make this fine great figure stand out as much as possible by grouping around it the most dry and arid material I have on the basis of the question. Unfortunately, I lack information. I should like to know, first of all, the degree of kinship connecting these three Sivers and the year of death of the *Landrath*, in order to understand the reason for his complete abstention from any participation in the legislative work of 1819—which with a single stroke of a pen cancelled the work of his entire lifetime.—Even though you say virtually nothing about it, I am sure that you must be overburdened with work and that your time is all taken up; so my idea is not to ask you to do research on my behalf. All I should like is this: if you happen to know anything about my three Sivers, whom I cannot get out of my head, please tell me; otherwise could you please

[183]The phrase is in German. (Trans.)

give me the address (with the Christian name and patronymic) of Count Sivers, director of a department in the ministry of the interior, whom I met at your place and to whom I intend to address myself for fuller information. I beg your pardon for having kept you so long on a subject which has nothing to do with your present cares. I feel myself quite egotistical with you and that is to some extent your own fault.

The newspapers yesterday brought me news of Tiutchev's[184] death. With him is extinguished the last ray of the *pléiade* of which Pushkin was the centre. It really was from him that he derived as an artist, while he was connected to Goethe because of his nature, which was open to every influence, being inspired by everything, though without the other's olympian arrogance, and possessing above all an inexhaustible store of cheerfulness. What is figuratively said of poets, comparing them to the stretched chords of an instrument which is always ready to resound at the slightest breath, could be applied to him without the slightest exaggeration. I have always been struck by his exceptional facility. The charms and the pains of poetic childbirth were to him equally unknown. His verses fell from his lips almost unconsciously, like fruit which ripens on its own and at the proper moment separates itself from the branch which bore it. A strange thing: his mother tongue was not familiar to him, he spoke it only with difficulty and this ignorance itself, together with a sound knowledge of French and German, led him to discover resources and precision of expression in Russian which no one before him possessed.

I am profiting from the holidays of my nephew (a pupil in one of the Moscow secondary schools, a very studious boy, possibly even too fond of his books and tending a little towards the German "scholar"[185]) by giving him a taste for the ideal. With this in mind, I set about rereading Schiller

[184] F. I. Tiutchev (1803-73). (Ed.)

[185] The word is in German. (Trans.)

and, once I found myself dabbling in it, I again dove in of my own will. I reread everything I could find on hand—poetry, memoirs, letters, etc. What a rich flowering, and what a wonderful wholeness in that great artistic, philosophic and social movement which makes the final years of the last century and the first years of the present one an age apart! You can feel Kant in Schiller and you meet Schiller in Herder. When you consider the men of that period and when you realize their strength and their work, it is impossible not to feel a little of that slightly incredulous wonderment you experience in reading the biblical tales of those patriarchs who crossed deserts on foot, who lived for two hundred years and who engendered children at one hundred and fifty. Are they really our ancestors,. and if so what happens to the theory of perpetual, immutable and necessary progress? What is going to become of the doctrine that world history is progress motivated by a sense of freedom, that every moment in history is the essence of all those which have gone before; and what about all the beautiful ideas that we have impressed upon ourselves since youth? *Sceptre and Crown* and the *Philosophy of the Unconscious* by Hartmann—there you have the quintessence of the Germany of today. It seems to me that something better could have come of that whole set of moments of the past.[186]

You must tell me whether you have received from Berlin the fourth fascicle of the *Okrainy, Protsess Rossii s Evangelicheskim soiuzom.*[187] Bock's successor wrote me almost two months ago that it was about to come out, I sent him the list of people in Petersburg to whom he was to send copies of it and since that time I have heard nothing about it. Yours truly.

[186]The last three sentences are in German. (Trans.)

[187]*Borderlands, Russia's Case against the Evangelical Union.* (Ed.)

BARONESS RAHDEN TO IU. SAMARIN

August 4, (1873).

I found your kind letter of July 19 when I arrived in Petersburg at the beginning of this week, and yesterday your second letter of the 26th also came. Above all, *thanks*; my heart is now at ease.

As I am always feverishly impatient whenever I need any sort of information, I wrote this morning to Livonia to get biographical and genealogical details about the Sivers you are interested in. Meanwhile, let me tell you what I knew vaguely and what I have just found confirmed in the work of Mr. Charles Blum: *Ein russischer Staatsmann, Denkwürdigkeiten des Grafen J. Sievers, etc.*[188] Kochubei's correspondent, the adversary of emancipation, is none other than the glorious governor of Novgorod, the devoted servant of Empress Catherine; it is he alone who was Count, it is to him that the estate of Bauenhof in Livonia belonged, it is again he who quarrelled with his old friend, the *Landrath* Frederick Sievers of Ranzen, a distant relative of his, I believe, over the peasant question. As far as the *Landrath* is concerned, I hope in a week or so to be able to furnish you with all that is known in the family about his life, his activity and his death. If you do not own Blum's work on Count Sievers, I could send it to you—at least the last volume of it, where I found all this. The present State Counsellor Richter died some years ago; he was married to the sister of Baron Budberg of Paris. After having served at length in the chancellory of Count Nesselrode, he retired to Riga where he held a rather inconspicuous post and where he died. Good evening—for now. With kind affection.

P. S. The Sievers of Wenden—that is, the director of the department of religious affairs, and his brother, the former governor of Moscow—belong to a completely different

[188] *A Russian Statesman, Memoirs of Count J. Sievers, etc.* (Trans.)

branch. In general the Sievers, whoever they may be, are not old. We Courlanders consider them of low nobility, of known origin.

I did not receive your number 4. Grot, who came back from Berlin ten days ago, did not find it there at Bock's. Why should I have any scruples about getting you all the information you want? It is all quite fair—even though I may have to answer for the deductions you draw from them. Farewell.

IU. SAMARIN TO BARONESS RAHDEN

Vassil'evski, August 24, (1873).

Soon after writing you last, I hurried to Serpukhov when I received a letter from my sister which much disturbed me about my mother's health. Reassured at least for now and back in the country, I found your two letters of the 4th and the 12th. A great many thanks for the trouble you took! How apparent it is that in temperament you are not one of us. If I had approached a Russian I should have waited at least six months, and even so God knows if I would have received any information that was at all precise. That for which I am indebted to you comes just in time to save me from a whole series of mistakes I was about to commit. On rereading my material, I noted at first that I had been wrong in giving to the *Landrath*, my hero, the title of count; he himself never took it. He signed himself simply Friedrich of Sievers or *Landrath* S. It was a couple of Russian letters and a couple of minutes of meetings of the Petersburg Committee which led me astray. It happened then that, for want of information, I took two other Sievers (the *Landrichter* and Count James) for one and the same person. Finally, I admit to my shame not even to have known of the existence of the fourth volume of the *Denkwürdigkeiten* of C. Blum. I have only the first three, which I have read and reread several times; always regretting that the editor had not touched upon the period in which I am interested. To send for and receive the fourth volume here would take at least two months (supposing that it is not on the banned list), so I shall accept with gratitude your proposition if you can let me have it until February; then I shall put it back into your hands personally.

I was in Moscow at the time the Emperor went through. The municipality is dismayed at the more than cold welcome given to its representatives. You probably know that at the grand reception in the Kremlin, His Majesty completely ignored the mayor and the deputies of the city and did not touch the bread and salt which were offered to him. People are examining themselves for faults to try to explain this glaring proof of disgrace and, not finding any, they seem ready to accept the governor's version who claims that the municipality should first of all have addressed itself to him to solicit permission to bid His Majesty welcome. It must be a new formality that no one to this day has heard of.

Let me thank you once again and clasp your hand with all my heart. Yours truly.

BARONESS RAHDEN TO IU. SAMARIN

September 14, 1873.

My thoughts have not left you since I found out you were sick,[189] and it is with ineffable impatience that I await news from you. It seems to me that by writing you I can reassure myself about your state; when you get these lines, you will be convalescent. Thanks be to God! Last week I sent

[189]During the trip which Iu. Samarin took from his property in Samara to Serpukhov, he hurt his leg. The wound brought on a long and painful illness which necessitated the invalid being carried to Moscow. (D. S.)

you the book you needed without enclosing any note because I was overloaded with tiring physical labour, and I wanted to have a couple of really free hours before me so as to speak at length with you about everything. And then Prince Dmitri Obolenski brings me the sad story of your accident and of your serious illness! You must already have been in pain on the 24th of August—why didn't you tell me about it? It isn't proper to quarrel with a sick person, but you deserve to be soundly scolded. What imprudence, what misplaced stoicism—and all that happening at the other end of the world, in a wilderness, where it is even impossible to get regular news from! You see, again it is "a matter of temperament" as you say; I need efficiency and accuracy in bulletins, my German affection is exasperated by these endless delays and, to take it out on someone, deluges Prince Obolenski with impatient questions and missives. You will at least come back to Moscow right away as soon as you can travel, won't you? Apart from your groundless fantasies, I have known you to be sick only once,[190] when you upset me a great deal; at that time your friends' anxieties surrounded you with a sort of exaggerated mystical halo, which I rather made fun of to myself. Today it is quite different; you are very naturally and gravely sick, I am very anxious about you and I pray God with all of the selfishness of a fond friend to restore you to health! Yours from my heart.

BARONESS RAHDEN TO IU. SAMARIN

September 27, (1873).

There you are in Moscow, my dear friend—and I breathe more easily now that I know you to be installed in a safe

[190]At the time when Iu. Samarin was a member of the "Editorial Commissions" charged with working out a bill on the emancipation of the peasants in 1859 and 1860. (D. S.)

place with the Faculty at hand. God be thanked, Prince Obolenski finally gave me good news, he even authorized me to write to you. I am going to do it often now—my letters will come to you like autumn rain, and you will have to resign yourself to it. It is to you that my thoughts turn when the work and the cares of the day come to an end; you keep me company in the evening without even realizing it. And how we speak about you, when "the friends" come to my place! So what do you do to make yourself so well liked! You treat everyone gently—affability is not *your* invention, but *you are yourself*, and that includes so many things that the affection which is borne you is both single and multiple. . . . That's what it means to be sick and to cause pain and infinite anxiety, it predisposes others to be so frank as to appall your modesty. And so I shall say goodbye to you for now, this morning. Yours truly.

IU. SAMARIN TO BARONESS RAHDEN

October 11, 1873.

I was extremely glad to read in the papers of October 4 Prince Urussov's report on the institutions of the late Grand Duchess. Knowing in only a very vague way of what you wanted and what you were hoping for in order to assure their future, I do not know whether you are satisfied, but it seems to me that the economic basis is quite broad and firm.[191] There is some talk of a public fund drive to raise the necessary sums; if you have recourse to it, make it last as long as possible and do not despair overly about the dearth of the offerings coming to you this year and next. The famine at Samara and Orenburg will make a terrible competition for you. The news coming out of these regions would make your hair stand on end. When I left the country last month, in the

[191]The last part of the sentence is in German. (Trans.)

district of Buzuluk people were fighting over acorns, which from the end of August were coming into the village markets from all over. What will it be like in winter? On top of that the present governor, an administrator of the new school, is showing his zeal. The recovery of tax arrears is being managed with a ruthlessness[192] which verges on madness. The peasant's last head of cattle is being sold by auction. The whole region will be completely ruined for a long time to come.[193] Things have come to the point where the president of the *Kazennaia Palata*,[194] the man especially charged with looking after revenue interests, has himself been obliged to protest.

Your last letter touched me deeply. You are absolutely right: I am fortunate in the friends I have—and I always have been, I should add deep down within me—very much more than I merit. Evidence of their concern which is clear everywhere I turn works a languorous charm on me, and I am completely disposed to let myself go to it. Help me resist the danger by sending me one of those fine dressing-downs you do so well. Please give me a good scolding.[195]

I finished the fourth volume of Sievers, but I do not have the nerve to send it back to you in the sad state to which it has been reduced. During my entire trip it did not leave my side. Let me replace it with a new copy I have sent for.

Do you have any reactions to the new publication of Strauss: *Der alte und der neue Glaube* (that is, really, *Unglaube*)?[196] Much could be said about this book, but it is time for my bandages to be changed and I hear the Faculty coming!

I clasp and kiss your two good hands. Yours truly.

[192]The three words are in German. (Trans.)

[193]The sentence is in German. (Trans.)

[194]Government revenue office. (Trans.)

[195]The sentence is in German. (Trans.)

[196]This last phrase in parentheses is in German: The old and the new faith (that is, really, lack of faith). (Trans.)

IU. SAMARIN TO BARONESS RAHDEN

Moscow, October 26, 1873.

Without your having told me I can see from here that your work is not leaving you a moment of leisure, and if in spite of that I decide to importune you with a new request, it is only because at the present state of relations between us I can certainly hope that you will not be embarrassed about turning me down. Again it is a matter of genealogical information.

1) In a letter of the *Landrath* Sievers to Prince Kochubei, dated April 6, 1803, he said to him, among other things: "There are high expectations (in Livonia) of the private counsellor of Vietinghof, the great patron of the opposition party (which is opposed to any reform in the agrarian question) and who, *by his mother-in-law*, believes himself in a position to make everything stay just as it is." I should like to know who this mother-in-law was. Would it not be Princess Lieven, the ex-governess of the Grand Dukes? The Vietinghof in question signed himself Boris. His party had delegated him to Petersburg to observe Sievers, to hurt him and to paralyze his influence.

2) At the same period a certain Richter was governor in Livonia. Would it be possible to find out to which of the branches of this large family he belongs?

If, when you have time, you were willing to get me the information I am looking for, you would be doing me a great favour. I really do not know to whom I could turn so as not to bother you.

My recovery is coming along slowly. The doctors still insist that I remain in bed, with my leg still, so as not to disturb the joining of the muscles which have been cut in two. I am using my leisure to put all sorts of notes and material in order, to study the chess games of the tournament in Vienna and to read the latest news from Germany. Have you read the latest publication of Strauss: *Der alte und neue*

Glaube as well as its epilogue?[197] It is curious as the last word on modern atheism and a great many good things could be said about this book, if only to underline the whole new set of superstitions which the negation of the divine principle necessarily gives rise to. It is a series of miracles wrought by matter.

Yesterday the election of a second candidate for the post of mayor has put an end to the election fever which for two weeks was disturbing our normal peace. The local authorities blame the municipal body a good deal, as if it were a crime of *lèse-nationalité*, for having elected a German (Schumacher). What do you think?

If you notice any improvement in my handwriting, give me a word of encouragement. Yours truly.

BARONESS RAHDEN TO IU. SAMARIN

November 8, (1873).

I have not yet received the requested information about the Richter family and I am getting impatient at waiting. So I want to make use of what I know about the marriage of the only daughter of the old Princess Lieven to write you at least a couple of words and to tell you that this time your inspiration has not misled you. The private counsellor Vietinghof, a Courlander, had the good fortune of making what was then called a good match and of marrying, along with a good, mindless woman, the magnificent protection of a stepmother who was all-powerful in the realm of awards and court honours. As far as her anti-liberal influence is concerned, I cannot yet tell you anything positive. The Richters are of the second class nobility; they have always served a great deal and have never been rich.—To be continued in the next episode.

[197] The word is in German. (Trans.)

Your letter, which was very well written with a calligraphic care which promises to give me a rival in this branch of the art, baffled me a little with the question with which it ends. You ask me if I have read Strauss' book: *Der alte und der neue Glaube.* I had already replied to the same question in a long letter in German in the middle of October. Is it possible you did not get it?

The autobiography of Stuart Mill is one of the most curious works you could imagine—you really should read it. Get a translation of the résumé, which is very well done, in the *Times* and in the *Saturday Review.* Kitty Tiutchev knows English so well that she could read you a sight translation. I think about you at every page of this extraordinary book.

Tell me that you are getting better; I am so sad and so weary without any particularly aggravating reason that I need some good news. Yours truly.

IU. SAMARIN TO BARONESS RAHDEN

Moscow, November 12, (1873).

Your letter of November 8 surprised me very much. Your second last letter was of September 27, and since then I have received nothing, and no letter in German of the middle of October has reached me. What could have happened to it? Did you send it by mail or did you make use of someone? I am not willing to give it up for lost, and I should like to have some details to be in a better position to carry out a search for it.

Since I wrote you, they have done an eighth incision on me deeper than the others. Everything points to this being the last; nothing, I hope, will impede my recovery this time, and by about the middle of December I hope to be on my feet. I am going to try to get those copies of the *Times* and the *Saturday Review.* With a dictionary in front of me possibly I can manage to decipher them. Yours truly.

BARONESS RAHDEN TO IU. SAMARIN

November 16, 1873.

If you are surprised, I am too—I wrote to you between the 14th and the 20th of October, but I cannot remember exactly what day; it was a long reply to several passages in one of your letters, so long that I put two stamps on it and so personal that I wrote it in German: my heart can express itself better in the language in which I pray. It seemed to me there was no risk in sending this voluminous epistle through the mail: firstly because *you are you* and *I am me*, secondly because if the worst came to the worst, a few pages of affectionate ideology would surely reach their destination. I see that I was wrong. Perhaps, too, some weary postilion threw my letter into a ditch somewhere. Pastor Dalton told me that, crossing Isaac Square on foot one day, he had picked up the handwritten debris of one of his theological articles sent by mail to his editor in Berlin, which had been lost without any trace and which he had had to re-write a second time, because in the necessary rush of his work he had not made a copy. Let us suppose the second case—it is impossible for me to write my letter all over again to you. Let us forget about it, just like any other perfectly useless piece of research if you think enough about it. Here I have gained information which has served only to strengthen me in the exercise of postal resignation.

The Richter family makes me unutterably impatient—no one knows anything *exactly* about its relationships and its genealogy; I am going to write to Berkholz so that he can enter the campaign. All my kindest regards. God be thanked that you are out of danger.

BARONESS RAHDEN TO IU. SAMARIN[198]

St. Petersburg, October 15, (1873).

You are absolutely right—you really have to hear the truth again some time! You are barely convalescing, are still a long way from being completely recovered, and already the old character is coming back and is conducting himself like a restored king, like a Bourbon, who cannot forget anything and will not learn anything. Your last letter which brought me so much joy, still moves me to reprimand you as really I should. Why did you write it at all? I had asked you to please remain in my debt, not to answer for as long as it might be a strain on you, for as long as you are not well. God forbid! With that German temperament, of which you actually have much more than I do, you want above all to straighten out accounts, and with a trembling hand you are doing the opposite of what I had asked! Please do forget completely the punctuality that friends observe, and allow those who have often been your debtors the luxury of giving freely, without your giving them a receipt out of a sense of duty and gratitude!

And now we come to the second point, which to my great horror I have found in your letter. You feel keenly the joy of being surrounded by expressions and tokens of love at a time of testing; you become gentle and are happy; all harshness, all severity disappears; a humble feeling of thankfulness pervades your being and it is strongly moved by feelings of love towards humanity . . . . This you point out to me—but right away you add that you are afraid of this, that you would like to reach as soon as possible the safety of a barren shore, where there is at least solid ground and a cool sense of balance! Please don't worry! You really aren't going to drown that soon! Just let yourself go—it is good to swim at high tide, try it today, if you have never done it

[198]The entire letter is in German. (Trans.)

before. . . . You provide a fine definition of the theological concept of love, in genuine technical terms and sublime eloquence; but when this concept becomes alive for you and begins to move gently and to breathe, when it alleviates your pain, makes a fire in the fireplace, watches through the night, and sings you to sleep with soft melodies, then you feel afraid and plead modesty in order to escape the feeling produced by this light and this warmth! You probably are secretly worried about the safety of your sharp logic—it could become dulled in this dubious atmosphere, and in the end you would be obliged to throw away the sharp *weapon* in order to use *power*! . . .

Now that is enough, otherwise I would condescend to speak about *my* old and new faith, and that would be superfluous; I am not familiar with Strauss's faith—and besides I do not have the time right now to read books which demand a state of battle readiness. For this reason I shall leave your *Okrainy* with the censor for a while—this is also a bit of cowardice on my part. The serious situation you are in has awakened so deeply in me the awareness of what you mean to me in so many ways, that I do not have the courage to let you hurt me, and that is what is going to happen! It will be just a few weeks till you are your old self again and by that time I am going to be over my weak nerves and I will devote myself to reading your work.

All my wishes with regard to the institutions of the Grand Duchess are fulfilled; September 29 was for me an indescribably sad day and at the same time a beautiful day. Now there still remains the worry about the clinical institute and the Administration.[198a] If you will allow me, I shall write to you shortly in detail about this latter point, I would appreciate very much having your opinion with regard to this important question. Just imagine, a few hours ago I received a letter from Stuttgart with new propositions: whether I could make a decision *after* taking care of all matters concerning the organization of the institutions? This persistence fills me with some anxiety; I am going to destroy it with silence, I am not going to agree to any possibilities, and therefore I ask you not to speak about it.

Prince Cherkaski must have told you about everything that people talk about, hope for and do in our capital and residence. I was very happy to note in him the same interest in the great church-state battle in Germany that I have. I can hear the swords clashing, so to speak. War was declared in the Middle Ages and it is only now, 600 years later, that the dice of fate are falling for the same stake. I have in my possession a copy of a very strange letter by the great Hohenstaufen, Frederic II, in which the description of the state of affairs is such that one could ascribe it to Bismarck.

What you tell me about the famine is terrible. Just imagine, there is a prevalent opinion here that all the reports from Samara are exaggerated and have their source either in the imagination of Tolstoy[199] or in the letters of the numerous tenants, who do not want to pay their rent. There is also some newspaper in which a landowner has given similar explanations. What is going to happen to alleviate this misery? To collect money at the last minute actually does not lead to anything. Are there no relief committees being formed in the neighbouring governments? Is there nothing one can initiate here and in Moscow? At first I did not want you to write and now I am asking you innumerable questions!

Farewell. I could go on talking like this indefinitely. May God keep you! Take care of yourself, see that you are well looked after and spoiled—but, above all, see that you get well again! Devotedly yours.

[199]Leo Tolstoy visited Samara Province in the summer of 1873 where he discovered a serious famine. After making an investigation he wrote a letter to the editor of *Moskovskie vedomosti* describing the terrible plight of the peasants and appealing for assistance. See L. N. Tolstoy, *Sobranie sochinenii, Pis'ma 1845-1886*, XVII (Moscow, 1965), 377-85. (Ed.)

IU. SAMARIN TO BARONESS RAHDEN

Moscow, November 17, (1873).

At last I have your long German letter in my possession and I think that from having read it over and over I know it by heart. The charm which I feel, reading you in German or in French, makes me reflect seriously about myself and about my compatriots in general. You have at your call all the resources of the two languages which you make use of and which become moulded without the slightest effort on your part to the most imperceptible movement of your thought. How far we all are, all of us including the most literate, from possessing our maternal language to the same degree. If I had to translate you I feel that, for lack of shades and half-tones, I would be forced to give up any hope of rendering many things which I can feel and admire in the original. There is much more I could add, but I can see you from here shrugging your shoulders, and so I shall stop. Here is the extremely simple explanation of the delay to which your letter was subjected. I inhabit a wing of my brother's house; in a couple of days he is to be back from Rome. He left orders with his steward to place any mail addressed to him in his cabinet. Our Swiss imagined, I am not sure why, that your letter was addressed to him, and it was only yesterday that the steward, in going through the mail, realized his mistake. Anyway, I am not complaining, because your letter could not have come at a better time. It was passed to me after a painful day, a sleepless night and a ninth incision necessitated by the return of the inflammation. It shows up in my writing, doesn't it? Yours truly.

P. S. Thank you for the book which you sent to me by the good office of Prince Shcherbatov, and which I am going to have picked up. Every day, since his return, he has been coming to see me and every time forgets to bring it.

BARONESS RAHDEN TO IU. SAMARIN

January 2, (1874).,

I have been wanting to write you for such a long time now. Up until now I have been held back by a tinge of embarrassment: I am still waiting for the information on the Richter family that Berkholz has not come through with, and I am depriving myself of the pleasure of telling you how grateful I am for your recovery, so as not to admit my involuntary unreliability! Really, it is all your own fault. You have on your conscience a certain compliment you paid to my alacrity; I did not want to fall beneath my first high accomplishments, and here I am remiss in a duty by which I set such great store! Oh the misery of being human! I miss seeing you again. Is Petersburg excluded from your future plans? When will you be able to walk and go outside at last? Now that I know that you are out of danger, I often have such a great desire to chat with you and to afford myself the royal luxury of honest conversation! And the New Year—I forgot, even though that is what forced my hand. May God bless you and keep you for your friends.

IU. SAMARIN TO BARONESS RAHDEN

Moscow, January 13, 1874.

I have not written you this last while in the hope of being able to see you and clasp your hand by about the middle of January, but all sorts of circumstances are forcing me to put off my leaving for Petersburg until February. Your last letter hurt my conscience. How could you possibly be upset at not having furnished me the information I asked you for, and which you yourself have not yet received! To set your mind at rest, let me assure you that there is no rush and even if the information I am waiting for should not arrive for another month or two it will still be in time.

My foot is performing all of the services which I ask of it in town quite well, which leads me to hope that later it will be the same in the country and while hunting. Goodbye for now. Yours truly.

BARONESS RAHDEN TO IU. SAMARIN

January 27, (1874).

Here at last is the very incomplete genealogical report which was sent to me from Riga. When you come to Petersburg I shall show you Berkholz's letter which explains his long delay.

I hope that you have had a good deal of contact with the Stanleys[200] and especially that, satiated with parties and magnificence, you will get here soon. Kindest regards.

IU. SAMARIN TO BARONESS RAHDEN

Friday, February 8, (1874).

I did not answer your last letter because I was expecting to leave within two days and to be able to thank you in person for the information you have gathered for me. Let me at least do it in writing. All sorts of odds and ends have held me back until now and I shall hardly manage to get away

[200] A. P. Stanley (1815-81) and his wife visited Russia in 1874 to participate in the marriage of the Duke of Edinburgh and the Grand Duchess Marie. He was an outstanding British divine and Dean of Westminster. He was an exponent of religious toleration and his first visit to Russia took place in 1857 when he collected material for a series of *Lectures on the Eastern Church* (London, 1861). (Ed.)

from them until the end of the first week in Lent. In any case they say that before the Emperor of Austria leaves, a new arrival would run the risk of knocking on all the hotel doors without finding anywhere to lay his head. I am very much tempted to impose on your good will once again in order to obtain some more information, but I shall certainly not do so until I have seen you and explained why I am always reduced to having to approach you. Prince Shcherbatov spoke to me about you. Yours truly.

IU. SAMARIN TO BARONESS RAHDEN

Hotel Demuth, Sunday, (February 17, 1874).

Here I am at your door at last! In order to lose the least amount of time possible, and especially so as not to disturb you in your various occupations, could you indicate to me the day and the hour which would be the most convenient for you? Today I shall pass a part of the afternoon with the Miliutins, and the 19th, after the founding dinner, with my old colleagues. Yours truly.

BARONESS RAHDEN TO IU. SAMARIN

April 14, 1874.

I sent your last question[201] to my poor correspondents in Riga with the formal admonition: "Have the courage to say no, if you are bent on leading the author of the *Okrainy* into little errors in fact and in names—oh, chivalrous revenge! But above all answer me, and do not make us wait futilely for what we could seek and find elsewhere!" Will that help?[202] I

[201] The phrase is in German. (Trans.)

[202] The phrase is in German. (Trans.)

am irritated by this long provincial silence and beg your pardon over and over on behalf of my compatriots. You will easily recognize by my impatience that I am far from having acquired the Slavic virtues. Your new illness in Moscow has again contributed to giving me a foul mood: for several days I have had fits of anger for which the responsibility falls on you; it was only a brief word from Princess L'vov which set me back into my poise of usual gentleness (?). If only that lasts!

You will find me in Petersburg until the first of June; your last stay here left me with the most pleasant memories, I like to think back over it; you can imagine the very great pleasure I shall have in renewing this good experience. Kindest regards.

BARONESS RAHDEN TO IU. SAMARIN

July 6, (1874).

Here is what I just received for you; I am taking the chance of sending it to Samara where I am guessing you are. As for me, after a short absence of fifteen days in Estonia, at the Keyserlings', I have again taken up my regular occupations, which are complicated by the arranging for a third popular kitchen at Vassili-Ostrov. The town is very dusty and very devoid of charms right now, yet I am better off there than at Oranienbaum or at Kammenyi Ostrov because there I am alone like a veritable anchorite in utter solitude.

Tell me what you are doing, I beg you: I have heard nothing about you nor about Dmitriev whom I was impatiently expecting in June. With kindest regards.

I am sending to you the explanatory letter of Berkholz. When you have the chance, give it back to me.

BARONESS RAHDEN TO IU. SAMARIN

August 12, (1874).

Here is the information you wanted; it seems to me that it is quite complete. Please do not trouble yourself about asking me for whatever you wish to know; even if it were not to help you out, which is always a great pleasure, I have such a burning respect for historic truth and any other kind that to clarify a fact, to restore a faulty date, to verify a recollection seems to me a real joy. In the Provinces, the few literate friends I still have share, I hope, my ideas in this matter.

In my own mind I have already replied to your interesting letter,[203] but I shall do it eventually as soon as my kitchens have become re-set in their winter routine and as soon as the imperial family turns its back on Petersburg; two rather dissimilar conditions, aren't they? But you have no idea how trips to Tsarkoe, Oranienbaum, Sergeevka absorb precious hours.

Farewell, I wish you the best thing there is in the world—peace.

IU. SAMARIN TO BARONESS RAHDEN

Moscow, December 31, 1874.

Before the year is out, let me clasp your hand once again and commend myself to your affection for the coming year, and for all of those which it may please God to grant me, or to impose upon me, "as long as sins will wait,"[204] as is said among us.

[203]This letter is not found among the correspondence which has been given to us. (D. S.)

[204]The saying is in Russian. (Trans.)

An article in a recent paper mentioned the financial result of your community dinners, and I am extremely glad about it. I am fully enough aware of the costs, the social milieu in which you are working and the variety of difficulties which array themselves against every good intention, to understand how much patience, goodwill, perseverance and resignation has been needed to manage not only to recover the expenses, but even to obtain a slight profit. Each one of these modest 400 rubles represents a portion of your life.

In a week or two Dm. Obolenski will pass to you a memoir,[205] which is much too long and very colourless, which I forced myself to write following a direct challenge from General Fadeev,[206] the adversary of Miliutin.[207] Yours truly.

BARONESS RAHDEN TO IU. SAMARIN

January 14, 1875.

How kind you are to tell me that you think of me with affection! I am deeply dependent upon it with a firm assurance, but every sign of this certitude still touches me and surprises me like something new, like an unexpected blessing. That is how, I think, one could distinguish true feelings: that they are incapable of wearying and that, eternally present, they are always new.

You say that my 400 rubles profit represents a portion

[205]This memoir was published in Berlin, in 1875, under the title *Revolutsionnyi Konservatism.* (D. S.)

[206]R. A. Fadeev (1824-83) was a well known military historian and publicist. See p. 21. (Ed.)

[207]D. A. Miliutin was a brother of N. A. Miliutin and an outstanding military leader and administrator. He introduced and superintended the liberal military reforms of the sixties. (Ed.)

of my life; in other days, when hours had value in my eyes, I should have thought so. Nowadays, the use of our strength for secondary works seems to me to constitute the crude web of our existence; the hand of the Master superimposes on this necessary base the colours, the harmonious design which gives the real value to the fabric. It is in the hours, possibly minutes, in which eternal feelings open up for us the horizons of the love of God. Irrespective of whatever type of work there may be, that is real life—does the rest deserve such a name?

I am going to start waiting for you, because I can selfishly remember your intentions last autumn. May God keep you! I am yours sincerely.

IU. SAMARIN TO BARONESS RAHDEN

March 22, 1875.

Today's newspapers announced the nomination of Grote as president of the Council, charged with the administration of the institutions of the late Grand Duchess. I think that you must be content and I am happy for you at this. An administrative council, among us at least, can have as its mission only to refrain from interfering with the individual action of the person who is willing to take on the real work. It can be hoped of Grote that he will do more, sparing you all the formal side of the job, accounts and so forth.

Could you possibly give me the address of Berkholz in Riga? I renewed my acquaintance with him during my last trip abroad, and he authorized me to write directly to him to get any information I may need. I want to try, by his agency, to obtain some data from Mr. Jung-Stilling, the author of a book on the agrarian question which you gave me some time ago. Yours truly.

BARONESS RAHDEN TO IU. SAMARIN

March 26, (1875).

I thank you for having shared in my satisfaction; yes, I am very happy at the choice of Grote, very happy at the way in which the Emperor commended the institutions to him: "What I ask of you is to put your heart into your work; when one knows how much the Grand Duchess Helen loved and cared for her work, one must see that it is only with the heart that one can completely fulfill her intentions." Isn't that fine and good?

Lent is passing on and you are not coming back; must I say farewell to you for good? Every time you have been here, I experience a keener desire to see you come back again—it is so long until the next winter! With kind and faithful regards.

IU. SAMARIN TO BARONESS RAHDEN

Moscow, May 26, 1875.

When you have a moment free, will you cast your eyes over the enclosed booklet.[208] I doubt whether there exists in any other language a translation which is as close to perfection; in any case you are in a much better position than I to thoroughly assess it. The author is the son of Madame Pavlov (née Janisch) who is very well known for her translations into three languages; it seems that it is an hereditary talent.

What are your plans for the summer? Will I find you in Petersburg until around the 10th or 15th of next month? I should like a word in reply so as to make up my mind on the choice of route to take to get to Berlin.

Yesterday Princess C. Cherkasski arrived in Moscow and is leaving again tomorrow for the country. She has managed to slim down which I had thought impossible, but seems to

[208] Probably the translation of *Faust.* (D. S.)

be in good humour. In short, I find her much better than I had expected according to the gossip and according to her writing. Yours truly.

P. S. I recently wrote a long letter to Mr. Berkholz in Riga, asking him to introduce me[209] to Mr. Jung-Stilling (the author of a book you gave me) with whom I should like to enter into direct epistolary contact.

BARONESS RAHDEN TO IU. SAMARIN

May 30, (1875).

Thanks—the translation seems perfect to me and the news of your coming arrival gives me infinite pleasure. I am counting on leaving the 15th or the 16th, depending upon when I am free.

Until we meet! From the 10th on I shall look for you every day. With kindest regards.

BARONESS RAHDEN TO IU. SAMARIN

August 28, (1875).

I found your parcel a couple of days ago as I came back from Tsarskoe, where I had been for quite a long visit, and from that first evening on, I plunged with delight into a reading of Vinet. A case of influenza helped, for I had to stay in my room more than I allow myself to in normal weather; everything lent itself to fulfilling the passion which occasionally drives me to read certain works which seize hold of me rather than make me study them. Right from the very beginning, the inside of the Vinet family charmed me, I found so many familiar moods there! Duty placed so highly;

[209]The three words are in English. (Trans.)

pleasure complacently ignored, like a vain and fleeting thing; those apparently severe relationships, so full of deep tenderness, whose sudden strong expression is as wonderful as a revelation. Then the study of and the enthusiasm for what is beautiful, the gradual development of intelligence in the midst of an exquisitely pure radiance, the incessant searching for God, as much in the intimate kinships of family and the friendships of youth as in the day-to-day labour of the man of letters. . . . All of this forms a whole which the most jaundiced reader could not help but be moved by! What about my heart then which rediscovers in this tableau the perfect ideal for the Protestant Church! It is getting there slowly—in spite of its errors, the gulf opened up beneath its feet by unbelief, the arid austereness of its service—only by virtue of its ardent love for *truth*, this way of naming God which is most dear to the German mind. To establish a *true* filiation between what one does, what one thinks and what one feels, and to feed one's sentiments at the living source of Eternal Truth, which is Eternal Love—what an ideal existence! It seems to me that Vinet was very close to this. You can see that you have made me very happy; I have scarcely finished half the volume and I cannot put off any longer my desire to thank you for it.

Where are you? When will you be coming back here? Up until now (except for my visit to a higher sphere) I have been living in a monastical solitude which I love. Farewell, thanks, I clasp your hand.

IU. SAMARIN TO BARONESS RAHDEN

Vassil'evski, October 12, (1875).

Without your suspecting it, I have spent the entire evening chatting mentally with you. For a very long time I had intended setting all my papers in order so as to spare those who will inherit my effects the trouble of sorting through them; this autumn, thanks to the bad weather, I have had the necessary leisure. Putting your letters into an envelope (after my death they will be given back to you by my sister) I reread them all from the first right to the last, and in this interrupted my work. Let me express to you the feeling of acute, profound gratitude I experienced, in refreshing my memory, for all the signs of affection you have shown me—and most particularly for the scoldings you have given me, the plain truths you have spoken to me, and which I believe I have been too long in appreciating.

In sending you Vinet's book I felt clearly that it was written for you. I certainly was strongly impressed with it, but I could not fully understand my impressions and, to tell the truth, I was hoping that you would come to my aid, straightening out and rendering clearly and precisely what was confused in my brain. It has already happened many times and this time again I got what I wanted without having asked you for it. How do you manage to hide . . . but I can see you from here shrugging your shoulders and I shall stop.

The sad news which has reached me in Moscow about our excellent friend C. Cherkasski doubtless reached you too; I do not yet know what has happened to her and I tremble at the idea of a nervous stroke. Aksakov wrote me that it is occasionally difficult to understand her when she speaks, her nerves are so very tense: "*Bez serdechnogo spazma nel'zia ee videt'*.[210] People are talking of her going abroad immediately and it appears that her sister, Countess Baranov, is to accompany her. Unfortunately I shall not see her before she leaves. From one day to the next there may be an interruption in communication between the right and left banks of the Volga, and for the moment it is impossible for me to come in from the country.

After a great many attempts I have succeeded in opening a course on religion, Sundays, for young lads of fifteen to eighteen years, who not only have finished their studies but

[210]"One cannot see her without feeling a pang." (Trans.)

have already had time enough to forget the little they had learned. Apart from that, I have my school where I give my class in religious history and catechism every day. That is running well and, let it be said just between us, I am having more success than I had hoped for. The prime requisite for elementary instruction is to manage to establish a sort of electric current between the pupils and the master: what is necessary on the part of the master is an immediate and exact perception of how each of his words affects and stimulates the young minds he has in front of him; and on the part of the pupils, a sustained attention which does not tire them. Could I finally at long last have found my vocation? Do not make too much fun of all this, or else I shall ask you for a reckoning of the number of little pastries you have sold over the last month. You should know that my teaching is not free either, as I charge a ruble per head. Experience has taught me that people take seriously only what is paid for with cash.

What are you doing, whom do you see, and what are you reading? I shall not be leaving the country until around the middle of November at the earliest; in December I shall be passing through Petersburg to get to Berlin. Goodbye, then, for about two months. Yours truly.

IU. SAMARIN TO BARONESS RAHDEN

Petersburg, Hôtel d'Europe, (30 December, 1875).

For a very short time and with great demands upon your time and patience.[211]

[211]The letter is in German. (Trans.)

BARONESS RAHDEN TO IU. SAMARIN

(December 30, 1875) 4 o'clock.

I have just come home and I am so happy! Are you going to be coming to see me this evening? I am counting on it and I am going to expect you from 9:30 on.[212]

IU. SAMARIN TO BARONESS RAHDEN

Berlin, Britisch-Hotel, March 4/February 21, 1876.

Gnädiges Fräulein! You will receive in a separate wrapper a page from the *Moscow Gazette*, No. 43, containing the end of a biographical report on the late Rukavichnikov (the founder and director of a reformatory). I was much impressed when I read this; unfortunately I did not keep the earlier issues, but you can easily find them. No one appreciated Rukavichnikov at first sight as much as Stanley; it is said (do I not have this from you?) that he probably thanked God for having shown him, in Russia, what a saint was. It seems to me that there is a sort of moral obligation to afford mutual support, especially in these times, for those insights of ours which revive our flagging faith in humanity, and I wonder if it would not be good to send Stanley, if not the complete biography of Rukavichnikov—he could make nothing out of the original, and translation of the whole would take too much work—at least an extract or even a few passages in good English? To undertake a task of this sort, and to carry it through, a task which is quite easy and for which two persons would be grateful to you, there is only *you*. Whether anything can be done there or not, what there is to be done first of all and how one should go about it, all of that you know better than I do and I willingly accept your opinion in

[212]The letter is in German. (Trans.)

advance, and unconditionally, as always. For my part it is not even a suggestion, but just a simple question.[213] I just had another idea: what if we spoke to the son of our late priest, E. I. Popov, in London?

What would I not give for a good, long evening in tête-a-tête with you across your tea table without even insisting upon the luxury of a slice of veal!

This last time I saw Berlin more closely than any year before, thanks to some new relationships in the circle of scholars and secondary employees; I followed the discussions in the chambers closely; I read a great deal and even (you are going to laugh) I was rash enough to accept the challenge of a young aspirant to a philosophy chair and to launch myself into a written discussion[214] in Moscow German about the origin of the concept God, the nature of miracles and the question: whether one can draw a firm, inviolable line between moral freedom on the one hand, and the necessity which is dictated by logic and nature on the other hand?[215] Although I caused a scandal, and properly, nevertheless I was not ejected (and that in itself is something for the bearer of culture[216]), but I am being threatened with a meeting with one of the great scientific and political authorities of the day, a very well known doctor whose name escapes me for the moment. Nothing better proves the impoverishment of moral life and the shrinking of intellectual interests, this crippling of the spiritual organ,[217] than the present power of slogans,[218] which no one fully understands, and the ease

[213]The preceding two sentences are in German. (Trans.)

[214]These articles appeared in the sixth volume of the complete collection of the *Works of Iu. Samarin*, pp. 478-523. (D. S.)

[215]From "in Moscow German . . ." the sentence is in German. (Trans.)

[216]The phrase is in German. (Trans.)

[217]The phrase is in German. (Trans.)

[218]The word is in German. (Trans.)

with which *all* of Germany lines up under the banners of the two presently opposing parties. Beyond them there is absolutely nothing and they are found everywhere, not only in the political journals and the deputies' speeches, but just as much in sermons, in the new biblical commentaries, medical reviews, public courses in astronomy, and so forth. According to the credo of the party which calls itself conservative, God and the *Hohenzollern*, revelation and monarchy, the immortality of the soul and the large estate ownership,[219] the sacraments and the lord's rights,[220] patronage, seigneurial jurisdiction, in fact even forced labour (if you really look at it closely)—all of that constitutes an *indissoluble* and *homogeneous* whole accepted as such by both parties. As far as the other party is concerned, that of the struggling culture, it is Jewish—that is all that need be said. You must know that today there is almost no Berlin any more, there is a new Jerusalem which is German speaking. When it is a question of Judaism, which rules in the chamber (which Bismarck *suffered*, all the while pretending to use it), which directs higher learning, which, somewhat like a family doctor, a private tutor or simply a neophyte's instructor, has taken with women the place of the seventeenth and eighteenth-century directors of conscience, which pays for and influences the majority of newspapers—it is not of course a matter either of the Old Testament or of a nationality raised to the height of a chosen race. It is something altogether impalpable and intangible, it is the purest essence that has ever existed of all of those elements which are fundamentally hostile to a Christianly constituted moral and social order. Quite certainly these elements are found more or less everywhere, but to perceive their presence, to extract them from the social mud and from the darkest corners of consciousness, to set them out in daylight, particularly to teach them how not to blush, in short to constitute them into a body of doctrine and into a

[219] The phrase is in German. (Trans.)

[220] The word is in German. (Trans.)

political party, what was necessary was what the Jews alone could provide: an infallible flair and a complete ruthlessness in the negation of that which exists. Only the Jews were in possession of this, or at least they possessed these qualities to an incomparably higher degree than all others, for this demanded an ancient, unbroken historical tradition going back to the beginning of the world, and a high degree of culture embracing an entire tribe, a culture which at the same time stands outside the Christian tradition (and I repeat, outside it, not just opposed to it.)[221] It is impossible not to admire the variety of forms and colours which this tendency has at its disposal, without its unity ever being broken. In politics—it is the worship of success and the cult of the golden calf; in philosophy—it is matter, which by its own strength rises to the highest form of consciousness;[222] in social questions—it is the whole body of historic institutions which are to be remade on the basis of *pure* Manchesterism, or the rise of productivity in a completely abstract sense, as the highest goal, for its own sake;[223] in the realm of the family—it is individual goodwill as the sole basis for all relations; in matters of education—it is the development and directing of instincts: drives and stimuli—nothing else, and as a goal, the combatting of the harmful ones with those that are useful.[224] That is what we have come to! Germany is the greatest threat facing my country's future, and yet I could not without agonizing heartache contemplate this dissolution, which comes about with the external appearance of a political power at its apogee. For every educated Russian, in my time at least, Germany is also a sort of homeland, from which he has long drawn nourishment.[225] Unfortunately, it

[221] From "... a complete ruthlessness ..." the text is in German. (Trans.)

[222] From the word "which" the sentence is in German. (Trans.)

[223] From "on the basis" the sentence is in German. (Trans.)

[224] Following the colon the sentence is in German. (Trans.)

[225] The phrase is in German. (Trans.)

is just that Germany, which has fed the men of my age, which is disappearing. When you ask where it is, they will laugh in your face; when you order the works of Lessing at a book store, they stare at you (such things are not in stock[226]) and at the same time send you on approval[227] the bulletins of the stock exchange. This is the phrase which has come back to me of its own accord on more than one occasion after conversations on various subjects: such a stubborn supporter of *our* views of the thirties could hardly be found among us; the man is in it up to his ears.[228] I accept the irony on my own behalf, and for yours even without waiting for any special proxy.

March 5. I have just reread yesterday evening's unfinished letter—my oculist recommended that I always get up from my writing table at midnight. I shall leave it as it is, because really it is only a matter of telling you that, after a great deal of labour and thought, I have finally perceived what you for a long time have known better than I. I let you have my impressions as they came to me and I shall change nothing of what I have written; but let me add to each of my words a constant mental reservation: these are only *impressions*; it is quite possible that I am completely wrong: it is more than probable that my views are very one-sided.[229] We Russians are paid to find out just how absurd a foreigner can become, after having spent two months in what is for him a completely foreign country, in wildly formulating generalizations.

I am staying here until next Sunday, just one week, after which I am going to spend three days at Paris with the Cherkasskis and then I shall be coming back to Berlin to set out again the same day or the next at the latest for Petersburg, and then Moscow. News of Princess Cherkasski is good.

[226]The phrase is in German. (Trans.)

[227]The phrase is in German. (Trans.)

[228]Following the colon the sentence is in German. (Trans.)

[229]The phrase is in German. (Trans.)

I have just received too a letter from Miss Tiutchev, who had charged me with a commission. She is in Nice and writes that she feels herself being reborn at the first puffs of spring. That is the least that spring can do in gratitude to a poet who has sung of it.

All good things come in threes.[230] There is a Russian proverb which says: God loves the Trinity. I am sending you a horribly motley letter, written in two languages; I have kept the third one to the end, that of my country, and the dearest to my heart, to repeat to you for the hundredth time that I am sincerely devoted to you and that I warmly clasp your loyal and faithful hand.[231]

Georg v. Samarin.[232]

P. S. By the way, have you come across the latest brochure of the ex-professor Walker recently published here and in which he relates, among other things, that he was surprised to learn from one of his colleagues that many members of the nobility in the Baltic Provinces really consider me a conservative, which, to their way of thinking, means an honest man? I strongly suspect you of having in the past written or else let drop a denunciation of me. May God pardon you![233]

[230]The phrase is in German. (Trans.)

[231]Following the colon the text is in Russian. (Trans.)

[232]The first six letters are in Gothic script; the next four are in Latin; the last three are in Cyrillic.

[233]This postscript is in Russian. (Trans.)

To the letter is attached a photograph of Lasker with the note: *Delegate Lasker: as a document in proof and illustration for my letter.* (D. S.)

BARONESS RAHDEN TO IU. SAMARIN

February 25, (1876).

I have only just now received your letter and I hasten to reply to it in two words, so that these lines may still catch you in Berlin. What a pleasure to think that you will not be there much longer! I so greatly needed your approval and counsel recently that I even wrote about it to your sister, who was good enough to pass on to me information of yours on the primary schools. I was daring enough to attack and combat—naturally without success—the bureaucratic knavery that is destroying us, and to call by their true names the tinsel of pseudo-liberalism and the humanitarian tendencies with which we are so dazzled. It was the council managing the Grand Duchess Helen's institutions which gave rise to that attack[234] on my part, and I am starting in all over again this evening!

Solitude is dear to me; I have become accustomed to it as to a second nature, but there are moments when being completely isolated in our firmest convictions is as painful as physical suffering, until a reaction sets in and this isolation becomes itself an additional source of strength.

What you tell me is so strikingly true—I am going to read and reread your letter while waiting for you to be here.

It can be taken for granted that I shall gladly make the extract you mention; I had already thought about it; only the long agony of Lady Augusta prevented me from writing to the Dean. Now that she has gone back to God and emptiness will close in around her grieving husband, it is good to offer him the consolation which fine souls find in sharing eternal thoughts and feelings. With the felicity of expression characteristic of Stanley, he not only believed he saw in Rukavichnikov a saint from the early days of Christianity, but he wrote in one of his speeches that he had found in the

[234]The word is in Russian. (Trans.)

face of a few persons, whom God had allowed him to meet in Russia, the reflection of those beatitudes which our Lord speaks of as the fruits of perfection. Once again, thanks—goodbye for a short while!

P. S. Kindest regards to the Cherkasskis. I am busy translating the *Zhivye Moshchi*[235] into German; we always present our best authors to Europe by their mediocre works—as witness the *Chasy*[236] of Turgenev, published in the *Deutsche Rundschau.* Goodbye for now.

IU. SAMARIN TO BARONESS RAHDEN

Berlin, March 11/February 28, 1876.

There is no one like you for punctuality! How could I have expected a reply? What information about the schools was it you wanted to have? I am surprised that my sister has not said anything to me about it at all. If you are in a hurry for it, you will have plenty of time to write me, either to Paris, rue Balzac, 4, or to general delivery, Berlin. Perhaps there are some data that could be gathered here. I must warn you though, that as far as schools are concerned I have examined closely only the most primary and thoroughly rustic ones; I have a little experience, but no firm ideas.

So, may God keep you, Edith Fedorovna, with your visor down, your lance couched, and above all, without any armorial bearings on your shield—as the proverb goes: In trying to teach a scholar you spoil him.[237] Yours truly.

[235]*Zhivye moschchi* (The Living Relic) was a tale written by I. S. Turgenev for *A Sportsman's Sketches.* It was first published in 1874 as part of a literary collection sold in aid of the famine victims of Samara Province. See I. S. Turgenev, *Pis'ma, 1872-1874,* X (Moscow-Leningrad, 1965), 191, 576, and 578. (Ed.)

[236]The short story *Watch.* (Trans.)

[237]The beginning of the sentence and the end, following the dash, are in Russian. (Trans.)

IU. SAMARIN TO BARONESS RAHDEN

Paris, Saturday, March 18.

I hasten to warn you that the *Zhivye Moshchi* have been translated into German and printed. It was Turgenev himself, with whom I spent last evening at the Cherkasskis', who told me.

In three hours I shall be leaving for Berlin. Princess Cherkasski is much better. Farewell for now! Your entirely devoted.[238]

[238]The last two sentences are in Russian. (Trans.)

INDEX

Aksakov, I. S. - 13, 13fn., 20, 23fn., 25, 80fn., 94fn., 131, 131fn., 150, 174, 208, 209, 209fn., 211, 212, 251
Aksakov, K. S. - 5, 5fn., 6, 9, 11, 13, 13fn., 23fn., 60fn.
Aksakov, S. T. - 5, 5fn.
Alexander I - 160, 160fn.
Alexander II - 4, 13, 14fn., 17, 18, 20, 71, 90fn., 91fn., 95, 98, 120, 121, 123, 125, 171, 173fn., 174fn., 176fn., 178, 178fn., 186, 215, 229, 248
Alexander III - 21
Anne Empress -63fn.

Bakunin, M. - 5
Baranov, Countess - 251
Barclay - 58
Bartenev - 113
Bebrinski, Count - 186
Beecher - 204
Belaev, I. D. - 62, 62fn., 63fn., 67, 70, 72
Belinsky, V. - 5
Berkholz - 236, 241, 242, 244, 247, 249
Bibikov, Governor-General - 12
Biering - 154
Bismarck - 70, 85, 165, 168, 191, 197, 239, 255
Bliudov, Anton - 124
Blum, C. - 227, 228-9
Bock, Bookseller - 166, 226, 228
Bock, W. - 30, 30fn., 81, 82, 83, 86, 87, 89, 92, 113, 114, 115, 157, 159, 171fn., 186, 190
Bratstvo - 97, 196, 205
Budberg, Baron - 227

Dahl, V. I. - 68, 68fn.
Dalton, Pastor - 118, 236
Darwin, C. - 184
Dashkova, C. R. - 197, 197fn.
Deubner, Pastor - 80
Dmitriev - 180, 182, 218, 219, 244
Dolgoruki, V. A. - 95, 95fn., 177, 229
Döllinger, J. - 140, 141fn., 149
Dostoevski, F. - 3

Eckhardt, J. - 86, 86fn., 172, 186
Edinburgh, Duke of - 242
Engelhardt, Professor - 129, 134, 139, 140, 141
Evangelical Alliance - 171, 176, 186, 226

Fadeev, R. A. - 21, 246, 246fn.
Fassanov, Arch Priest - 193
Fersen - 58
Fowle - 204
Francis-Joseph, Emperor of Austria - 243
Frederick, Prince - 197
Frederick II (Hohenstaufen) - 239

Gagarin, Sister - 215
Gallagan, G. P. - 124, 125fn.
Gluck, C. - 200
Goethe, J. - 225
Gogol, N. - 5, 180fn.
Golovnin, A. V. - 58, 58fn. 59fn.
Gorchakov, A. M. - 85, 85fn.
Gradovski, A. D. - 23fn.
Granovsky, T. - 5
Grot - 228
Grote - 157, 247, 248
Guizot, F. - 95
Gulliarov-Platonov - 66

Hardenberg, K. - 166
Hartmann - 226
Haxthausen, A. F. - 70, 70fn.
Hegel, G. - 7, 40, 183
Helen Pavlovna, Grand Duchess - 14, 14fn. 25, 26, 27, 35, 36, 37, 38, 39, 40, 61, 62fn., 64, 65, 66, 67, 68, 69, 69fn., 73, 75, 78, 79, 82, 84, 85, 106, 107, 114, 122, 123, 124, 150, 181, 182, 188, 201, 207, 208, 212, 214, 215, 217, 218, 220, 221, 231, 238, 247, 248, 259
Herder, J. - 226
Herzen, A. I. - 4, 5, 23, 60, 60fn., 82
Hilferding, A. F. - 206, 206fn., 207

Ianishev, Father - 154, 155
Iaroslav, I. - 62
Iavorsky, S. - 6, 7, 106

James, Saint - 141
Jeanne d'Arc - 167
Jesuits - 65, 67, 105
Jesus - 99, 142, 204
John, Saint - 145fn.
Jung-Stilling, F. - 94, 247, 249

Kant, I. - 105, 134, 183, 226
Karakozov, D. V. - 178
Karamzin - 126
Katkov, M. - 3, 5fn., 86fn.
Kavelin, K. D. - 20, 198, 199, 199fn.
Keyserling - 244
Khomiakov, A. S. - 6, 6fn., 7, 9fn., 12, 19, 20, 22, 23fn., 31, 32, 33, 61, 61fn., 84fn., 96, 98, 99, 103fn., 108, 113, 115, 124, 126, 127fn., 129, 132, 133, 134, 142, 143, 144, 151, 152, 157fn., 159, 180, 188
Khotek, B. - 164, 164fn.
Kireevski, I. V. - 6, 6fn., 20, 22, 23fn., 144
Kochubei, Prince - 223, 227, 233
Korff, N. A. - 209, 210fn.
Koshelev, A. I. - 12, 13fn., 19
Kossovich, Professor - 38
Kotliarevski, Professor - 129

Lanskoi, S. S. - 36fn.
Lasker - 258fn.
Lemaistre de Sacy - 140
Leont'ev - 38
Lermontov, M. - 5
Lessing, G. - 257
Lieven, Princess - 233, 234
Locke, J. - 183
Luke, Saint - 146
Luthardt - 140
L'vov, Princess - 244

Marie, Grand Duchess - 242
Martin - 140
Mary, Empress - 26
Mary, Princess of Mecklenburg-Schwerin - 207
Medem (de Medem) - 192
Mengden, Baron - 181
Merkel (Ianau?) - 49
Michael Pavlovich, Grand Duke - 14fn.
Miklukho-Maklai, N. N. - 169, 169fn., 170, 189, 206, 207
Miliutin, D. A. - 25, 39, 246, 246fn.
Miliutin, Lise - 123
Miliutin, N. A. - 17, 17fn., 25, 36fn., 79, 120, 121, 121fn., 126, 221fn., 243
Mill, J. S. - 183, 235
Milton, J. - 104
Moses - 146
Mozart - 200
Mueller, M. - 20

Napoleon, Louis Bonaparte - 119, 163, 165
Narichkin, B. - 92
Naville - 171, 172
Nechaev, S. G. - 184, 184fn., 188
Nesselrode, Count - 227
Nicholas I - 11, 70fn.
Nicodemus - 104
Nolcken - 86

Obolenski, Princess Dolly - 207
Obolenski, D. - 94, 94fn., 96, 107, 118, 126, 158, 187, 205, 230, 231, 246
Odoevski, V. - 19fn., 61, 98, 106, 213
Oettingen, Professor - 151
Ogarev - 97
Orange, Prince of - 182
Orlov-Davidov, O. I. - 208, 209fn.
Ossinin - 66, 67, 68
Overbeck - 65

Palmer, W. - 102, 103fn.
Panin - 208

Paul, Saint - 82, 104, 107, 139, 141, 146, 148, 149
Pavlov (nee Janisch) - 248
Perfil'ev - 213
Peter I - 63, 67
Peter, Saint - 146
Pilate - 204
Pobedonostsev, K. P. - 66, 68, 125, 125fn., 208
Pogodin, M. P. - 4, 5
Popov, E. I. - 254
Pressensé (de Pressensé) - 172
Priev - 184, 184fn.
Prokopovich, F. - 6, 7
Pushkin, A. - 225

Raevski - 155
Rahden, E. P. - 3, 23, 23fn., 25-34, 35, 92, 157, 260
Redkin - 68
Richter - 223, 227, 233, 234, 236, 241
Rostovtsev, Ia. I. - 15
Rukavichnikov - 253, 259

Samarin, D. F. - 23, 25fn., 26fn.
Samarin, Iu. F. - 3-24, 25fn., 26, 27, 28, 29, 30, 31, 32, 33, 34, 35, 59, 60, 62fn., 65fn., 74fn., 75fn., 84, 90fn., 91fn., 98fn., 115, 116, 127fn., 145fn., 151fn., 157fn., 171fn., 178, 178fn., 187fn., 213, 221fn., 229fn., 230fn.
Samson - 224
Scharnhorst, G. - 166
Schedo-Ferotti (F. I. Firks) - 58, 58fn.
Schelling, F. - 183
Schiller, J. - 225, 226
Schirren, C. - 30, 30fn., 115, 116, 119, 121, 122, 157, 164, 171fn., 186
Schönlein - 166
Schumacher - 234
Semenov - 68, 69, 169, 170, 208
Shcherbatov, Prince - 120, 213, 214, 240, 243
Shuvalov, Count Peter - 182, 186
Siever (Sivers) - 58, 86, 223, 224, 225, 227, 228, 233
Sievers, G. - 81
Sigismond-August (Sigismond II, King of Poland) - 41
Slavophil - 3, 5, 6, 9, 12, 13, 17, 22, 206fn.

75 01845

Solov'ev, S. M. - 5fn.
Stahl, Helen (Countess of Hauterive) - 183
Stankevich, N. - 5
Stanley, A. P. - 242, 242fn., 253, 259
Stegemann - 166
Stein, H. - 166
Strauss, D. F. - 232, 233, 235, 238
Struve, P. - 20
Suvorov, A. - 38, 39

Titov - 78
Tiutchev, F. I. - 225, 225fn.
Tiutchev, Kitty - 235, 258
Todtleben - 58
Tolstoy, D. A. - 58fn.
Tolstoy, L. - 3, 239, 239fn.
Trepov, F. F. - 72, 72fn.
Turgenev, I. S. - 68, 68fn., 260fn., 261
Turr, General - 165

Urussov, Prince - 207, 231
Ustinov - 184, 184fn.

Valuev, P. A. - 36fn., 59fn., 182
Vassil'chikov, Pierre - 176
Vassilchikov, Princess - 122
Vietinghof, Boris - 233, 234
Vinet, A. R. - 249, 250, 251
Vinogradov, P. - 23fn.
Vladimir, Grand Duke - 207
Vladimir, Saint - 10
Voght, K. - 183
Voltaire - 167

Walker - 258
William I, Emperor of Germany - 197
Wurstemberger - 196
Würtemburg, Princes - 114
Würtemburg, Queen of -215

Zasulich, Vera - 72fn.

UNIVERSITY
OF BRISTOL
LIBRARY
W.M.L.

UNIVERSITY OF BRISTOL
WITHDRAWN
10 0200831 0
TELEPEN
UNIVERSITY OF BRISTOL
LIBRARY